T0340358

'That our lives become increasingly complex is part of our common experience. How to navigate complexity, however, is another matter. It is here where we need reliable and insightful guides. Chris Mowles has provided such a brilliant guide. True to form, this is a multi-dimensional guide, ranging from the self, trough organizations, to the world at large. With every chapter, the reader is encouraged to complexify his/her understanding – new ideas and questions crop up, judgment is sharpened and a new sensibility emerges. This is an highly enlightening book fit for our challenging times.'

Haridimos Tsoukas, *University of Cyprus and*
University of Warwick, United Kingdom

'Chris Mowles provides us with a useful antidote to the notion that complexity thinking can solve "wicked problems". This book takes seriously the social relations which shape organisations, and people's day to day lived experience. It provides readers with different ways of thinking about continuity and change, and some very practical ways in which managers and leaders can behave differently.'

Chris Roche, *Professor of Development Practice and*
Director of the Institute for Human Security and Social Change
at La Trobe University, Australia

'Professor Mowles' work offers those who care about organizational life the chance to consider the impossibility of controlling outcomes or predicting the future. Within his descriptions and stories of leading and participating, I have found a rewarding and refreshing invitation to pay more attention to the present, to value emotion, confusion or difference and be re-invigorated when collective thought and discovery result in changed minds and renewed agreements for action.'

Cathy Risdon, *Professor and Vice Chair, Director, Health Services,*
McMaster University, Hamilton, Canada

'Over the past few years, there has been a major shift in the research culture of universities. Research fundamentally motivated by innate human curiosity has been subjugated to research driven by strategic objectives chosen by university management. Researchers are fired because they do not align with strategic objectives, because they dare to critique management orthodoxy. Chris Mowles' book is extremely important because it resists this destructive trend and makes a serious contribution to keeping critical management traditions alive.'

Ralph Stacey, *Founder of the Doctor of Management*
Programme at the University of Hertfordshire, United Kingdom

COMPLEXITY

This book interprets insights from the complexity sciences to explore seven types of complexity better to understand the predictable unpredictability of social life. Drawing on the natural and social sciences, it describes how complexity models are helpful but insufficient for our understanding of complex reality.

Taking an interdisciplinary approach, the book develops a complex theory of action more consistent with our experience that our plans inevitably lead to unexpected outcomes, explains why we are both individuals and thoroughly social, and gives an account of why, no matter how clear our message, we may still be misunderstood. The book investigates what forms of knowledge are most helpful for thinking about complex experience, reflects on the way we exercise authority (leadership) and thinks through the ethical implications of trying to co-operate in a complex world. Taking complexity seriously poses a radical challenge to more orthodox theories of managing and leading, based as they are on assumptions of predictability, control and universality. The author argues that management is an improvisational practice which takes place in groups in a particular context at a particular time. Managers can influence but never control an uncontrollable world. To become more skilful in complex group dynamics involves taking into account multiple points of view and acknowledging not knowing, ambivalence and doubt.

This book will be of interest to researchers, professionals, academics and students in the fields of business and management, especially those interested in how taking complexity seriously can influence the functioning of businesses and organizations and how they manage and lead.

Chris Mowles is Professor of Complexity and Management at Hertfordshire Business School, University of Hertfordshire, UK.

KEY IDEAS IN BUSINESS AND MANAGEMENT

Edited by Stewart Clegg

Understanding how business affects and is affected by the wider world is a challenge made more difficult by the disaggregation between various disciplines, from operations research to corporate governance. This series features concise books that break out from disciplinary silos to facilitate understanding by analysing key ideas that shape and influence business, organizations and management.

Each book focuses on a key idea, locating it in relation to other fields, facilitating deeper understanding of its applications and meanings, and providing critical discussion of the contribution of relevant authors and thinkers. The books provide students and scholars with thought-provoking insights that aid the study and research of business and management.

Sustainability
A Key Idea for Business and Society
Suzanne Benn, Melissa Edwards and Tim Williams

Human rights
A Key Idea for Business and Society
Karin Buhmann

Complexity
A Key Idea for Business and Society
Chris Mowles

For more information about this series, please visit: www.routledge.com/Key-Ideas-in-Business-and-Management/book-series/KEYBUS

COMPLEXITY

A Key Idea for Business and Society

Chris Mowles

Routledge
Taylor & Francis Group

LONDON AND NEW YORK

First published 2022
by Routledge
2 Park Square, Milton Park, Abingdon, Oxon OX14 4RN

and by Routledge
605 Third Avenue, New York, NY 10158

Routledge is an imprint of the Taylor & Francis Group, an informa business

British Library Cataloguing-in-Publication Data
A catalogue record for this book is available from the British Library

Library of Congress Cataloging-in-Publication Data
Names: Mowles, Chris, author.
Title: Complexity : a key idea for business and society / Chris Mowles.
Description: Abingdon, Oxon ; New York, NY : Routledge, 2022. |
Series: Key ideas in business and management |
Includes bibliographical references and index.
Subjects: LCSH: Complex organizations. |
Organizational change. | Organizational sociology.
Classification: LCC HM786 .M69 2022 (print) |
LCC HM786 (ebook) | DDC 302.3/5–dc23
LC record available at https://lccn.loc.gov/2021030901
LC ebook record available at https://lccn.loc.gov/2021030902

ISBN: 978-0-367-43385-7 (hbk)
ISBN: 978-0-367-42568-5 (pbk)
ISBN: 978-1-003-00284-0 (ebk)

DOI: 10.4324/9781003002840

Typeset in Bembo
by Newgen Publishing UK

CONTENTS

PREFACE

This book has been a long time in the writing, although it was only relatively recently commissioned by Routledge. The invitation came after a long period sketching out something to write and then the commitment I gave to the publisher spurred me on to stop dithering. In categorizing the book into seven types of complexity, I am conscious how one type blurs into another: the reader will find that I write about practical judgement, for example, in at least three chapters. Equally, themes like power come up in a number of chapters, as does the idea of the thoroughly social self. The categories are to a certain extent arbitrary. Then there are also types of complexity that I haven't done full justice to. Time, for example, is fundamental to a complex understanding of social life, given that complex systems are 'path-dependent': what has happened has a big influence on how things are now, what can happen. Although we often miss the complex interconnectedness of people, things and events, there are certain junctures, like the Brexit vote in the United Kingdom, for example, where whole nations, can become something radically different. Today isn't always yesterday plus or minus 5%. So apologies for what the book doesn't cover in depth as much as for what it does.

I first tried out the ideas for the book three years ago at the Complexity and Management Conference, an annual event held with my colleagues who teach on the Doctor of Management programme at the University of Hertfordshire. The occasion was the retirement of the founder of the programme, Ralph Stacey. In his final public lecture, he gave a very moving overview of why he had become preoccupied with the complexity sciences, why he had moved from a career in the City of London to becoming an academic and how fulfilling that had proved both in terms of his achievements and his generative relationships with colleagues. It was the relationships which he valued the most. He talked about the continuous satisfaction he had gained from watching sometimes less formally educated students go on to complete their doctoral degrees and be presented with their doctoral certificates in St Alban's cathedral.

Ralph said he was ready to retire and also sounded a note or warning about what universities are becoming. He was concerned about the marketization and instrumentalization of everything, which involved treating students as customers and promising them the world. Rather, he thought of universities as the institutionalization of curiosity, where everybody, teachers and the taught, is involved in the struggle to discover what we know and the way that we come to know it. We both agree that even in a Business School, knowledge is not a commodity, but a social achievement which involves struggle, discussion, getting lost and disappointment as well as joy. To know, you have to experience not knowing: achieving anything worthwhile, whether in taking a degree or doing something else that involves hard work and application, often involves feeling blown about. This is hard to capture in student satisfaction surveys.

I know from my own experience of taking over from Ralph as director of the programme ten years ago how much of my time is increasingly spent tied up with filling in forms, accounting for how I spend my time and 'making the numbers.' All universities have become radically different over the last 30 years of Ralph's career, and even in my relatively short period as an academic, the dynamic has amplified. I am not longing for a golden age of academia, partly because I wasn't there to experience it. But I share Ralph's concerns about what I sometimes experience as the brutal instrumentalization of everything we have cause to value, not just in universities and beyond. When everything becomes a metric, it can feel like we are hitting the targets but missing the point.

I think orthodox management practice and discourse has a particular role to play in the way we talk about and live our lives, in an age where we are encouraged to think about our individuality as a brand which needs refreshing, our bodies as though they need optimizing for effectiveness and efficiency and our relationships as though they are businesses. Management, business and economic vocabulary pervades our everyday lives, and when it does so, it smuggles in other assumptions, in effect an ideology, about our relation to the world and to each other. Instead of resonant bodies in relation, we become instruments to one another. Thinking differently about management, talking differently about it, practising managing and being managed as though it were a highly social and improvisational activity which takes place in groups containing plural points of view might make a difference to how we come to think about ourselves and our complex problems. It may also make us critical, in the sense of questioning and making judgements, which can sometimes be a dangerous disposition, even in organizations that consider their staff to be their 'greatest asset.' I have the strongest aversions to organizations where we are invited to be positive, to believe in the vision and to leave our politics at the door.

For this reason, I think the complexity sciences and the insights we can develop from them to think about managing and being managed offer a dose in humility about how the world works and our place in it. For me, to take insights from the complexity sciences seriously invites us to decentre ourselves, to take note of the radical contingency of life and to be less determined to subdue the natural and social worlds to extract more use from them. It is an invitation to reflect more and become reflexive about the complexity of the dilemmas we face and to try harder to make meaning together. If the last 16 months of the pandemic have taught us anything, it is surely to do with the interdependence of our lives and that there is no trade-off between human flourishing and productive economic activity. The first leads to the second. For me, human flourishing involves asking questions continuously about who we are, what we think we are doing and who we are becoming.

Chris Mowles
Oxford, 28 May 2021

ACKNOWLEDGEMENTS

This book is dedicated to Ralph Stacey who died while this book was going through the production process. There are no words to convey how much I owe Ralph – he taught me how to think and to see the world anew. And to my friend Nick Luxmoore, who died much too young, and whom I miss. He would have been pleased for me that I finally completed it, and would have teased and cajoled me into having a book launch.

The book would not have been possible without the support and encouragement from, and endless conversations, with my good colleagues Kiran Chauhan, Emma Crewe, Karen Norman, Nick Sarra and Karina Solsø Iversen. I am indebted to you all for your commitment to the Doctor of Management programme to keep it going as an important countercultural research community. You help keep critique and alternative ways of working alive.

Thanks too, to the intriguing students who continue to turn up on the programme and for the interesting things they keep finding to write about. Their theses are an endless source of fascination and continue to provoke my thinking. The community who participate in the annual Complexity and Management Conference also help us keep going and refresh us.

To the late Doug Griffin and Patricia Shaw, my thanks are due for what you created for my colleagues and I to inherit.

To Nikki, Rosa, George, David, Kristy and Kellan who have been with me every step of the way. Many thanks to Nikki for her critical engagement with my chapters.

To Margaret and Tony who started me off, and to whom I owe everything.

All shall be well, and all shall be well, and all manner of thing shall be well.

1

INTRODUCTION

The predictable unpredictability of the world

I first came across the complexity sciences in the mid-1990s. I had recently become a manager in the public sector and managerialism, the ideology that holds that management tools and techniques are applicable everywhere and to all society's problems, had been washing through all state services. There are a variety of socio-economic and political causes for the emergence of managerialism, but the idea that the public services, even social work and education, should be run on business-like grounds took hold and has been promoted by governments of all complexions until the current day.

In fact, I was a beneficiary of the wave of new public management. I had recently successfully applied for a manager's job in the Social Services Department despite never having qualified as a social worker, a highly unusual event. I was made a manager by the Director of Social Services who was not a social worker either. He was originally a town planner who had acquired a management qualification and decided to climb the greasy pole of management, whatever the specialism of the department he ended up managing. The Director took a chance on me when I put in for the job of social worker team manager, although I didn't really expect to get it, precisely because I didn't know what social work involved and had only joined relatively recently as a community worker. He was convinced that social work needed the firm smack of management, and the fact that I was reasonably bright and ambitious, and not of the tribe, was a good reason to promote me. Among my social work colleagues, this appointment created consternation. But I was young, and impervious. I wore a suit to work for the first time.

The Department was reorganized, we were introduced to new terms like line management, management supervision, targets, key performance indicators and purchaser–provider splits (accompanying the marketization and privatization of services, it was necessary to separate out previously integrated 'purchasers' of services from 'providers' of services). All the new managers, whether they had been around in

DOI: 10.4324/9781003002840-1

the service for a long time or not, were sent on a Diploma in Management Studies (DMS) course at the local university. It was a two-year, part-time programme which could lead to an MBA if you went on to complete another year of study. I learnt about marketing, finance, strategy, human resource (HR) management (a new term for me at the time). We were taught about the history of industrial relations and that we had now learnt to do things differently and better. Interestingly, leadership had not yet become a topic that required a separate module, at least not in this particular regional university. The absence of leadership as a principal theme in any management programme is hard to imagine now.

Two memories stand out for me from this course, which I took over 25 years ago. The first was how we rebelled as a group during the HRs module. All the students knew each other, more or less, and although we took our studies seriously, we also thought it a bit of a game to be learning this new way of speaking, which pointed to a new way of being. We made jokes about it and we resisted being corralled unreflectively into using the new management terms and the subsequent change of identity that we anticipated it might entail. We picked up that the academic in charge of the HR module didn't seem to like public sector workers much from the way he dealt with us, and we returned his ambivalence. He intimated to us that we were naïve and perhaps a little pampered and didn't know what the harsh 'real world' of private sector companies was like.

He may have had a point, at least as far as his second assumption. On one occasion, he had some role-play activities prepared for us which involved some of us being managers and the rest being recalcitrant workers. We felt set up, and none of us put our names forward to play the managers. We got our recalcitrance in first. He was incensed. He huffed and puffed, he waited for us to cave in, but eventually he backed down and came up with something else for us to do. For me, this was one of the most profound learning experiences of the course, as I reflect back on it now. We were on a course where we were exposed to the tools and techniques of management to optimize, to create alignment and to cohere. It is a particular way of exercising power. And yet, the particular circumstances led to a temporary breakdown of relationships until the lecturer was obliged to acknowledge the power position he was in. We weren't undergraduates and there was a limit to the degree to which he could coerce other adults of a similar, sometimes greater age and experience than him, to do what they didn't want to do. I hope in the rest of this book to dwell further on the complexity of everyday organizational life, which involves this kind of negotiation of power and politics and doesn't always turn out as expected. That's what makes it complex and gives a partial explanation of why the tools and techniques might be necessary but are never sufficient to get done what you need to get done as a manager.

The second memory of attending the DMS is the profound impact on me of the strategy module where I first came across the work of Ralph Stacey. Ralph was one of the early pioneers of insights from the complexity sciences and their implications for the management of organizations. He and his colleagues developed a perspective combining the sciences of complexity and social theory, building on

Stacey's previous work, which they termed complex responsive processes of relating (Stacey et al., 2000; Stacey, 2012; Stacey and Mowles, 2016; Mowles, 2011, 2015). As little as I had been exposed to strategy before the DMS, it made everyday sense that you couldn't undertake a journey unless you had a map to chart the territory (and all the other spatial metaphors that usually accompany common-sense strategizing). And yet, here was a scholar, among the other more orthodox literature we were exposed to, saying that one of insights from the complexity sciences held that the future is unknowable. What was a manager to do, then, and what was the point of strategy if this were true? I must admit that at the time I found Stacey's work intriguing, but frustrating. In every other module, including this one, I learned frameworks and grids, often those two-by-two Cartesian co-ordinate diagrams. When you were asked to evaluate your own organization using a two-by-two, you often located it in the bottom left-hand quartile, and the job of the manager, then, was to 'move' it to the top right-hand quartile, where the axes you valued were both 'high.' Or, you chose a 'direction' and you then followed the logical milestones towards the vision you had had and corrected your course along the way. Stacey refused to give this kind of comfort. Cleaving to the radical implications of the complexity models, which he argued demonstrated stable instability, or predictable unpredictability, it was necessary to think differently, pay attention differently, but to leave behind a dependence on tools and techniques, which might be helpful for encouraging thinking, but no more than this. The frustration with Stacey's handling of complexity, and the curiosity to find out more about what he meant, remained an itch I was yet to scratch.

For the next few years I became the dedicated manager, and then a restive organizational consultant, fired up by my DMS, mostly convinced that I could predict and control and guide the organization according to prereflected targets. I could manipulate a group during facilitation to achieve what we had set out to achieve and develop good organizational strategies. However, I soon found out that things often didn't work out as intended. For example, I supervised the managers of two children's homes and a youth justice team, and the young people attended to by the social workers were about as respectful of my teams' targets and strategies as we had been as a group of mature students of the university lecturer who wanted us to role play. This is not to say we had no influence over what happened to the young people looked after by the local authority, or that we were completely ineffective. It's just that it was hard work. We had to improvise continuously, we had to manage up in terms of our managers' expectations and sometimes we had to cover over what was really going on to achieve our targets. I had to find justifications for being called out regularly in the middle of the night because the young people looked after in one of the homes had set off the fire alarm in the children's home, which meant that the fire service were obliged to attend.

I worked in an organization which had been converted to managerialism and there was no other way of talking about what we were doing than by using the accepted language embraced by the senior management team. Only among ourselves at our particular managerial level, middle managers, did we sometimes let our hair down at the pub, or after work and talk about what we knew was really going on. We talked one way in public meetings and another way when we were among trusted friends. The split between the public and private discussion of what's really going on at work is a theme I return to in the book when I address the role of gossip.

When I became a consultant, I kept busy and in work by reading the next best thing. There is no shortage of fads and fashions in the consultancy world, and perhaps my main advantage (my unique selling point [USP] as I learnt to say on my marketing course on my DMS) was that I had read the next latest books some weeks or months ahead of the people who contracted me to do strategy with them, or facilitate some kind of awayday. It looked as though I might know what I was talking about, so performance and confidence in my performance was all. Except that I knew I was winging it, I experienced disruptions, unexpected and unwanted outcomes of awaydays where things just hadn't worked out as I had planned; I began to lose confidence in what I was doing. This led me back to Ralph Stacey, whom I had encountered in my management course. I wrote to him to inquire if he offered an academic programme to develop the ideas I had come across nearly ten years previously. He did. I joined the Doctor of Management (DMan) programme at the University of Hertfordshire. And here we are.

One of the things that struck me as a doctoral student engaging with the perspective of complex responsive processes and reflecting back on my days caught up in the fever of managerialism firmly exercising my right to manage was that I had forgotten what I had learnt about life previously. Prior to being a community worker and social work manager, I had worked for years in international development as an aid worker and volunteer. In one job, I was in a war zone trying to help Palestinian refugees. The lives of refugees are precarious in a country, Lebanon, where the day-to-day politics is volatile: uncertainty rests uneasily on uncertainty. I had an itinerary and I had plans, but my plans were often disrupted as I worked out what to do next with local people who had much more experience than me. I experienced bodily and on a daily basis that life was uncertain. I learnt reflection and reflexivity, terms which we return to in this book, through watching and learning from my local colleagues. I remember standing atop a lorryload of mattresses and food supplies and taking turns to pass them down the hubbub of Palestinians who had recently been driven from their homes for the nth time. Later on, I met up with a dear local friend who had not been involved in what was enfolding. She herself was a refugee from the same group who were mobbing the truck for supplies, so it wasn't that she didn't care. But why had she not been there alongside me with her own organization, helping the refugees? She told me:

> this always happens when the refugees are driven from their homes. I have seen it many times. The international organisations like yours always feel they need to be seen to be doing something, so they rush out and buy things that the refugees don't actually need. But if you're giving away things for free, who wouldn't want to take them? But actually they have carried enough

with them for now and may even be able to return quickly. The real needs will start in a week's time, if they can't return, by which time we would have spent our budget if we had just responded as you and your organisation did.

I realized that I had got caught up in the heat of the moment and was amplifying a dynamic which may not have been helping the situation unthinkingly. The ability to reflect in the confusion and intense emotion of getting swept up in something that matters has preoccupied me ever since.

Overview of the book

I want to return to the frustrations I felt on reading Stacey's work, to forgetting and to the importance of reflection and reflexivity at the end of this introduction. But for now, I give an outline of the chapters and what the reader will find in them.

So, in Chapter 2, I explain the models in more depth and their limitations; in Chapter 3, I explain why I think taking complexity seriously implies a different theory of action; in Chapter 4, I write about the implications of complexity for our sense of self and our identities; in Chapter 5, I explore some ideas on complex communication; in Chapter 6, I think through the implications for knowing about a complex world; in Chapter 7, I work out a more complex understanding of leadership; and in Chapter 8, I address the ethical difficulties of living in a world which may always escape our understanding.

This is not a book about the pandemic, but it strikes me that the last 18 months have given us a unique opportunity to notice just how unpredictable, and ungovernable, the world can be. So, as I explain briefly what the reader will find in each chapter, and how it contributes to the overall argument, I bring in a few real-world examples, based on my experience of the pandemic in the United Kingdom to illustrate why I think each aspect of complexity is important.

Chapter 2 – complex models

There are minority disciplines in science which develop non-linear models of phenomena in nature and society. The point is not to predict the outcome, but to notice qualitative changes over time and novelty which arises from the self-organizing properties of the agents in the model. In this chapter, I explain the spectrum of models used in the sciences of complexity, which have emerged coterminous with the development of computers, and what they demonstrate. I try to point to their limitations as well. Scientists have long been fascinated by complexity in nature and increased computer power has enabled them to model complex chemical reactions (Prigogine, 1997), the neural activity of the brain (Solms, 2021) or ant colonies and traffic flows within cities. Meteorological probability models are used on a daily basis to give us our weather reports. The Santa Fe Institute, which was set up in 1984 by the seminal thinkers in the complexity sciences, Murray Gell-Mann (1994) and Stuart Kauffmann (1995), continues to host researchers who do a wide range of important work on real-world problems using real-world data to populate their models.

Over the last 30 years, there has been a movement away from just adopting the models in a restricted sense towards combining insights with social sciences which are also preoccupied with social complexity. The perspective of complex responsive processes was one of the first coherent bodies of thought to articulate the social and psychological implications of taking complexity seriously. My experience of becoming more familiar with the complexity sciences and the social theories we have developed to adopt a complexity framework, as Byrne (Byrne and Callaghan, 2014) phrases it, is that once you are thinking with a different paradigm, you see the implications everywhere. It's hard to switch off.

For example, I cannot remember a time when there has been so much discussion of complex models of reality, and when they have had so much influence over the daily lives of billions of people on the planet. During the pandemic of COVID-19, computer modellers, epidemiologists, virologists and quantitative sociologists have been constantly on the news explaining their work and their thinking, trying to predict how the pandemic will unfold, even how people will behave, to try and keep citizens safe.[1] The models were crucial in persuading reluctant governments that mitigations strategies would not work once significant community transmission had occurred (Ferguson et al., 2020); so, lockdown and social distancing became inevitable. The models themselves had to be built in real time to help inform policy and so were not subject to the usual rigorous testing that comes from peer review. They are used as the basis of making predictions anyway.

The models differ in terms of their sophistication and the assumptions around which they are built. It has also become clear that some models are more trusted than others by authority figures and the media based not just on the efficacy of the model but the prestige of the institution producing them and the credibility of the scientists fronting them. Equally, the models are only as helpful as the assumptions and quality of data which go into them, which can have real-world effects in terms of government decision-making. Abstract modelling can also trump more practical ways of knowing to everyone's detriment.

Meanwhile, organizational practices which have been adopted because they are efficient and effective, rooted in economic models of equilibrium, have proven fragile in an emergency. Health service in the United Kingdom, which, like most public services, has been subject to year-on-year cuts with the stripping out of beds, staff and equipment, proved itself unable to cope in the initial months of the pandemic. Efficiency and effectiveness may be relevant criteria for the operations of markets, but our health system has fallen foul of the fact that actually we needed some redundancy in services to take up the slack of the surge in demand, particularly during a crisis. A variety of different services in the United Kingdom temporarily put aside working assumptions about how to operate and housed the homeless, built new hospitals, offered GP consultations online, reconfigured services and moved to video teaching. Models of working, which were taken for granted and based on economic theory, became exposed as vulnerable and inadequate and were transformed in the new circumstances. It is too early to say whether changes will endure.

The pandemic has revealed how important modelling of the real world is to help inform our actions but at the same time shown just how imperfect and incomplete they are. Science is enmeshed in other human activity like politics and ethics, and the way we try to think about current problems is heavily informed by the way we have dealt with previous problems, and not always helpfully.

Chapter 3 – complex action

Put simplistically, most theories of action assume that things happen because of the will and charisma of heroic individuals, sometimes groups of clever individuals, who strategize together and impose their plans on others. If you make this assumption, you pay a lot of attention to the characteristics and inner mental states of these remarkable individuals and see if you can identify similar traits in others. Or, you think about how you can 'create the conditions' for the magic to happen through enthusiasm, or passion, being positive or inviting belief in the vision. Another way of thinking which dominates organizational scholarship is that what happens in organizations arises from the sum of behaviours of individuals understood as discrete and closed off from each other. Based on this assumption, you then take an interest in the variables of these behaviours and recommend ways of influencing individuals so that the aggregate pattern of what they create together is more optimal. Both these theories of action are significant and helpful for thinking about what goes on in organizational life, and in society more generally. I have attended meetings in organizations in which I have worked where I have felt uplifted and remotivated by focusing on the potential of what we might achieve together. Equally, I understand that it matters what we each do at work for the good of the collective.

But, a third set of assumptions that I explore more extensively in this chapter investigates the dynamic between the individual and the group and how they mutually co-constitute each other. As individual employees, we form the pattern we refer to as organization and, in turn, we are formed by it, which has consequences for our identity. I assume that there are simply too many variables to take account of no matter how many we identify, and non-linearity means that small changes can escalate into big effects, and big interventions can result in very little change at all. We can't know in advance the consequences of our actions, and even having acted, we don't know what the ripples will be.

Similarly, during the pandemic, no matter how complex the circumstances, how incomplete the data or our understanding of what is going on, we have all had to act anyway. We have also experienced how not acting is also a form of acting which may have dire consequences for populations when the government dither over locking down or restricting travel. Acting and not acting have had ripple effects throughout the pandemic in the United Kingdom, as well as policymakers' assumptions about what people will and won't tolerate in terms of their patience with lockdowns, or following rule-based prescriptions. Politicians' own theories of actions have been on public display. It became obvious in March and April last year that despite grand claims about the UK's pandemic preparedness, the country wasn't prepared: the nation had no working test and trace system. This led to the UK Health Secretary making escalating and arbitrary claims about the number of tests which would be carried out by a particular time as though simply to command it would make it happen. This led, in turn, to exactly the kind of gaming behaviour that I described in my experience as a new manager in the Social Services Department many years ago, presenting things to the good to cover over what was really happening. To fulfil the promises he had made, the Department started including the number of tests which had been posted out, not just ones which had been completed, in the count.[2]

The effect of non-linear interactions during the pandemic has been very obvious: a minority of people panicking to buy toilet rolls and aspirin with the anxious anticipation of shortages amplified by the media; it quickly escalates to become a global pattern of shoppers stripping the shelves of both perishable and non-perishable food stocks. Just-in-time supermarket supply chains take time to respond to the sudden shortage, and a cycle of glut and famine continues until things settle down. It seems that we do not just make up our minds on our own but are influenced by what other people think, what our particular society expects of us and constrained and affected by what everyone else is doing around us.

Some of the most important research which has been done during the pandemic has been micro-studies, which complement the generalized, abstract population-wide models which we discussed in the outline to Chapter 2. For example, the choir practice which took place at Skagit County, Washington, in March 2020 led to important significant insights into the importance of aerosol transmission of the disease and the importance of face masks and physical distance. A total of 61 people attended the 2.5-hour choir practice and 53 people became infected (Hamner et al., 2020). Three patients were hospitalized, and two died. In other words, paying attention to what people are doing in particular circumstances at particular times is invaluable data for understanding how local action contributes to global population-wide phenomena.

Chapter 4 – the complex self

Sociologists still debate which is more important: is it the individual or the group? This is not an arcane discussion, but it makes a difference to how governments make policy, how managers manage organizations and how we think about ourselves and our dilemmas. If as a government, you think that the group is the most important, you might target your policies at improving infrastructure and services for communities and regions rather than giving individuals' tax breaks. If as a manager, you assumed that individuals were prior, you might develop a lot of staff support in the form of well-being seminars and individual resilience training, rather than worrying so much about the working practices and demands of the organization that lead people to seek well-being classes in the first place. This chapter explores the importance of the paradox of thoroughly social individuals, who are shaped by the society into which they are born, and whose individuality is created by the groups they are part of. They are an 'I,' a 'me' and a 'we' at the same time. The chapter goes on to discuss the consequences of our highly individualized times for the way we think about ourselves and the resolution of our dilemmas, particularly in organizations.

As for the pandemic, questions of identity may also have played into people's reactions to the risks they might be running, when they challenged the rules or refused to comply with them, such as not wearing face masks, for example. If you think of yourself as an independent and discrete individual, fully in charge of your own destiny, why would you need the government to tell you how to behave? A substantial minority of people have experienced the imposition of society-wide rules as a serious assault on their liberty. While a fierce individualism may encourage resilience, it may also lead to magical thinking that somehow one can overcome the circumstances through sheer strength of will.

Meanwhile, the last period has immersed us in a generalized uncertainty not just about making plans, but has provoked existential questions about whether we will live or die, whether or not we will be able to make a living, whether or not we will be evicted from our homes and what it means to be in relation with others, no matter how attenuated the relationship mediated by video meetings. It has caused many to question their identities, what they are doing with their lives and how to make their lives more resonant.[3] Whether experiencing extreme hardship as a consequence of widespread crisis or not, there are few among us who have not been bounced into reflecting on our lives to make sense of them and the meaning of the crisis we all share, as a result of a change in the relationships we have with others. In contradistinction to the independent individual mentioned in the paragraph earlier, for some the pandemic has reinforced their need for interconnectedness through the experience of its dilution. Some people have missed their bodily sense of interdependence which is not possible in the same way over a video call or isolated from others.

Public discussion during the pandemic has brought front and centre the debate about whether one achieves greater freedom through recognizing the sovereignty of individuals, or whether individuals can only realize their freedom by acknowledging their interdependency with others, a matter we return to in this book.

Chapter 5 – complex communication

This chapter explores why it is that no matter how clearly a manager thinks she has communicated her message, no matter how clear the policy or procedure is, there will always be misunderstanding, misjudgements and unintended consequences. Meaning is not decided by one party or another engaged in communication but arises in the gesture and response between the parties taken together. Although managers can be very influential in creating narratives about who 'we' are as an organization, and what we are trying to achieve, any narrative will be interpreted by unique individuals with their own life history, who will make different things out of it. Managers can learn a lot by paying attention to conversation because we talk our organizations into being. Being able to persuade is a key part of being a good manager. When we talk differently about what's going on, we change and talk the organization into being a different organization.

During the pandemic, communication, the government's narrative, has been an important part of generating trust, mediating the exercise of power and getting people to cohere and comply. It is not enough just to ask your citizens to trust you, you have to persuade them using rhetoric. In highly developed societies, where it is difficult to fully recognize the large variety of groups which make it up, it is much easier to appeal to symbols that have resonance and which embody what G.H. Mead (1914, 1932) referred to as 'cult values.' These are the values that we all have to recognize to remain a member of this particular group. In the United Kingdom, the National Health Services (NHS) has been described as being the closest the British have to a national religion.[4] So, one of the UK's key messages was that we should all stay home and protect the NHS. No one would want the NHS to be overwhelmed, but in the United Kingdom, the institution has a particular symbolic significance and the appeal has significant resonance for that reason. Appealing to a cult value could also be a way of covering over less salubrious motives and actions: for example, the test and trace system in the United Kingdom is referred to by the government as 'NHS Test and Trace,' although it is privatized to corporate contractors. So criticizing the test and trace system is tantamount to criticizing the very essence of what British people care about: it is above reproach.

The UK government's communication strategy also reveals their assumptions about action, covered in Chapter 3. Depending on whether we are assumed to be asocial or prosocial animals influences the policy as to whether we need to be scolded and shamed into conforming, by pointing to 'COVID-idiots' who break the rules, or whether more traction is gained by referring to the overwhelming majority of people who complied despite very difficult circumstances.[5] Communication also reveals power relationships: it's hard to encourage others to keep the rules if, as in the United Kingdom, senior government advisers are then caught breaking them.

The pandemic has demonstrated the limitations of relying on rationality and science alone as a form of communication to large numbers of people, particularly in polarized times.

Chapter 6 – complex knowledge, complex knowing

In fast-moving and highly uncertain environments, how do we navigate what we know and what we don't? In the absence of sufficient facts, where we still need to make decisions and go on together, how do we find out what to do? This chapter explores the different traditions of thinking which pay more attention to flux and change and call into question how we know what we know. This is not the same as saying that anything goes, but that some schools of thought might be more helpful than others in surfacing what we take for granted, and thus potentially preventing us from repeating past mistakes. Knowledge is produced by humans arguing together in groups, so it is always infused with power relations and moral questions: discussing together keeps hold of the generative tension of what we need in the here and now as an interpretation of a more generalized dilemma. The chapter discusses the role of groups in making managers more critically reflexive.

During the pandemic in the United Kingdom, it has been rare for a politician to make a claim about a new policy initiative related to the pandemic without appending the clause, 'guided by the best available science' or 'guided by the evidence,' which has predominantly been the science of modelling. But governing in the pandemic has given us plenty of material to demonstrate the science is not only a unitary discipline which produces incontrovertible evidence, but also how scientific discourses are taken up in the social sphere and contested. Contestation has arisen within the scientific community itself between different disciplines of science and between modellers developing different models. There has been disagreement between scientists about whether we should lock down or not, and for how long. The disagreement has sometimes become personal, for example, about whether the absence of evidence is the same as the evidence of absence, most notably on the wearing of face masks.[6] Failing to find randomized control studies which proved that masks worked, some eminent scientists at the University of Oxford concluded that they didn't. Meanwhile, other scientists drew on other studies and real-time practical examples, ignoring the so-called hierarchy of evidence, to claim that there was a sufficient amount of alternative evidence to say that masks work, for example (Greenhalgh, 2020). In terms of arguments within the scientific community, there seems to be a feeling among public health scientists, who from the very beginning of the pandemic have consistently argued for their mantra of test, trace and isolate, that they have been marginalized.[7] Just as there is a hierarchy of evidence, so there is a hierarchy of scientific discipline: scientists are also human beings struggling for recognition.

Meanwhile, and to the contrary, conspiracy theories abound about whether the virus actually exists or not, whether the vaccines are safe and how much the whole pandemic is a hoax to take away liberty and human rights. The dominant narrative of science, judicious decision-making calls out a counter narrative of domination, oppression and conspiracy of 'them' against 'us.'

Even scientific advice is conditioned by politics. In the United Kingdom, the government is advised by an umbrella body called SAGE, from which branch many subgroups, such as modelling and social behaviour. Yet, there is also a group titling itself 'Independent SAGE,' chaired by the ex-Chief Scientific Adviser to the government, which comprises many eminent scientists who also give advice to the government and to the public. What we mean by independence is qualified. To understand the complexity of what we face, it has proved important not only to combine abstract knowledge embodied in the sophistication of mathematics but also to look at real-world examples of what has actually happened onboard a cruise ship, or when a choir sang together and many people became infected (what I refer to later as combining the perspective of the airman and the swimmer).

Chapter 7 – complex authority

Organizations are overwhelmed with contradictory and often fad-driven thinking about leadership. This chapter explores what leadership might mean in a complex environment, particularly given the evolving argument in the book about the importance of the paradox of the individual in the group. How much do leaders influence groups, as opposed to the other way round? The discussion involves thinking about how unconscious processes get amplified in the group context and can play to our tendencies to become dependent on authority figures, thus inhibiting our own agency.

Leadership has emerged in all kinds of surprising ways in the current pandemic, both to encourage and to break our sense of dependency on idealized individuals. In terms of the latter, young medics have gone to work in hospitals just as they are graduating, supermarket workers have continued to turn up to help feed the population every day and underpaid carers have continued to care for the vulnerable despite lacking the support and PPE they need; community groups have rallied in their communities to support and aid their neighbours. Leadership doesn't always emerge from people we call leaders.

As an example of our dependency on leadership figures, in the United Kingdom, our principal authority figure, the Prime Minister, was largely absent for the first few months for good reason and bad. Leading up to the emergency, he didn't attend cabinet meetings planning for the crisis. During the beginning of the pandemic, he ignored his own government's emerging advice about not getting close to COVID-19 sufferers and contracted the virus himself and nearly died. Subsequently, he was absent through recovery and paternity leave. Johnson's return was greeted by politicians within his own government as a 'boost for the country,'[8] where Johnson's body and the body politic become synonymous. In the meantime, and in the United Kingdom, we co-created an amplified idealization of Captain Tom Moore, a 99-year-old, who has raised more than £30 million for the NHS by walking 100 laps of his garden in anticipation of his 100th birthday, and who subsequently recorded a song which went to the top of the charts. It may be a helpful comparison to think about how different leaders around the world responded to the pandemic: Johnson, Bolsonaro and Trump on the one hand, and Ardern and Merkel on the other, and whether leadership is also gendered. How might we think about their leadership in terms of their acting into the expectations of their particular communities (as well as the difference in their gender)?

The pandemic has created fertile ground for us to reflect on the exercise of authority in a group, and the extent to which conditions of uncertainty call out the very dependency that we might seek to overcome.

Chapter 8 – complex ethics

If there are too many variables to measure, and we cannot know what has been going on, let alone what is going on, making choices about what to focus on and why as a manager in an organization involves questions of ethics. This chapter treats the complexity of competing valuations of the good which arise in any problematic situation. Any way of managing, whether by metrics, command and control or operating as a co-operative involves choosing certain values over others, including some points of view, and excluding others. One way of uncovering the concrete particulars of specific situations is through narrative. The chapter develops a discussion about how to keep many points of view in play as possible with a view to informing action.

In everyone's lives, and for every community, there have been a variety of competing goods. Locking down keeps us safe but threatens our livelihoods; sealing off care homes prevents infection but makes our elderly relatives deteriorate because of their isolation; clearing hospitals for the treatment of COVID patients has increased waiting lists for more 'routine' yet serious illnesses. In the United Kingdom, the government risked giving more people one shot of the vaccine, rather than giving fewer people two as the regimen originally specified. There is no one best way, or even an obvious way, and sometimes the only way to go on together is take as many goods into view and to make the best judgment at the time. This may mean being alert to narratives which try to unify unthinkingly, which are helpful on the one hand, but may be a way of heading off criticism or denying difference on the other.

Narrative descriptions of the state of NHS emergency wards at the height of the pandemic, the suffering of family members unable to console their loved ones, the insights gained from listening to people in communities narrating in particular how the pandemic has affected them, has enabled us all to have a much more concrete grasp of the goods in play. Narrative, context and detail which are polyvocal and plural have combined as an essential medium for grasping ethics.

With so much at stake, it has been a time where we need better to account to one another about what we are doing and why and perhaps to make more visible some of the assumptions we make in doing so.

Seven types of complexity – combining natural and social sciences

Throughout the book, I make a variety of arguments drawing on the complexity sciences as a source domain, and by analogy. I extrapolate further to think about how a complexity framework might explain what's going on in society more generally, and in organizations where people are managing and being managed. My colleagues and I at the University of Hertfordshire are by no means the only academics to be doing this. Social scientists like David Byrne (Byrne and Callaghan, 2014) and Brian Castellani (2018) take a mixed methods approach: not only do they develop and use complexity models but they also draw on social theory to complement their findings. In Byrne's case, he turns to critical realism and in Castellani's case, to poststructuralism, social psychology and globalization studies. Similarly, Boulton et al. (2015), whose book I draw on in Chapter 2, complement their detailed understanding of the complexity sciences by turning to the social sciences and the humanities to theorize about organizational life.

In the last 30 years, since the original pioneers of the complexity sciences tried to hammer out the implications of the complexity sciences rigorously, and with direct reference to the detail of the models, the term has been taken up much more loosely. Sometimes, it has been instrumentalized. So complexity can just mean very, very difficult circumstances; or academics might claim that we can harness complexity for the good of the organization (thus assuming that complexity is good) with particular frameworks, or a particular style of leadership; or they might claim that complexity thinking applies some of the time in circumstances of the manager's choosing. Some academics claim that the complexity sciences are so diverse and the terminology so exotic that there is nothing we can learn from the complexity sciences that isn't already available in sociology, anthropology, social psychology and social theory. As Anderson noted 30 years ago (1990), there is no unifying theory of the complexity sciences, and this is still true, so perhaps they are more confusing than illuminating. Other disciplines are interested in the same set of phenomena, whether they draw on the complexity sciences or not. For example, economists John Kay and ex-Governor of the Bank of England, Mervyn King, have just brought out an excellent book on the radical uncertainty of large-scale human problems (Kay and King, 2020).

To sum up this brief overview of the book, the perspective of complex responsive processes developed by Stacey and colleagues tries to link some of the insights we derive from the complexity sciences, which I explain in Chapter 2, by drawing on process sociology, pragmatic philosophy and group analytic method. I assume, in the light of process sociology, that everything is in flux and change, and our fluctuating interdependencies are the engine of social stability and instability and shape our identities. I assume, after the pragmatists, that we are social through and through; we are selves because there are other selves, and our paradoxical ability to take ourselves as an object to ourselves enable the mind, self and society to emerge. And, I assume after group analytic theory that the best place to realize oneself as an individual is in a group. Becoming more skilful in groups is a prerequisite for becoming more fully ourselves, and, as a by-product, better managers. I explain as I go through the book how I arrive at these insights.

The four traditions of thought, complexity sciences, pragmatism, process sociology and group analytic theory/practice permeate my understanding of complex social reality, and you will find the scholars who make up these four thought collectives in each chapter.

Thinking without a bannister: the importance of reflection and reflexivity

So as awful as it has been for the last year and a bit, we have had as much evidence as we need to confirm our experience that life is both predictable and unpredictable. The second pole of the dialectic, unpredictability, can take very radical and existential forms. All of us have had direct experience that whatever we think of as developed society cannot be taken for granted. The pandemic has pulled back a curtain to reveal the fragility of 'normality,' which is usually sustained by a constant and dynamic improvisation. The very long chains of interdependencies, social and economic, which sustain societies can tip over into near collapse but may also recover because human beings are adaptable and have the capacity to co-operate. But we have all been confronted with the contingency of human life. The last year has been a general, society-wide experience of destabilization. In recovering, our patterns of co-operation and improvisation may return, but they may also change radically if history repeats itself but never exactly in the same way.

I mentioned earlier that to learn what I did on my DMS, and in my enthusiasm to get on in the world, I ended up forgetting, or perhaps covering over, my previous experience. Almost nothing in my life had worked out exactly as I had planned it, and if it had, it might not have been nearly so interesting. Serendipity, bad luck, bad timing or the influence of factors outside my control had often interfered with plans I had made or objectives I wanted to achieve. And yet, some of the most important things which have happened to me have done so just as much despite my plan as because of it. What would it mean for the richness of our lives if we could predict and control everything?

None of us has been able to forget that life is both stable and unstable this year. The last period has propelled much of the world into a state of radical complexity and uncertainty, the kind of uncertainty which citizens of less developed countries in the world are much more used to, as I mentioned in my passage about working in Lebanon. The precariousness of the ground we stand on has been much more in evidence for everybody. Even then, the privileged have done better than the marginalized, as they always have done (Bambra et al., 2020) and perhaps always will do in times of crisis. We are not, and never have been, 'all in this together,' and as I write this, the Global North is making progress in subduing the pandemic just as the Global South becomes overwhelmed, sometimes for the second or third time. Countries in the former have ordered twice or three times the numbers of vaccines they need, while countries in the latter struggle to vaccinate even their most vulnerable. There are always insiders and outsiders as some groups work to gain advantage over other groups.

I think this is something that most managers who have been around the block know intuitively, because they are human beings first and managers second. When I give talks to groups of managers about the implications of taking the complexity sciences seriously, there are as many nods as there are frowns. The nods are perhaps acknowledgement of putting into words what people already know. What I think the frowns are about is the destabilizing challenge to a discipline and an orthodoxy that pretends to be more in control than is possible, as I hope to show. It is not possible to predict the future, to 'create cultures,' to choose a leadership style and to transform someone else: that's because these involve other people who have the annoying habit of behaving in ways which thwart our intentions towards them, whether we think of ourselves as well motivated or not. And, an additional frustration might be that I have no particular tools or techniques to offer as a replacement for the ones which are currently inadequate.

What I do have to offer is a theory of thinking and action, based on the idea that thinking and action are two sides of the same coin. To think differently about the world, to pay attention to what's going on around you and to become reflexive about this results in acting differently, and I hope, more skilfully. It is neither easy, nor straightforward, but is a necessary response to the everyday complexity with which we have to deal. With the variety of intractable, and yes, complex problems we have facing us, we are required, in Hannah Arendt's terms (2018), to learn to think without a bannister. This means accepting that some of the tools we have developed to date may have helped in the past but may not help us with the problems we face in the present. That's the challenge about thinking and acting with complexity in mind.

Notes

1 This current period of attending carefully to scientific thinking and models, debating them and acting on them has been in stark contrast to our recent history in the United Kingdom. During a long and protracted wrangle about whether we should or should not continue to be members of the European Union (EU), we were encouraged by some politicians not to trust expert opinion derived from economic models which purported to show the dire consequences of our leaving the EU. A prominent British politician claimed that 'we have had enough of experts.'
2 The UK government was criticized for its claims by the UK Statistics Authority: www.bbc.co.uk/news/health-52889103.
3 Resonance, mutuality and sociality are themes I return to again and again in this book.
4 The quotation is attributed to former Conservative Chancellor, Nigel Lawson.
5 This latter point I derive from following Prof Stephen Reicher, a member of Independent Sage and social psychologist, whose work I reference in this book in the chapter on complex authority, Chapter 7.
6 *British Medical Journal*, 2020; 371: m4586.
7 In the United Kingdom, Prof Devi Sridhar, Chair of Global Public Health at the University of Edinburgh, and Anthony Costello, Professor of Global Health and Sustainable Development at UCL, have been leading advocates of the much less glamorous activity of putting public health workers on the ground in the messy social activity of talking to people infected with the disease to find out who they have been in contact with.
8 www.bbc.co.uk/news/uk-politics-52431913.

References

Anderson, P. (1990) Complexity theory and organisation and organization science, *Organization Science*, 10(3):216–232.
Arendt, H. (2018) *Thinking without a Bannister: Essays in Understanding 1953–1975*, New York, NY: Knopf Publishing.
Bambra, C., Riordan, J.F. and Matthews, F. (2020) The COVID-19 pandemic and health inequalities, *Journal of Epidemiology and Community Health*, 74(11):964–968.
Boulton, J., Allen, P. and Bowman, C. (2015) *Embracing Complexity: Strategic Perspectives for an Age of Turbulence*, Oxford: Oxford University Press.
Byrne, D. and Callaghan, G. (2014) *Complexity Theory and the Social Sciences: The State of the Art*, London: Routledge.

Castellani, B. (2018) *The Defiance of Global Commitment: A Complex Social Psychology*, London: Routledge.

Ferguson, N., Laydon, D., Nedjati Gilani, G., Imai, N., Ainslie, K., Baguelin, M., Bhatia, S., Boonyasiri, A., Cucunuba Perez, Z., Cuomo-Dannenburg, G., Dighe, A., Dorigatti, I., Fu, H., Gaythorpe, K., Green, W., Hamlet, A., Hinsley, W., Okell, L., van Elsland, S., Thompson, H., Verity, R., Volz, E., Wang, H., Wang, Y., Walker, P., Winskill, P., Whittaker, C., Donnelly, C., Riley, S. and Ghani, A. (2020) *Report 9: Impact of Non-Pharmaceutical Interventions (NPIs) to Reduce COVID-19 Mortality and Healthcare Demand*. Available at: www.imperial.ac.uk/mrc-global-infectious-disease-analysis/covid-19/report-9-impact-of-npis-on-covid-19/.

Gell-Mann, M. (1994) *The Quark and the Jaguar*, New York, NY: The Freeman Press.

Greenhalgh, P. (2020) Face coverings for the public: laying straw men to rest, *Journal of Evaluation in Clinical Practice*, 26(4):1070–1077.

Hamner, L., Dubbel, P., Capron, I., et al. (2020) High SARS-CoV-2 attack rate following exposure at a choir practice – Skagit County, Washington, March 2020, *Morbidity and Mortality Weekly Report*, 69:606–610. doi:10.15585/mmwr.mm6919e6.

Kauffmann, S. (1995) *At Home in the Universe: The Search for the Laws of Self-Organisation and Complexity*, Oxford: Oxford University Press.

Kay, J. and King, M. (2020) *Radical Uncertainty: Decision-Making Beyond the Numbers*, London and New York, NY: Norton and Company.

Mead, G.H. (1914) The psychological bases of internationalism, *Survey*, XXIII:604–607.

Mead, G.H. (1932) Scientific method and the moral sciences, *International Journal of Ethics*, XXXV:229–247.

Mowles, C. (2011) *Rethinking Management: Radical Insights from the Complexity Sciences*, London: Gower.

Mowles, C. (2015) *Managing in Uncertainty: Complexity and the Paradoxes of Everyday Organisational Life*, London: Routledge.

Prigogine, I. (1997) *The End of Certainty: Time Chaos and the Laws of Nature*, New York, NY: The Free Press.

Solms, M. (2021) *The Hidden Spring: A Journey to the Source of Consciousness*, London: Profile Books.

Stacey, R. (2012) *Tools and Techniques of Leadership and Management*, London: Routledge.

Stacey, R., Griffin, D. and Shaw, P. (2000) *Complexity and Management: Fad or Radical Challenge to Systems Thinking*, London: Routledge.

Stacey, R.D. and Mowles, C. (2016) *Strategic Management and Organisational Dynamics: The Challenge of Complexity to Ways of Thinking about Organizations*, 7th Edition, London: Pearson Education.

2

COMPLEX MODELS

Radical challenge to management orthodoxy

There is a bird sanctuary north of where I live in Oxford. Otmoor is a restored flat wetland area of about 400 acres and is a Site of Special Scientific Interest (SSSI) between Oxford and the market town of Bicester. For about six weeks in December and January is the best time to go and see the murmuration of starlings which happens around dusk. It's always cold but this doesn't deter the many booted and bescarved enthusiasts, warmly wrapped up against the chill and equipped with binoculars, who come to witness this spectacular natural event. Tens of thousands of starlings, some in small groups, some in much larger flocks, arrive over the wetland ponds from all directions, then begin their strange and beautiful aerial ballet. They swoop, they soar, one minute a dense mass, the next separating out into two perhaps three fizzing, unevenly sized but connected balls of birds. Dazzling and shimmering, the mass of starlings is never at rest, and never predictable in the turns it takes. It is quite hard to judge the start and the end of this dramatic display, but by the time the sun has set, all the starlings have peeled away to roost. They will appear again the next day, but there is no guarantee that they will create the same dynamic and explosive patterning – murmurations don't happen every night.

The murmuration has become emblematic of a general interest in complexity, and a picture of one is quite likely to be on the front cover of a book, to adorn a blog post or to precede a seminar on complexity and its relevance to social life. With caveats, I sometimes use a video of the Otmoor murmuration myself with groups of managers or students. But the phenomenon is both helpful and unhelpful for thinking about organizational complexity, the topic of this book; it is a starting point for unpicking some of the radical implications of complexity thinking, which I explore below, but it has its limitations too, which I reflect on after that.

The flocking pattern that we can see in nature, murmurations, shoals of fish, has been modelled on a computer by Reynolds (1987). Populating a computer programme with agents, strings of code, which he termed 'boids,' Reynolds

DOI: 10.4324/9781003002840-2

programmed them with three simple instructions: keep a minimum distance from other boids and objects in the environment; match the speed of other neighbouring boids; and head towards the centre of the cluster of neighbouring boids. These three instructions guiding each individual agent/boid are sufficient to produce the overall flocking pattern once the computer programme is begun and is an example of a simple complex adaptive system (CAS). A CAS is an agent-based computer programme and has proved particularly helpful for thinking about phenomena in the natural world which involve many interacting 'agents' (ant colonies, neurones in the human brain), and by extension, the social world, although we have to be careful about how we translate a computer programme for thinking about social life. It is helpful because, rather than being an aggregate model simulated at the global scale with equations, the CAS models detailed patterns of activity arising from interacting agents. There are some problems to explore with how much computer models can be applicable to human activity, but the move from CAS to ants, fish, brain activity or human beings by analogy is easy to understand.

For the time being, let's dwell on how this particular example of a CAS is helpful and thought provoking as a challenge to some of the traditional ways we are encouraged to think about stability and change, order and disorder and, by extension, the relationship between the individual and the group in society more generally. Later I go on to discuss its limitations.

So the first thing to notice is that the murmuration modelled as a CAS is never at rest: it never reaches an equilibrium point but oscillates as a flock for as long as the programme is running. The pattern of the flock evolves and changes because the boids are programmed with non-linear equations which simply iterate and reiterate but are never 'solved.' Each adjustment to the neighbouring boid is simply followed by the next adjustment in the light of the last and in relation to what neighbouring boids have done. The murmuration is an ever-changing pattern.

The second thing to think about is that the flocking movement has the quality of predictable unpredictability about it. We know the boids/birds are going to flock, but we don't know exactly what the flocking behaviour is going to look like: it's going to be both familiar and unfamiliar. There is a general recognizable character to flocking, but it is never repeated exactly the same way again, neither within the same episode nor between different episodes.

The third characteristic related to how the boids are interacting is that each boid places constraints on its neighbouring boids and is, in turn, constrained by them, in terms of the rules that they are following. The flocking arises as a 'negotiation' of the conflicting constraints and adaptations that each boid needs to make to follow the rules.

A fourth quality of the population of flocking boids is that the patterning of the flock arises because of what all the boids are doing together, acting locally. There is no chief boid, no group of boids directing all the other boids what to do. After the CAS has been programmed governing the activity of individual agents, there is no second-by-second plan of how the flocking movement will unfold. The exact pattern of the flocking behaviour is unknowable even to the programmer. The agents are said to be self-organizing, which is not the same as saying that anything goes but is the pattern of negotiating constraints locally, which I described earlier, and uninformed by a controlling boid or group of boids.

Finally, there is a paradoxical movement between local and global patterns. How the boids interact locally with each other forms the global pattern of flocking, but at the same time the global pattern of flocking constrains how the boids interact locally. This isn't a movement of first one, then the other, but happens simultaneously as an imminent property of this particular form of CAS. Local forms global, while at the same time global forms local.

How might any of this be helpful to managers in organizations?

Just to take a step away from the model for the time being to consider the first characteristic I have described earlier that the model is never at rest, never reaches an equilibrium point. What we might think of as the orthodox literature on organizations encourages us to think about stability and change as two separate states. I would argue further that the orthodox literature predominantly valorizes change and often contrasts it unfavourably with stability. I do so tentatively; however, an article by Burns (2004) gives an overview of three decades of change literature, arguing that even one of the grandfathers of step models to change, Kurt Lewin (1947), was fully aware that stability and change are inseparable. Nonetheless, the predominant way of thinking in much management literature is to take for granted his unfreeze, change and refreeze model or organizational change. These days, simple change is often considered inadequate and has become a desire for 'transformation.'

Moving on to the second characteristic that the pattern arising from the boids' interaction is both predictable and unpredictable at the same time. We know they are going to flock, but we don't know exactly what the flocking pattern is going to be. To make an analogous claim about social life, what we might think of as every day organizational routines are accomplished by staff working broadly in a predictable way, but each time they undertake something that involves other people, they have to improvise, adapting and responding to the people they are dealing with. If there were no broadly predictable pattern to social life, sometimes achieved through enormous precision of timetabling, or just-in-time deliveries or repetition and habit, it would be hard for us to function. We are born into a world of existing habits and particular ways of conducting ourselves which we call culture. But the social regularities we perceive, which can sometimes be rendered statistically, arise in unpredictably predictable ways and sometimes endure quite large shocks, which tip them into a different pattern. As I write these sentences, much of the world is enduring some kind of lockdown, or slow release because of the pandemic of COVID-19. All kinds of taken-for-granted social patterns have been disrupted as people stay at home and refrain from their usual routines, such as going to work and sending their kids to school. The shock, in its turn, produces new patterns which many people will create and recreate as they become more normal. Whatever happens, we all improvise and make workarounds, sometimes quite large ones, all of the time, to accomplish what might look like a predictable social pattern.

Improvisation and adaptation lead me into the third characteristic of the model I itemized earlier that of the mutual constraints that that the boids place on each other, we place on each other, to achieve a social routine or pattern. One way of thinking about this mutual constraint shaping our mutual adaptation, which I explore further below, is an interdependency, even a power relationship depending on how we define and think about power. I mentioned earlier that we are born into a world where there is already a play going on, conducted in a particular language or languages and particular ways of understanding the world that we call culture. We might think of these as constraints in the sense that we can't behave in just any way: we are all acculturated enabled and constrained by rules of politeness, turn-taking and what is socially acceptable for 'us.'

Fourth, it is the characteristic of the boids' simulation that there is no central point of control, no plan for the murmuration's development. In broader society, in organizational life, we might entertain the idea that we do what we do because politicians legislate, or our managers or leaders tell us what they want. They shape society or the organization according to their will. This is partially true: those in positions of authority do have particular influence and sometimes the power to command what we spend our time doing or not doing. But what we actually do will depend on the specific context we find ourselves in with other people trying to get the work done, or trying to work out what these general rules mean for us in the here and now, as we make sense of the instruction in the context of what the particular situation requires. Oftentimes, there are conflicting sets of rules: what we think society requires, what our organization seems to demand of us, what we need to do in the here and now and what we ourselves can live with. In our day-to-day lives, we are not following rules, except in the broadest sense, and at work we are probably only dimly aware of what the organizational strategy actually says. So to draw on the model of flocking birds, whatever happens, happens because of what everyone is doing and not doing together, making the best sense of what it is they think they are there to do, senior management team or no senior management team. What we might think of as the organizational plan or strategy emerges from the interweaving of everyone's activity responding to sometimes conflicting rules, plans and constraints. Stating it this way in no way denies that managers have more influence than others to encourage their staff to act according to particular instructions. I do not claim that management is an irrelevance. But I am making a claim that the stable instability of every day organizational life arises from the self-organizing activities of what everyone is doing together to get the work done.

The last quality I mentioned about the model, the paradoxical movement between local and global, with local activity producing global patterns which at the same time constrain local interaction speaks to one of the most important questions in sociology and organizational theory. We might think of it as the structure/agency question, or the relationship between the individual and the social;

how we account for the way human beings know how to behave on the one hand, how they are acculturated, yet reproduce and change the culture they are part of at the same time. We will need to keep returning to this question again in this book because it generates a lot of fierce argument among sociology and organizational scholars. Put simply, the two poles of the argument are that everything comes down to individuals and their particular choices and mental states, or everything comes down to structures, the culture of an organization, for example, or class, or perhaps the way that capitalism creates inequalities. In mediating these two positions, I am not going to posit splitting the difference with some kind of half-way house, but to keep returning to the question to see if we can achieve a good enough explanation of how we encounter long-term trends in social life on the one hand but account for agency on the other. In doing so, I will be framing it as a paradox, an unresolvable contradiction which iterates and reiterates.

Taken together, the extrapolations I have made from the boids simulation could be considered a profound challenge to a number of management orthodoxies because they offer a different understanding of stability and change and the role of the manager. They call into question how much of our lived experience is predictable and controllable, how much is down to individuals and their attitudes and how much we can stand outside the environments we operate within. Management is a discipline predicated on the idea that managers decide, are in control and can change things at will: they have a variety of tools and techniques to turn the organization from one state to another and to plan, predict and keep things running smoothly. The alternative perspective, extrapolating from the model, is that the organization arises because of everyone's activity, which, because it brings about a colliding of intention and understanding, is both predictable and unpredictable of outcome. The organization is in a constant dynamic state: even those situations which appear stable are dynamically maintained. Organizational work is accomplished by people acting locally with a small handful of other people, and their activities contribute to the organization understood as a whole, just as the whole organization defines and shapes their work. The achievement of work is possible through people placing and negotiating, sometimes conflicting constraints on each other (including managerial constraints) as they try to follow abstract organizational plans and injunctions. How they understand these constraints is influenced by their life experience, how they have come to value certain things over others and how they understand what is demanded of them.

Thinking about the model again

But we need to steady ourselves before rushing to conclusions. It's important to notice how I have argued here. I have drawn on a computer simulation to make claims about society more generally and management in particular. It's a model which a computer programmer has developed with some simple instructions to the agents or 'boids': once the model is running, the programmer plays no further part as the pattern iterates and reiterates. There are quite a lot of limitations to the model as it stands, which we need to identify if we are serious about drawing some conclusions about social life, and we should consider the limitations of models more generally. First, and in this particular model, all the boids are the same and are following the same simple instructions. This is quite far from removed from the social world where we are all different and find it hard to follow rules in the same way, no matter how clear they are.[1] Second, the only pattern that the boids follow is flocking: the boids don't change and flock is all they do. This is not an evolutionary model to the extent that no 'learning' takes place which moves them on from following the same three simple instructions. Third, and arising from the second limitation, there is no historical context to the flock as there is to human beings in societies or in organizations. The boids come into the flocking pattern all the same, and they are unaffected by the context in which they are flocking. Next time all the birds/boids assemble, they will flock again.

Any perceptive reader might conclude that these limitations of the boids model were enough on their own for organizational scholars to be modest in their claims about what such models of complexity allow us to carry over to the social world. But since the early 1990s, a variety of organizational scholars have argued that insights from the complexity sciences, in the form of simple rules, can be applied directly to organizational life. A recent example of this in the health domain is Reed et al. (2018) who evaluate health interventions in complex environment and derive 12 'simple rules' for evaluators to follow in evaluating complex health practices. There is nothing in them to take exception to; indeed they sound like good pieces of advice, but of a highly abstract kind: for example, they contain injunctions to 'understand processes and practices of care; understand the types and sources of variation.' These highly generalized recommendations are helpful but only take you so far as both Wittgenstein and Charles Taylor (1999) have identified: there is nothing so clear about a rule which makes it obvious for you to know what to do without negotiating with other people. Following a rule is a social practice. Other organizational writers, without directly adducing the complexity sciences, argue that cutting through increasing organizational complexity is best achieved by following simple rules so that organizational life doesn't become overly complicated. A relatively recent example of this latter category of books is Morieux and Tollman's (2014) volume which claims that managers can manage complexity and not make it complicated by adopting six simple rules, again of a highly generalized kind.

I mentioned earlier that over the last few decades there has been much greater emphasis on the notion that individuals and their psychological states and choices figure much more prominently in theories of governance, which, in turn, are reflected in theories of management. If you think that the world arises simply and only because of the aggregation of the activities of discrete individuals, then the notion that you would get them all to act differently according to a preferred set of rules becomes very appealing. I cover this in more depth in the next chapter. Complexity models which, in effect, have often been programmed using relatively straightforward algorithms easily lend themselves to this simple, perhaps overly simple, translation to the social sphere.

So before going any further with this investigation, it is worth exploring complexity modelling in a bit more depth to see what kind of intellectual assumptions are in play, and what kinds of problems the models are intended to shed light on.

Varieties of complexity models and how they are constructed

There are a variety of ways to model complex behaviour and the boids simulation is just one of them. In a helpful chapter on the complexity of complexity models, Boulton et al. (2015) describe, in detail and stepwise, the intellectual assumptions and the mathematics involved in developing non-linear computer-based models which attempt to model complex reality. Peter Allen, one of the joint authors, who worked with the Nobel Prize–winning chemist, Ilya Prigogine, and his colleagues are reliable guides for helping us think about the relevance of complexity models for understanding social life. Boulton et al. show how making increasing simplifications in models, averaging away from diversity that one might find in the natural or social worlds, allows the models to be more predictive but only by covering over important details. But the most interesting models, from the point of view of thinking about social and organizational life, are the agent-based evolutionary CASs models. The evolutionary models are more sophisticated than the boids simulation I have just talked about because the agents are heterogenous and interact in a non-average way. As I go on to describe, this leads to novelty emerging in the form of new agents demonstrating new behaviours.

We will follow Boulton et al.'s stepwise classification of complexity models which proceeds from most to least complex because this will prove a useful way of understanding the origin of complexity vocabulary, so that we can better assess its relevance to thinking about organizations. There is something of a thicket of terms derived from these complexity models which are sometimes liberally applied to organizational settings and can sometimes cover over their precise derivation from the models.

Let's start with what the pragmatic philosopher and psychologist William James referred to as the 'blooming, buzzing confusion' (James, 1890/2007: 488) of reality. There are a variety of ways of engaging with the richness and variety of life without building models: we can describe it, for example, and render it in prose, either as a literary undertaking or as piece of research using qualitative methods. I give an example of this in Chapter 8 on complex ethics using narrative. But for model-building, Boulton et al. (2015: 79) argue that the first step is to choose a boundary to decide what is inside and what outwith the focus of study. This seemingly simple task of choosing what to include and exclude, even if only temporarily, can sometimes be very difficult. The extent to which social life can be thought of as boundaried is still contested. But for the moment, then, having chosen a boundary, Boulton et al. then recommend that we choose the types of things we want to include in the model, including the possibility of later introducing new types of things. When rendered mathematically, different entities interreacting in non-average ways over time can create structural change where new types of entities and behaviour can

emerge either because of the diversity of interaction conditioned by chance variation, and/or because of the introduction of new entities. The boids model we
referred to earlier is also an agent-based model, but one where all the agents are
the same and are doing the same thing. The only thing which emerges from the
pattern of local interaction is flocking. But heterogeneity of form and behaviour
between forms allows for the emergence of new types of form and behaviour, and
the disappearance of others.

One of the first examples of evolutionary modelling where new forms emerge
is the Tierra simulation developed by Ray (1992). In Tierra, 'agents' made up of 80
digits were given the instruction to self-replicate, a process which was complicated
by the programmer introducing random fluctuations into the procedure, to emu-
late chance mutation in nature. As the agents copied themselves, some sequences
of code might be randomly flipped thus producing slightly different forms. In addition, Ray introduced a 'grim reaper' function to remove mostly older agents as they
queued to use computer time. Competition over scarce resources was simulated by
only allowing a certain amount of computer processing time for each iteration of
the simulation. Over time, the original agents 'mutated' and new forms emerged,
which began to simulate a 'parasite-host' dynamic that could only continue as long
as the 'strategies' of the hosts and parasites were not so successful as to wipe each
other out. Further iterations of the programme produced 'hyperparasites' feeding
off the parasites. In further iterations of the model, Ray switched off the random
flipping of code and noted that new forms continued to emerge. From this, we
might conclude that diverse agents interacting in diverse ways are enough for novelty to emerge in this model: Darwinian chance mutation was not necessary for the
system to take on a life of its own.[2]

Ray's model was an attempt to simulate evolutionary processes in nature which
depend upon the relationships between diverse agents in co-operation and competition with each other. Chance and randomness were also critical to the simulation.
So in reflecting on these types of evolutionary models, including those that Allen
has built himself (1997), Boulton et al. conclude that:

> non-evolutionary models without 'noise' will tend to run smoothly towards a
> single trajectory, giving the illusion of predicting the future precisely. In con-
> trast, evolutionary complex models will consist of a basic core model plus vari-
> ation and noise, together with the exploration of new ideas, and new things
> might 'invade' it. Therefore it will show a possible spread of futures towards
> different possible 'attractors' – that is, towards qualitatively different outcomes.
>
> *2015: 84*

Notice the difference between these models simulating novelty and change and the
boids model I described earlier, and further below, where all of the birds remain the
same throughout, and no adaptation or instability takes place. The former models
are path-dependent: that is, what is going to happen is dependent on what has
already happened.

Simplifying by assuming stability of the elements and average behaviour between them

Boulton et al. argue that these evolutionary complex models are difficult to build and show many possible futures, and for these reasons, decision makers facing policy choices are more likely to commission models which have more simplifications, but which also give greater predictability. The simplifications they have in mind are dropping assumptions about the possibility of changes in the elements and making the model probabilistic. This means that no new variables emerge, and thus existing ones don't disappear either. With a mathematical technique known as the Master Equation developed by Prigogine and colleagues (Allen, 1988), the model can demonstrate not just one most likely outcome but takes into account 'all possible sequences of events according to their relative probability' (2015: 86). The authors point out that this reverses the idea that the distribution is calculated from a fixed average, to one where it is calculated from the distribution of its actual behaviour at a particular point in time. The added detail of the Master Equation enables the system to alternate between different possible outcomes, rather than just one. Where the system ends up depends on what has happened in detail before the point of change, i.e., it is path-dependent, dependent on its history. The advantage of using the Master Equation, according to Boulton et al., is that it keeps structural stability but nonetheless shows the possibility of the system moving spontaneously between more than one equilibrium point. It does so because of the non-average micro-behaviour included in the Master Equation.

Simplifying by assuming structural stability

There are further simplifications to be made to models to make them more manageable, but at the same time make them less rich in terms of representing the 'blooming, buzzing confusion' of the world. So, according to Boulton et al., the next simplification is to assume a stationary state for the model, where the macroscopic variables basically stay the same. The model tends towards an equilibrium state and instead what comes into focus is the dynamic between the individual elements. Such assumptions make it possible to model power laws, tipping point events which can be statistically calculated and can demonstrate the point at which the system can reach a critical point and tip into another state. The simplest example is the point at which piling up individual grains of sand provokes an avalanche. Similar claims have been taken up in the field of evolutionary biology to describe the 'punctuated equilibrium' theory of evolution, which assumes long periods of stability punctuated by short periods of radical activity. Boulton et al. note that the idea of power law distributions, that sizes of cities, or companies or frequency of earthquakes are thought to follow a particular inverse square law where the sequence of different-sized cities is calculable, for example, have proved very powerful for some people as exemplifying complexity theory. But the authors go on to question whether power law principles really do apply in real world contexts. They point to the limitations of power law principles, not least because the mathematics treats each city or company as though it were discrete and independent of each other, and also independent from the wider environment in which it sits. This may be true of grains of sands but is less likely to be so of populated cities situated in a dynamic environment.

Simplifying by assuming the most probable events

Boulton et al. describe a variation on the simplification of stationarity in complexity models, which is to drop the Master Equation which calculates all possible states according to their probability, to modelling the most likely state of the variables. These are known as dynamical systems and can demonstrate the impact of different interventions by running the model several times with different parameters and initial conditions. Meteorological models are good examples of dynamical systems which take a handful of interdependent variables such as wind speed, pressure, temperature and humidity at different points over time to produce what is known as a strange attractor, the technical term for a mathematically chaotic pattern. In a mathematically chaotic pattern, short-term forecasts are possible, but the further into the future the model is run using current data the more likely small differences will have escalated into qualitative changes in the overall pattern. This is popularly known as the butterfly effect, where a butterfly flapping its wins in Sao Paulo, thus producing minute changes to air pressure, is said to cause a storm over Miami. To chart such a development, however, would require measuring all perturbations with infinite precision, since in non-linear systems, even a small change can escalate into a big change over time. Although weather forecasting has improved dramatically in the last 20 years, the UK Meteorological Office no longer predicts 'ice cream summers' from the spring.

Systems dynamic models are helpful to decision makers because they can compare different policy interventions by varying the initial starting conditions, but Boulton et al. also discuss their limitations. There are only a handful of variables which can be experimented with, which is a long way away from real-world problems which may have multiple interlocking variables, and many which are not at all obvious. Moreover, they assume average categories and average interactions between categories.

Advantages and disadvantages of drawing on complexity models

Boulton et al. show how complexity modelling is a sophisticated science involving complicated mathematical calculations which nonetheless and inevitably carry with them simplifying assumptions about the world. The attraction of these complexity models, which have increased in intricacy coterminous with the development of computing, is that they are able to simulate dynamic processes in nature and in social life in a more realistic way than has been previously possible. Modelling has really come into its own in the last year with competing models of the pandemic, for example. In their evolutionary agent-based form, they produce qualitative changes over time with unpredictable outcomes, which are unpredictable even to the programmers of the model. In other forms, using further simplifications, they are helpful to policymakers and politicians to think through the implications of following one approach rather than another, demonstrating that slight changes to variables/inputs might lead to very significant changes over time. They demonstrate that the more simplifications are made, the easier the models are to handle and to use for making broad predictions about what might or might not work for, say, policy interventions or the spread of infection during the pandemic, but the less they capture about the messiness of lived reality. In non-linear models, small variations in detail can make big variations to the trajectory of the model over time, so averaging is not an inconsequential detail.

I am using the word 'realistic' in an everyday sense here, rather than suggesting any philosophical underpinning. This is just to convey the idea that our felt sense of making our way through life is that things don't work out exactly as we would expect them to because of chance, because our plans intersect with other people's plans, because we change our minds and because we chose to accept or refuse one opportunity rather than another. Neither examples in nature nor our participation in social life leaves us in much doubt that life is complex and unpredictable, and the last year has provided a very stark example of that. The complexity models based on non-linear formulae, where there is no longer proportionality between cause and effect, help provide some insight into how the unexpected can happen, and further data to think about in terms of policy formulations. But although they might approximate more closely to life as we experience it, they are still models, algorithm-based simulations based on computers, and there is a limit to what they can tell us about real life, just as there is with any modelling approach.

It may be that organizational life, with its vast underpinning of consultancy, executive education and business school research, is more prone to following fads and the next 'best thing' than many other areas of social life, but the complexity sciences do lend themselves to widespread and sometimes naïve adoption in the discourse. This arises for a number of different reasons.

First, management is a practical, not to say instrumental, discipline more inclined of late to adopt step-models or recipes for success. We discussed previously why recommendations for following 'simple-rules,' particularly dominant in the boids simulation, might have particular appeal in an organizational environment. Similarly, the most ubiquitous model for taking up the complexity sciences is a two-by-two grid that creates four categories to place social reality in (Glouberman and Zimmerman, 2002): simple, complicated, complex and chaotic. A variety of consultancy forms have taken up this formulation and claimed it as their own. These Cartesian co-ordinates, like the Ansoff and Boston Consulting Group matrices, are widely used in business schools and perhaps for that reason are recognizable to managers. Maybe there is something soothing about the familiarity of these grids, that social reality can be subdivided into four, and that managers can choose which segment the think they are in. It is important to reflect upon what makes complexity complex, what are its qualities and characteristics, but this particular matrix puts the manager back in control of deciding what kind of social reality they face. Another way of putting it is that managers can decide that in particular circumstances, complexity is not at issue. In this book, I take a very different – and I would argue more radical – view that human interaction is always complex.

Second, it may be the fact that because the complexity models are run on computers and algorithmically driven lends them special appeal to those who aspire to management being a scientific discipline. There may be a post-platonic yearning that models based in mathematics express some kind of truth: they can at the very least be very helpful depending on how we think about and use them. In Chapter 1, I drew attention to the prevalence of mathematical modelling which has dominated discussion of and the response to the pandemic in the United Kingdom. The current UK government turned to algorithms to make assessments of end-of-school exams for 18-year-olds, with disastrous results, and now intend to do the same thing with planning regulations. As another example, there are a number of doctors who offer service at my local General Practice surgery: with some, when I describe my symptoms, they consult a checklist and tell me that my 'score' means that I am on the threshold of some medical intervention or other, such as being prescribed statins for cholesterol.[3] Others may know about the guidelines but hold them lightly and respond to me using their own practical judgement about what they know about me in relation to all the other patients they have seen with my condition. To be clear, contemporary life would be impossible without models and algorithms, which involve reducing sometimes complex processes to rules. They operate to good effect in our mobile phones, our computers, inform our choices when shopping online and, as Boulton et al. demonstrate, help inform policy decisions. At the same time, there is growing resistance to the proceduralization of professional life (see, for example, the conversation with anthropologist and social scientist James C Scott: Gabay, 2016) and a big debate about whether judgement, and even ethical choices, can be outsourced to computers, or robots used in care, for example (Stahl and Coeckelbergh, 2016). Trust in mathematics, in algorithms, may arise from admiration and may also arise from the feeling that social life is just too complex and we need to outsource our difficulties. We humans are fallible, but we haven't given up on the dream that we can come up with the perfect answer.

Third, the variety of models I explained briefly earlier with Boulton et al.'s help produce a thicket of exotic terms like strange attractors, edge of chaos and tipping points which lend themselves to the fad-driven world of management consultancy. There is wide recognition that the leadership and management discourse turns on the continuous invention of new ideas and concepts of shaky provenance (Collins, 2013), which supports a whole ecology of business schools and consultancy practices. It might be intriguing to use the consultancy services of a consultant who promised to keep your organization 'at the edge of chaos,' although this has no meaning in practical terms.

So far, I have tried to explain the complexity sciences, the assumptions which inform the models, their limitations and the selective ways in which they might be adduced in the management literature. It behoves me, then, to say how I am going to draw on them, and to do so, I am going to take a detour via Edgar Morin.

Taking the insights further

The French philosopher Edgar Morin (2005) gives the complexity sciences credit for posing a profound challenge to the assumptions of prediction and control in the natural sciences. He notes that there were a number of breaches to narrow scientistic thinking in the 19th and 20th centuries, beginning with the development of the second law of thermodynamics that posits that systems degrade over time; entropy. Up to that point, he argues, the laws of physics were thought to be reversible in time. Next came quantum theory, and the idea that the researcher can influence the outcome of the experiment, which problematized the idea of separating the knower from the known, which is taken as a core principle of the scientific method. A much bigger breach in thinking occurred when scientists in the Santa Fe Institute from 1984 onwards developed dynamical systems, which produced alternative ways of modelling natural phenomena. As we have seen, these did not depend upon theories of equilibrium and also undermined the central notion of determinism: novelty emerged in the programmes which went beyond the simple rules according to which they were operating. However, in doing so, he argues the Santa Fe models only challenged the classical natural science paradigm so far, because the scientists developing complexity models made very few knowledge claims about the significance of what they were doing. As an example, an eminent complexity scientist like Murray Gell-Mann (1994) interpreted the complexity models from within the orthodoxy of their natural science discipline. Gell-Mann understands novelty as a series of 'frozen accidents' which occur in an otherwise predictable and rule-bound environment.

Morin encourages us to go beyond what he understands as a still restricted view of what the complexity sciences might mean for our understanding of the world. Rather, he thought that we need a general theory of complexity, one which enables us to raise more profound questions about how we come to know the world in which we participate:

> Restricted complexity made possible important advances in formalization, in the possibilities of modelling, which themselves favor interdisciplinary potentialities. But one still remains within the epistemology of classical science. When one searches for the "laws of complexity", one still attaches complexity as a kind of wagon behind the truth locomotive, that which produces laws. A hybrid was formed between the principles of traditional science and the advances towards its hereafter. Actually, one avoids the fundamental problem of complexity which is epistemological, cognitive, paradigmatic. To some extent, one recognizes complexity, but by decomplexifying it. In this

way, the breach is opened, then one tries to clog it: the paradigm of classical science remains, only fissured.

2005: 6

Morin puts forward the idea that although the sciences of complexity made possible more dynamical models of what we observe in nature, nonetheless they made no dent on the claim that nature's laws, as complex as they are, could be discoverable.

Morin's idea of general complexity, on the other hand, is to take the ideas further, as we try to do in this book, and think about their philosophical and social relevance. This means opening up further questions about how we can come to know the world we participate in (epistemology) and our theories about what we take reality to be (ontology). A complex system modelled on a computer might depend on simple, deterministic rules to function, but that doesn't mean that we can draw the same conclusions about nature and our sociality.

The principle of disjunction, of separation (between objects, between disciplines, between notions, between subject and object of knowledge), should be substituted by a principle that maintains the distinction, but that tries to establish the relation.

ibid.: 7

Notice that he frames the challenge as a paradox, that we should maintain the principle of separation between disciplines at the same time as trying to identify the relation between them, which is one of the arguments that we try to establish here. Morin makes a strong claim that a general idea of complexity, one that takes science as well as philosophy and the humanities seriously, bringing subject and object, separation and unity and knower and the known, into paradoxical relation.

WHAT IS MEANT BY 'SCIENTISM' OR A RESTRICTED VIEW OF SCIENCE IN MORIN'S TERMS?

The eminent evolutionary biologist and New Atheist Richard Dawkins promoted his new book, *Science in the Soul: Selected Writings of a Passionate Rationalist*, on BBC radio. He discussed the role of scientific method and evidence, particularly in relation to the Brexit vote. He began by saying that nothing as important as staying in, or leaving the EU should hinge on a binary yes/no vote. But he then went on to extol the virtues of scientific method, which in his radio interview, and in the introduction to the book, he argues should be the preeminent method for making decisions about the world, including Brexit. We should seek out the evidence, public and private, and make our decision according to that. For Dawkins, scientific method is predicated on removing prejudice and gut feeling, indeed all feelings, from rational decision-making and is as relevant to making political decision-making as it is to discovering more about the natural world. The best example of a method which does this is the double-blind randomized control trial, the gold standard of medical research. He declared that he didn't want his politicians to be emotional, but rather he wanted them to make the best possible decision, rationally, and on the basis of the best possible evidence.

Further, in the introductory chapter to his book, he praises scientific method and compares philosophy unfavourably with chemistry. It might be the case, he says, that a philosophy department will advertise for a professor of continental philosophy, but can you imagine a chemistry department advertising for a professor of continental chemistry? Science is everywhere the same, in Delhi or in London. In setting out his argument like this, Dawkins reveals himself to believe in a unified theory of science. Scientific method is equally applicable in social and natural settings: all biology is reducible to chemistry, and all chemistry to physics. He believes that comparing chemistry and philosophy, one way of theorizing against many ways of theorizing, casts philosophy in an unfavourable light, and in so doing, he makes an ideological claim on his readers.

But here I want to examine Dawkins' claim in the light of the topic in which he introduced it – the Brexit vote, because this is an area of extreme complexity which does not lend itself to simple answers or simple methods of inquiry. In what way would it make sense to say that our approach to the decision to leave or to stay in the EU could be made scientifically, rationally, without emotion and according to the best evidence? This is particularly the case when the very reason we had the vote in the first place was driven by value and emotion-laden questions of identity, and what we take to be moral ways of organizing our society, as well as for reasons of political strategy and competitive advantage. What kinds of evidence are available in such a political and contested context, where everything is in flux? And if the answer to these questions is no, it is not possible to decide using the method Dawkins recommends, or only a partial yes, what other ways are available to us to make up our minds, given that not voting would also have had consequences? Not to act rationally does not imply acting irrationally, and nor is the only response to emotion-laden questions to try to expunge emotion altogether. Rather than assuming that emotion is always unhelpful, it might be more productive to think systematically about what all the emotion might be about.

I think this is an important example given that, on a smaller scale, this is the kind of dilemma which faces managers in organizations on a daily basis, particularly in human services, where sometimes none of the options are good ones, the evidence is partial or non-existent, every aspect of the problem is contested, but a decision is needed anyway. Particularly in the public sector where workers are often asked to do more with less, or are facing austerity budgets, it would be hard to produce evidence in Dawkins' use of the word, to know what to do next. This is not to imply that evidence, as much as it exists, should not inform policy, but that it is necessary but insufficient.

In terms of the Brexit vote, no country has ever left the EU before: there are no prior examples to assess. And if there had been examples, would the specific circumstances of the United Kingdom and its history make them irrelevant? Second, there are an infinite number of variables, political, social and economic, which make it impossible to isolate any single process and argue that if X then Y. A number of economic institutions model possible outcomes, but all are limited and based on assumptions which need further exploration; they are likely to be based on extrapolations of what we currently know. There are too many variables to build into a predictive model of what is likely to happen in such a complex situation. And with such a wealth of possibilities, and so much data to choose from, it is difficult to develop a neutral model which is free of ideological assumptions.

In situations, where we are trying to make up our minds about something, both complex and unknown, where the evidence, such as it is, is partial, and to present it involves making choices which inevitably reveal value positions, how might we proceed?

Taking a pragmatic perspective on a situation like the Brexit vote assumes that there is no value-neutral position, no God's eye view, but rather that every position in a politically contested situation is a value position. What is important, then, is not to claim objectivity but to try and make as many of one's value positions and assumptions clear. In terms of method, sometimes it is only possible to do this in relation to other people's value positions and through inquiry. In other words, by asking questions of one's 'opponents,' not as a way of defeating their argument, but rather making it clearer both to you and to them, it might be possible to develop a deeper understanding of claims and clarify one's own position in relation to the arguments made. The movement is dialectical: making your position clearer to you helps me make my position clearer to me. This would also involve investigating each other's evidential claims as to whether, say, immigration does or does not undercut wages, as far as the data can support this investigation.

Rather than denying emotions as being helpful in this situation, it might be interesting instead to consider my own emotional response to the claims being made about what it means to be British, to 'take back control,' to be independent and to evaluate whether I experience resonance or not. To what degree do I identify with the 'we' identity which is being evoked? In other words, my emotional response is further 'data' to consider in knowing how to vote for what I consider to be best for 'us.' This is not necessarily an isolated activity but could be a further theme to explore with my own particular thought collective or community of inquiry.

Dawkins argues that there is only one scientific method based on rationality, objectivity and squeezing out emotions, and that this method helps us in all situations, even the Brexit vote. We might think of this as taking a restricted view of science in the way that Morin means it. This is what he means by 'scientism.' In contrast, I have made a case for dialectical engagement, historical and sociological investigation, judgements of character and taking emotions seriously, both mine and other people's. A pragmatic approach to complex decision-making involves systematic thinking using whatever thinking tools might be useful in the circumstances. There is no one best way. In other words, events like the Brexit vote, or every day complex situations faced by managers in organizations, require a variety of methods to know how to go on. There is no position which offers a privileged perspective on the messy situation I find myself in with others, 'objective' or other. Instead, the best that can be achieved is a reflexive engagement with what we think we are doing and who we think we are becoming, and a greater wisdom about and insight into what we feel about who we are becoming.

Summary of the argument and key implications for managers

In this chapter, I have tried to explore what it means to draw on the complexity sciences critically. Understanding them in depth and how they operate does demand some application and helps determine what kinds of assumptions are adopted in the models and their limitations. Boulton et al. (2015) provide a thorough guide for those who are interested in the mathematics and insights into what the different manifestations of modelling are helpful for. To sum up, I take further guidance from Paul Cilliers (1998: 3–5), an early pioneer of exploring the complexity sciences and their relevance to organizational life, who produced a more concise explanation of the characteristics of complex systems. This description collapses a number of distinctions made patiently by Boulton et al., but I think is helpful as a simple overview of why we might be interested in agent-based complexity when it comes to thinking about what goes on between us. However, I am going to take a major departure from two of the characteristics to make some broader claims about social life.

To return to Cilliers' helpful simplification:

a. Complex systems comprise large numbers of interacting elements.
b. The interactions are dynamic and rich, or a larger number of sparsely connected elements can replace fewer richly connected ones.
c. The interactions are non-linear so that small causes can have large results and vice versa.
d. The interactions are mostly short range, although they can have influence in a few short steps to other more distant elements.
e. The effect of an activity can loop back on itself in amplifying or dampening ways.
f. Complex systems are open to the environment.
g. Complex systems are far from equilibrium: equilibrium is equivalent to death.

h.   Complex systems have a history which is integral to understanding what is happening now.
i.   Each element only responds to information available locally and has no insight into the patterning of the whole population of elements.

Social life, like the description of complex systems itemized by Cilliers, also has large numbers of interacting 'elements'; we call them people. And all the people have different life histories. Their interactions can be dynamic and rich and are mostly local, but they can influence others more weakly by other media. As we will explore later in this book, their interactions are non-linear where a minor interaction can have a large effect and vice versa, and patterns of behaviour can mutually amplify or dampen down.[4] The way we behave together, our culture, has a history which partly informs who we are and who we are becoming but doesn't necessarily determine it.

So to take up insights from the complexity sciences to help leaders, managers and consultants make sense of their organizations requires two major moves away from the bare characteristics of CAS as they stand, unless we are going to undertake modelling. The first move is to make the social sciences much more central to our interpretation of complex situations as a number of scholars have done including, and in particular, my colleagues (Stacey et al., 2000; Stacey, 2012). As I mentioned, models of pandemics, brains and even workflows can be immensely helpful in making sense of what's going on and modelling the possible effects of different interventions. But instead, in this book, encouraged by Edgar Morin and guided by my colleagues at the University of Hertfordshire, we pay attention to rich interaction between unique human beings using all the resources at our disposal: insights from the complexity sciences along with sociology, philosophy, social psychology and anthropology, even group analytic theory to try and make sense of the complexity of organizational life. One way of thinking about this is that we are using the complexity sciences by analogy (Stacey, 2012), where we take the known properties of one domain and apply them to an unknown domain. We hold the natural and social sciences together as a way of bringing the full armoury of thinking to bear on the difficulties we encounter of being together. Or, to borrow from Karen Barad (2007: 88) the theoretical physicist, who claims that arguing by analogy is too weak a way of writing about the entanglement of the knower and the known, we argue by diffraction. What I think she means by this is something similar to Morin's proposal, that we find additional ways of accounting for the way the world becomes with our participation in it. This involves bringing together an in-depth knowledge of the particular scientific practice we draw from, as well as describing the concrete contextual situation we are interested in, and what people are doing there. This means bringing together the world we are interested in, and what we do as participants in the world making and interpreting it.

The second move is to make two departures from Cilliers' list at points (f) and (i), partly in the spirit of the earlier reflection on bringing disciplines together through a general understanding of complexity, or a refracted one. I am not going to assume, as at (f) in Cilliers' list, that what human beings do together in any way forms a system, no matter how open the boundary. This is a departure that Stacey in particular has been keen to emphasize. This is not to say that sometimes it is helpful to frame an area of inquiry by focusing on an organization, for example, or a specific field of activity. In this sense, I agree with the sociologist Norbert Elias when he argued that parts and whole thinking is an idea imported from biology which doesn't apply to thinking about human beings. He holds that 'using the term whole, or wholeness, is simply using a mystery to solve a mystery' (Elias, 1978: 73). Nor am I assuming in quite the limiting way that Cilliers does, that the elements of the system have no insight into the whole population of elements, as he does at (i). I referred to this earlier as the structure/agency debate, where I explained that I am taking a paradoxical position. That is, in human terms, we are born into a world where there is already a play going on. We learn the language, we imbibe the culture and we take up or reject the roles we are invited to assume. In that sense, then, we do have insight into what's going on in the whole pattern, although it is not complete. But I assume it to be a paradox: we are formed by the social pattern into which we are born but we form it both at the same time.

The paradoxical position I am sketching out, and which is inherent to the perspective of complex responsive processes, is that individuals form social structures, but social structures form individuals, sometimes referred to as interactionism or elisionism (Sawyer, 2005). This position needs further exploration. I do this in the next chapter on complex action. But in brief, the position claims that it is neither one pole, nor the other, but both at the same time. The perspective is perhaps summed up best by Norbert Elias, a sociologist whose thinking has informed the perspective I have taken, who titled one of his works *The Society of Individuals* (2001). In the opening chapter of this volume, which is given the same title as the book, Elias argues against both poles of the argument, individualism vs structuralism, and claims that it has to be both at the same time: the 'I' and the 'we' are two sides of the same coin. The paradoxical position is not meant in any glib way (Mowles, 2015): in fact, the idea of a paradox is quite difficult to get your head around, since the idea of paradoxa means against common sense. But many of the authors I draw on in this book use paradoxes extensively to describe some of the deep contradictions of human existence that we are able to take ourselves as objects to ourselves, for example, that our individuality is made manifest by our membership of different groups (Elias, 2000: 543)[5] or that we are able to detach from our involvement, we can reflect and become more reflexive, to be involved more intensely.

For managers reading this chapter and reflecting on the implications of the complexity sciences for their ways of managing, all is not lost. I am not suggesting that there is no need for managers. I hope I have merely tugged away at and partially unravelled some of the more obvious taken-for-granted assumptions about management. These are that managers can predict and control, that management can be a scientific discipline understood narrowly as a natural science like physics and that if managers do take complexity seriously, they can choose when it applies and when it doesn't and that there is some neutral, controlling position for them to adopt. Thinking through the implications of the complexity sciences worries away about what we know, how we can know it and what we take our social reality to be. I hope to address all of these questions as the book unfolds.

Notes

1 This will be very obvious to anyone who has tried to run this boids simulation as an exercise in a group of people in a workshop setting. The exercise breaks down very quickly, even if people are trying to co-operate (which inevitably, some of them aren't), because everyone interprets the rules differently. This tells us a lot about human agency, meaning-making and imagination, phenomena which will preoccupy us in this book.
2 Whether chance mutation is or isn't required for evolution to take place is still contested among evolutionary biologists according to complexity scientist Melanie Mitchell (2009). She classifies evolutionary biologists into three schools: adaptionists who believe chance mutation is primary; historicists, who give primacy to historical accident; and structuralists, such as Stuart Kauffman, who give primacy to the evolutionary potential of self-organization.
3 Heart surgeon Atul Gawande (2011) wrote an influential book about the importance of checklists for medical interventions, which is contested by some medical practitioners, who consider it necessary but insufficient, or who claim that it proceduralizes practical judgement.
4 This is an effect that the sociologist Anthony Giddens (1993) referred to as the 'double hermeneutic,' where descriptions of social behaviour are then adopted by people and start further to shape social behaviour.
5 Elias (2000: 543):

> The coexistence of people, the intertwining of their intentions and plans, the bonds they place on each other, all these far from destroying individuality, provide the medium in which it can develop. They set the individual limits, but at the same time give him greater or lesser scope.

References

Allen, P.M. (1988) Dynamic models of evolving systems, *Systems Dynamics Review*, 4(1–2):109–130.

Allen, P. (1997) *Cities and Regions as Self-Organizing Systems: Models of Complexity*, London and New York, NY, Routledge Gordon and Breach Science Publishers.

Barad, K. (2007) *Meeting the Universe Half Way: Quantum Physics and the Entanglement of Matter and Meaning*, London and Durham, Duke University Press.

Boulton, J., Allen, P. and Bowman, C. (2015) *Embracing Complexity: Strategic Perspectives for an Age of Turbulence*, Oxford: Oxford University Press.

Burns, B. (2004) Kurt Lewin and the planned approach to change: a re-appraisal, *Journal of Management Studies*, 41(6):977–1002.

Cilliers, P. (1998) *Complexity and Postmodernism*, London: Routledge.

Collins, D. (2013) *Management Fads and Buzzwords: Critical-Practical Perspectives*, London: Routledge.

Elias, N. (1978) *What Is Sociology*, London: Hutchinson and Co.

Elias, N. (2000) *The Civilising Process: Sociogenetic and Psychogenetic Investigations*, Oxford: Blackwell.

Elias, N. (2001) *The Society of Individuals*, London: Continuum Books.

Gabay, C. (2016) Sisyphus on the mountain: a conversation with Professor James C. Scott, *Development and Change*, 47(4):861–875.

Gawande, A. (2011) *The Checklist Manifesto: How to Get Things Right*, New York, NY: Profile Books.

Gell-Mann, M. (1994) *The Quark and the Jaguar*, New York, NY: The Freeman Press.

Giddens, A. (1993) *New Rules of Sociological Method: A Positive Critique of Interpretative Sociologies*, Cambridge: Polity Press.

Glouberman, S. and Zimmerman, B. (2002) Complicated and complex systems: what would successful reform of Medicare look like? Discussion Paper No. 8: Commission on the Future of Health Care in Canada, Plexus Institute. URL: www.plexusinstitute.org/resource/collection/6528ED29-9907-4BC7-8D00-8DC907679FED/ComplicatedAndComplexSystems-ZimmermanReport_Medicare_reform.pdf.

James, W. (1890/2007) *Principles of Psychology*, Vol. 1, New York, NY: Cosimo Classics.

Lewin, K. (1947) Frontiers in group dynamics. In: Cartwright, D. (ed.), *Field Theory in Social Science*, London: Social Science Paperbacks, pp. 1–29.

Mitchell, M. (2009) *Complexity: A Guided Tour*, Oxford: Oxford University Press.

Morieux, Y. and Tollman, P. (2014) *Six Simple Rules: How to Manage Complexity without Getting Complicated*, Cambridge: Harvard Business Review Press.

Morin, E. (2005) Restricted complexity, general complexity. In: *Presented at the Colloquium "Intelligence de la complexite: "epistemologie et pragmatique", Cerisy-La-Salle, France, June 26th, 2005"*. Translated from French by Carlos Gershenson.

Mowles, C. (2015) *Managing in Uncertainty: Complexity and the Paradoxes of Every Day Organisational Life*, London: Routledge.

Ray, T. S. (1992), 'An approach to the synthesis of life', In: Langton, G. C., Taylor, C., Doyne Farmer, J. and Rasmussen, S. (eds.), *Artificial Life II*, Santa Fé Institute, Studies in the Sciences of Complexity, vol. 10, Reading, MA: Addison-Wesley.

Reed, J., Howe, C., Doyle, C. and Bell, D. (2018) Simple rules for evidence translation in complex systems: a qualitative study, *BMC Medicine*, 16:92. https://doi.org/10.1186/s12916-018-1076-9.

Reynolds, C.W. (1987) Flocks, herds and schools: a distributed behavioral model, *ACM SIGGRAPH Computer Graphics*, 21(4):25–34.

Sawyer, R.K. (2005) *Social Emergence: Societies as Complex Systems*, Cambridge: Cambridge University Press.

Stacey, R. (2012) *Tools and Techniques of Leadership and Management*, London: Routledge.

Stacey, R., Griffin, D. and Shaw, P. (2000) *Complexity and Management: Fad or Radical Challenge to Systems Thinking*, London: Routledge.

Stahl, B. and Coeckelbergh, M. (2016) Ethics of healthcare robotics: towards responsible research and innovation, *Robotics and Autonomous Systems*, 86:152–161.

Taylor, C. (1999) To follow a rule. In: Shusterman, R. (ed.), *Bourdieu: A Critical Reader*, Oxford: Blackwell, pp. 29–44.

3

COMPLEX ACTION

The uncertain outcomes of individuals negotiating in groups

The previous chapter was a discussion of the complexity sciences, how they are useful for thinking differently about stability and change in organizations but may be at the same time misleading if we think they are directly applicable in an instrumental way. Computer-based models are only models after all, and all models are simplifications, no matter how helpful they are in supporting us to think differently. In this chapter I take Morin's invitation seriously, and the perspective of complex responsive processes of relating, to take a general view of complexity, that is, to bring in the social sciences to help us reflect broadly on why human interaction always has unpredictable consequences.

We live in highly individualized times where we are encouraged to think of ourselves as separate and closed off from others. There has been a dramatic falling away of membership of and identification with collectivities such as trades unions, community groups and voluntary associations in the last 30 years or so. The hollowing out of collective identification is a phenomenon remarked upon by a wide variety of sociologists beginning with Robert Putnam (2000) in his book *Bowling Alone*, a major study of the waning of American community participation. Perhaps it is more accurate to say there has been a hollowing out of particular forms of collective identification which is gradually being replaced with other forms: for example, we are said to live in an age of 'identity politics' where people identify according to characteristics of the self, such as race, ethnicity, sexual orientation or gender. Sometimes people try to take account of a whole variety of identifications, which is known as intersectionality. This latter phenomenon has led to collective action, in the short and longer term but has been much more obvious in spontaneous manifestations of collective identification such as Black Lives Matter protests.

There are a number of reasons for individualization, but one significant factor is our increased sense of ourselves as discrete individuals closed off from other selves, a trend which has been accelerating since the Enlightenment and informs

DOI: 10.4324/9781003002840-3

our identities and our theories about the world (Taylor, 1989; Elias, 2000). This emphasis on individualism, not to say competitive individualism, has become more significant in the last 30 years or so commensurate with political and economic policies which privilege this point of view. Nonetheless, both Taylor and Elias explain how this assumption that we are separated off from each other, which is a felt identification, is a relatively recent development in the course of human history. Unsurprisingly, the taken-for-granted emphasis on individuals and individualism informs the theories we find most prevalent in understanding stability and change in organizations, and the role that we have in participating in them.

There are two dominant ways of understanding how change comes about in organizations in orthodox management discourse, which have different interpretations of this individualistic perspective, and a third way which is a substantial but minority interest and which underpins the principle assumptions in this book.[1] The first two privilege the role of the individual, and the third places much greater emphasis on the indivisibility of the individual and the group maintaining that there is no self without the existence of other selves. These radically different premises contribute to completely different perspectives on understanding stability and change.

Magico-mystical thinking

The first theory prioritizes the role of heroic and charismatic individuals who bring a magical essence to organizations and help galvanize things and turn them around. Airport bookshelves are full of books like this, either documenting the heroics of big personalities who have led big American corporations, or encouraging managers and leaders to search for the hero inside themselves. Pragmatist philosopher John Dewey and his intellectual collaborator Arthur Bentley referred to this as the theory of self-action, which they thought of as 'a pre-scientific presentation in terms of presumptively independent "actors", "souls", "minds", "powers" or "forces" taken as activating events' (Dewey and Bentley, 1945: 246). In other words, there is something almost magical which happens, especially when particular people are involved in an organization which doesn't require any further explanation. There is still something very seductive about charisma, even if it's negative charisma, as we can see from the pattern of electing demagogues and authoritarians across the world.

Equally, a modern-day equivalent of Dewey and Bentley's idea of self-action might be the mobilizing of neuroscience by organizational scholars to claim that certain ways of behaving in organizations are 'hard-wired' into us. The brain and its functioning become the only explanation we need to grasp, a root cause of what is going on. I am not suggesting that the way our brains are wired, individually or collectively, has nothing to tell us about why things happen the way they do, but it is an insufficient explanation on its own (Smith, 2019). As another trend, the contemporary encouragement for individuals to be positive emerging from the appreciative inquiry (AI) (Cooperrider and Srivastva, 1987) and the positive psychology industry (Seligman and Csikszentmihalyi, 2000) could be considered manifestation of theories of self-action in organizations where special powers are ascribed to individuals and their positive state of mind. As a cancer survivor who was always enjoined to be positive as a way of defeating her illness, the journalist scholar Barbara Ehrenreich (2010) has been a particular critic of the limitations of this way of thinking. Ironically, although it suggests that being positive can invest individuals with magical powers, it can also be experienced as a kind of tyranny. Critics of AI (Fineman, 2006) have consistently pointed out that positive and negative feelings are always interconnected and to focus primarily on the former at the expense of the latter is to demonstrate a lack of criticality.

Assumptions about our agency and how change comes about can have real-world effects on the way people are treated and the expectations which are placed on them. For example, the Department for Work and Pensions in the United Kingdom has used positive psychology techniques as a way of encouraging job seekers to find work. Here is an example of the kinds of encouragements one unemployed attendee was given on an unemployment training programme, which she recorded in a diary, as told to researchers Friedli and Stearn (2015):

- Go hard, or go home.
- My only limitations are the ones I set for myself.
- Failure is the path of least persistence.
- Success is getting up one more time than you fall down.
- It's always too soon to quit.
- Nobody ever drowned in sweat.
- The sin isn't falling down but staying down.
- No one can make you feel inferior without your consent.

These edifying quotations are supposed to stir the unemployed person into finding work through self-belief, as though there are no structural or economic obstacles to doing so. It also locates all the responsibility for what happens with the individual. In a context where people are rewarded or sanctioned for adherence to the training programme, this attempt to instil positivity in workshop participants comes very close to what the eminent organizational scholar Edgar Schein (1999) described as 'coercive persuasion,' or a form of brainwashing.

Again, what I present here as a critique of positive psychology is not the same as saying that the way we perceive the world and how we feel about ourselves has no implication for how we participate in it. I merely point out that constant inquiry into our mental states, and the injunction to see all things as positive, may be unrealistic and perhaps less productive than inquiring into what's going on for others and society more generally. The 'inquiry' part of AI is much more obvious to me than is the 'appreciative' part. Insisting that employees remain positive and upbeat may also have ethical implications in organizational life, as Edgar Schein suggests. There are also studies which suggest that a negative emotional reaction to particular circumstances, such as serious illness, is entirely appropriate and is a good predictor of psychological health and adjustment (Coifman et al., 2016). A variety of scholars have taken the contemporary phenomenon of positivity seriously to suggest that it has become a general trend formed by increased individualism, but it also amplifies individuality at the same time (Davies, 2015; Spicer and Cederström, 2015; Cabanas and Illouz, 2019). As critical scholars, they also claim that it represents a manifestation of contemporary capitalist relations where individuals and their choices are considered preeminent. I explore the effects of this preoccupation with the positive and 'well' self in the next chapter on the complex self.

Disaggregating and recombining

The second common assumption, consonant with the observation of the critical scholars mentioned in the paragraph earlier, and particularly in the literature that is widely published in academic journals, is that what happens in organizations does so as a consequence of the aggregation of discrete, autonomous individuals bumping into each other in more or less rational or utility-maximizing ways. These autonomous individuals are largely unchanged by the interaction. Dewey and Bentley described this assumption as a theory of interaction and I began to explore the consequences of this in the last chapter. A recent policy manifestation of a preoccupation with individual choice is *Nudge Theory* (Thaler and Sunnstein, 2008) which has been adopted by the UK government. This patterning of unchanged agents was also modelled by the birds/boids flocking simulation which I also discussed in the last chapter. For Dewey and Bentley, this is a Newtonian view of the world arising from an assumption of unchangeability. According to Dewey, Newton 'set up permanent substances, the particles or atoms having inherent mathematical properties as ultimate realities' (Dewey, 1929: 186). Particularly for those scholars who build models of social interaction, assuming no change to the 'agents' makes the mathematics much easier to deal with.

The pragmatic organizational scholar Barbara Simpson (2016) notes that there are various formulations of this idea of interaction in the leadership literature, where it produces thinking about fixed categories, or entities, such as leaders and followers. Agency is not just inherent in self-actors but is directed towards entities through routinized practices, or communities of practice. Simpson says: 'the common ground in all inter-actional approaches to leadership is that entities come first, and the connections or networks which animate these entities are secondary.' Meanwhile, the sociologist Emirbayer describes how the theory of interaction underpins quantitative sociology where there is an assumption that fixed entities with variable attributes interact, in causal or actual time, to create outcomes, themselves measurable as attributes of the fixed entities. Variable-oriented researchers employ a variety of quantitative methods to test their causal hypotheses, including multiple regression, factor analysis and event history approaches. Interactional thinking and methodology is very helpful in helping study phenomena but it is still a simplifying approach, perhaps necessary but insufficient for understanding social life in all its complexity.

There are many contemporary examples of this way of thinking about organizational change and the role of individuals and their aggregation. One commercial consultancy company I came across recently offers to intervene in organizations to improve organizational culture, through the 'application of neuroscience,' and by identifying eight factors which can be measured in individuals and then improved, including phenomena such as trust and openness. This company mobilizes both types of individual theories of change, the magic bullet of 'neuroscience' and the aggregating of individual choices. Notice too that the idea of trust is individual rather than relational. Their method is 'fun, fast and engaging' and involves sending three-minute motivational videos to individual employees' mobile phones. This is a classic example of the promise of 'big data,' where an organization is understood simply as an aggregation of all of the activity of discrete individuals and collecting data about individuals leads to insight about the group. The video also presents the idea that the high trust operating in one team is copiable to another, just as one would copy and paste a formula from one spreadsheet cell to another. The company supports the idea that improving the whole, the structure, means improving the discrete parts, the agents, that is to say the staff.

Transaction and transformation

The sociologist Norbert Elias (1978), as a precursor to Emirbayer, notices that what gets lost with a focus on individuals and their attributes is the centrality of relationships:

> In other words, present forms of sociological analysis make possible the separation of interrelated things into individual components – 'variables' or 'factors' – without any need to consider how such separated and isolated aspects of a comprehensive context are related to each other. At all events, the relationship appears to be an afterthought, an addition, tacked on later to intrinsically unrelated and isolated objects.
>
> *1978: 116*

It is these relationships, and the effects they have on transforming individuals and being transformed by them, which informs the third theory of organizational stability and change, which Dewey and Bentley refer to as transaction. Dewey and Bentley's concept of transaction is close to the idea of transformational teleology that Stacey et al. (2000) describe in their book on complexity (see endnote 1 in this chapter). I explore transaction/transformation later.

The first difficulty with the term transaction in an organizational context is that it calls out the distinction between transactional management and transformational leadership originally coined by Bass (1985). The transactional/transformational formulation is now a trope and a taken-for-granted assumption in a lot of discourse on leadership and it's important not to get distracted by what we might consider a simplistic dualism. This is not the way that Dewey and Bentley intended the term of course. Rather, they thought about it in contrast to the two previous theories, the first of which implies some kind of magico-mystical force, the second implies fixed entities bumping into each other in different combinations and recombinations. Recombining entities into different patterns is not the same as transformation with its focus on relationships and their transformational potential.

By transaction, I think Dewey and Bentley are trying to account for the entanglement of 'agents' which we described in the complex adaptive systems (CAS) models in Chapter 2, where the agents form the global pattern and are formed by it both at the same time, but where they are also potentially transformed in the exchange. Remember that in the evolutionary CAS models I described in Chapter 2 heterogenous agents interacting in non-average ways produce novel forms over time. Dewey and Bentley's idea of transaction involves this idea of evolutionary transformation and also includes objects in nature and time. The nexus of human, objects, context and time create an event which is also thought to have agency in Dewey's metaphysics. As Brinkmann (2013) points out in his book on Dewey, the concept of transaction tries to overcome a number of dualisms such as the knower and the known, the mental and material, the inner and the outer:

> Transaction is the procedure which observes men (sic) talking and writing, with their word behaviour and other representational activities connected with their thing-perceivings and manipulations, and which permits a full treatment, descriptive and functional, of the whole process, inclusive of all its 'contents', whether called 'inners' or 'outers', in whatever way the advancing techniques of inquiry require.
>
> *Dewey and Bentley, 1949: 123*

In inventing a neologism like 'thing-perceivings,' Dewey and Bentley are trying to model exactly what they are trying to describe, that the perceiver and the perceived, the knower and the known are inseparably linked. As Brinkmann reminds us, whatever we call reality, as far as Dewey and Bentley are concerned, it is all of a piece. There is no inside and outside, or something above, below or beyond our perception of it. It arises from our everyday dealings with each other. Of course, reality is independent of the perceiver, but without the perceiver the object is not brought into knowledge. In this sense, Dewey's view of the world is based on realism. Brinkmann notes that Dewey's theory of transaction tries to accommodate objects in the same way that Latour's (2005) actor-network theory does, and we have previously considered how Karen Barad (2007) tries to explain a similar phenomenon. Objects cause us frustration, and 'the object is that which objects' (1922: 191), that is to say, things in the world push back at us and do not just exist in our thoughts about them, which would be an idealist position. Idealism is at the root of AI and other forms of positive psychology where it is assumed that the way we think about the world makes the world. Dewey's idea about transaction also involves the important dimension of time, most helpfully developed by his friend and colleague George Herbert Mead (1932/2002). In complex theories of action, time plays a threefold role: we act in the present by interpreting the past and in anticipation of the future. This is an alternative to the contemporary preoccupation with an idealized future that seeks to escape from an embarrassing past.

Game analogies

So if it's an insufficient explanation to think that organizations change through the magic of charismatic and transformational individuals, or forces such as positivity (although we can all think of the difference a charismatic individual can make both for good and bad), and if it is more complex than assuming that fixed entities interact in recombinant ways, if they are correctly reprogrammed, how else might we construe change? Continuing with the analogy of the iterating and reiterating CAS models in Chapter 2 and turning to the social sciences, another way of thinking about the stable instability of organizational life is to use the idea of the game. This is not meant in any pejorative sense, that it's 'just' a game, but that game analogies offer us a model for thinking about the dynamic interplay of co-operation and competition between human beings, and as a way of describing activities which are never at rest. For example, sociologists Norbert Elias and Pierre Bourdieu both draw on the analogy of the game, as does the pragmatic philosopher G.H. Mead, to help us think about how we are socialized into acting and responding in social life. They write about how we contribute to the game yet are shaped by it both at the same time. As we play the game of social life with others, we learn about ourselves and them: how we think about ourselves and what we are doing is potentially transformed in the act of trying to get things done with other people. Elias in particular was concerned to work against what he termed 'process reduction' (1978: 116). That is, our language and concepts are often much more suited to talking about entities in a state of rest rather than being able to describe the world in a state of flux and change. An example that Elias gives is 'the wind is blowing' – but there is no wind without blowing. The process has been turned into an entity. Similarly, if we think about a game of cards, there is no game without the participation of each of the card players taking turns.

Perhaps it's best to start with Mead (1934) since he helps us think about how we are originally socialized through play and games, which begins when we are young children. At first, Mead argues, as children we play alone, perhaps by copying others in simple role play, being a mother or father, a doctor or a police officer. This activity is mostly imitative so that children can learn to understand the role they are adopting and call out the responses in themselves that the role calls out in others. This is 'the simplest form of being another to oneself' (1934: 151) as Mead describes it. This skill, being able to anticipate how we might act, and what is expected of us by being able to assume in ourselves the role of others, is at the heart of the socialization process.

The next step in Mead's explanation of social and psychological development is to take part in an organized game. In order for us to do that, we have to understand what everyone else in the game is doing so that we know how to act. Take hide and seek, for example. It's impossible to play that game unless you understand the different roles of the people hiding and the person seeking, as anyone who has played with young children not quite ready to make that conceptual leap can testify. Through play, and then games, Mead argues, we are able to infer our part in social life and have an insight into the parts that others play. We have a sense of what he calls the 'generalized other,' which is a general sense of the social game that everyone is playing and their roles in it. To be able to develop, this generalized sense of what is going on enables us to participate and to anticipate what others might do, and, therefore, the range of options available to us in our action. It is also a form of social control – if you like, our developing generalized sense of what the game is about, what the rules are, also conditions our responses in the game. The reader may remember that in the last chapter on complex models I took issue with Cilliers' schematic of complex systems when he argued that individual interacting elements have no insight into the pattern of the system as a whole, at least as far as it pertains to us. If we adopt Mead's perspective, we wouldn't be able to participate in social life unless we had some insight into what was going on and could broadly anticipate what others might do. This, for me, is where comparisons between complex systems and social life break down.

Continuing with Mead, the older we get, the more able we are to understand quite complex configurations of activities where we have a role, others have a different role and together we contribute to what Mead referred to as a social object (1925). By social object, he meant a particular patterning of activity, some-times involving very large numbers of people playing different roles and antici-pating the roles of others, which we recognize as a routine in social life. The routine, or pattern, is both stable and unstable because it is always produced and reproduced by particular people in a specific context. For example, a university is a social object in Mead's terms, i.e., it is not an object in nature but one which arises in a specific location involving different actors, students, teachers, administrators and researchers. Universities carry out many activities in common, may even teach very similar courses, but each university is very different with its unique history, location and personnel. Through our socialization processes, we learn how to participate in the social object we call university, or hospital or workshop, although our participation will always be unique. The social object itself will always be unique, even though it has many characteristics in common with other manifestations of that social object.

It's important to get hold of the social and relational aspect of what Mead is suggesting here (Mead knew Dewey well and was a long-term friend and colleague, so they had an intellectual project trying to understand social evolution in common) along with the other sociologists I'm about to introduce. Our participation in the game of social life is only possible because we internalize a generalized sense of what it is going on. It forms and shapes us: it makes us who we are. We are not, then, pre-shaped billiard balls colliding into each other and unaffected by the exchange. Rather, as we interact, and from the moment we are born, who we are and what we are becoming is shaped and may be radically changed by our relationships with others. This is what I think Dewey and Bentley mean by transaction, or what other scholars including Stacey et al. (2000) mean by transformation as a theory of social change. Human interaction is complex and potentially transformational because it enacts the paradoxical dynamic of forming and being formed through which we become, in Mead's words, 'organic' members of society (1934: 159). There has to be something generalized at the heart of our personality structure which we share in common with others in order for us to recognize each other, but at the same time, we are unique individuals with our own dispositions and histories. It is the paradoxical tension between the two, the individual and the group, that can cause evolution in us along with evolution in society.

The idea of the game, then, presents us with an image of something which involves multiple players, is never at rest and has rules which broadly dictate what moves are and aren't permissible. To take a step further, I am also claiming that there is also no standing outside of the game, as though somewhere on the sidelines, shouting instructions to everyone else from a God's eye view. But it is also the case that some people can influence the game better than others and have developed an enhanced capacity to predict moves in the game one or two steps ahead. But this is not the same as thinking that they are in charge of what happens, or that they will always be right about how the game is going to evolve. In social life, and over time, the rules of the game, what we might think of broadly as cultural norms, change, and will be different from context to context, and from country to country.

I point to this complex dynamic to show how no one person, or group of people, is entirely in control of the game since they have to adapt and change in response to each other and the warp and weft of their interdependencies. This is what makes it complex and unpredictable. Even if it is just a game of two players, such as the game of chess, the pattern evolves in a way which neither of the players can have previsioned. It is so much more complicated if we imagine that the game of life involves millions of interdependent people:

> Imagine the interlocking of the plans and actions, not of two, but of two thousand or two million interdependent players. The ongoing process which one encounters in this case does not take place independently of individual people whose plans and actions keep it going. Yet it has a structure and demands an explanation sui generis. It cannot be explained in terms of the 'ideas' or the 'actions' of individual people.
>
> *Elias and Dunning, 1986: 52*

Elias' theory of social development has a number of characteristics in common with that of Mead and Dewey. The first is that he doesn't break the link between what human beings are doing in their interactions and how much larger patterns in social life become visible. In other words, there is no need for an intermediary concept like a system, for example. According to Elias, human beings don't form systems, but their activities do produce dynamic regularities, tendencies to act in Mead's terms, which sometimes persist for decades, and which have real-world effects. The second similarity is that the pragmatist philosophers and Elias make the link between these dynamic patterns of action and social control, particularly in Elias's case, with self-control. For Elias, the development of societies, what he terms the civilizing process,[2] has brought about much greater interdependence between people as more and more of them are required to regulate their actions in highly differentiated ways. But at the same time, this increasingly intricate improvisation and coordination requires us to self-regulate, what Elias calls 'more or less automatic self-control, towards the subordination of short-term impulses to the command of a long-term view' (2000: 380). In other words, we learn to exercise self-discipline in anticipation of being shamed. But our improvisation with one another is in constant motion, we are invested in the outcome, and as with all games, there are 'rules' of engagement, which in the first instance we might think about as codes of politeness, turn-taking and cultural norms, which are then layered over by institutional codes and rules, and ultimately laws. For Elias, this ensemble of norms/institutions/codes, what he terms the *habitus*, shapes the 'we layer' of our personalities, how we identify with our group of groups.

According to Bourdieu, a contemporary of Elias, and one who also uses the term *habitus* and who also thinks in terms of game analogies, we develop an embodied sense of how to act. He terms this a 'feel for the game' (1990: 108), which is largely unreflective. For both Bourdieu and Elias, we can become more aware of the way we play the game, and the way we are played by the game because of our capacity for reflexivity, which we will explore in the chapter on the complex self. Equally, there is more to inquire into if we want to answer the question of what changes in our dealings with each other if we are to offer an explanation about what gets transformed for us with a transactional/transformational understanding of social change. To offer a quick insight before we get to the relevant chapters in more depth, what changes is meaning and identity: changes in organizational life involve both a change in conversation and a change in the way we understand ourselves in relation to others. We define and redefine ourselves through social activity.

This leaves us still to explain what is happening at the point of interaction with others which causes these sometimes enduring patterns in human activity.

Negotiating constraints in organizations

In Chapter 2, on the complexity sciences and in relation to the boids/birds model, I talked about the concept of self-organization, which I described as the way the individual agents negotiate the mutual constraints that they were given in their local context. In the case of the flocking model, these constraints were quite straightforward preprogrammed rules dictating speed and orientation. In a social context, we also have to negotiate constraints of a much more complex kind, so it's worth thinking about what form these take and what the medium is for negotiating them.

In the paragraphs earlier, I have referred a number of times to influencing the game of social life, or being influenced by it. I have also talked from a social perspective about our interdependencies with each other – to draw on Elias's thinking, as highly social beings, we have need of each other for nurture, for love, for recognition and for reward. Elias construes this interdependency as a power relationship, which is a function of all human relationships. One way of thinking about power through Elias' eyes is as the determinant of how mutual constraints are negotiated. It is important to understand that from Elias' point of view, power is not a thing, but a quality of a relationship, or set of relationships. An ensemble of power relationships, Elias referred to as a figuration, a word he coined to denote the fluid, interlocking activities of people engaged in competing and co-operative activities. Elias was a keen swimmer and was also interested in sport, deriving his insights about dynamic social processes from analogies with team games and then extrapolating to society more broadly:

> If groups or societies are large, one usually cannot see the figurations their individual members form with one another. Nevertheless, in these cases too people form figurations with each other – a city, a church, a political party, a state – which are no less real than the one formed by players on a football field, even though one cannot take them in at a glance.
>
> *1986: 199*

Bourdieu, too, regards power as essential for understanding the movement, or lack of movement, in social relations, although he tends to express it more in abstract terms, such as symbolic power or cultural power. While for Elias, power enables as much as constrains, for Bourdieu, power often has the quality of domination. As a post-Marxist, Bourdieu understood power in terms the accumulation of capital and was as interested in asking why patterns of domination stay the same, rich over poor, educated over uneducated, as much as why things change. Both sociologists are interested in the way power has a granular quality to determine our relationships with each other and inform our everyday dealings.

NEGOTIATING POWER RELATIONSHIPS – THE INTERWEAVING OF INTENTIONS

I was working with a group of managers and we had been discussing how a lot of managerial work is about dealing with uncertainty. Things don't work out quite how you planned, surprises come out of left field and your boss, or the organization with which you are working closely, has just decided that something else is now a priority. What you came in to do in the morning has somehow gone off course by the afternoon, but you're still responsible for your first priority. This was the link I had been making previously to the complexity sciences: I had been arguing that small changes can amplify into big differences, and social life arises in the interplay of differing intentions. But how do you know how to respond and what to pay attention to?

I suggested that we might work together with uncertainty with the group as an experiment the next morning, if they were up for it. We would meet with no agenda as such and the only task would be for the 26 of us to sit together in a room for an hour and a half and talk about how we cope with uncertainty, making links with organizational life and noticing at the same time how we were dealing with the task together as we were dealing with it. I was explicit about the fact that this was a group method developed by the Institute of Group Analysis as a way of paying attention to process from within the process itself, including how we negotiate our differences. I told them that I would participate with them, but that I wouldn't be in charge. I warned them that they might find it a bit uncomfortable and anxiety provoking, but they were a group of social work managers and no doubt they would have been in situations like this before.

They said they would like to try it.

When we started the next morning, we sat together and I briefly reminded them what we had agreed to do. Hardly had I finished speaking before one person had come up with the idea of a round of introductions (26 people, three minutes each, that's almost all the time used up already), and another suggested we make a list of themes and then prioritize and vote on them (this is in a country where there is a lot of devolved democracy and a lot of referenda). Within a minute, someone had leapt up to grab a marker pen and started writing down suggestions about what we might talk about. One way of understanding this last move was as a power gesture to claim authority.

Suddenly, there was a crisis of confidence. The themes that people suggested were quite broad and actually not very related to the theme of dealing with uncertainty that we said we would talk about. The person who wanted a round of introductions lobbied again for his idea, and meanwhile, my colleague, with whom I was co-leading the workshop got caught up in a discussion with another group member because he felt guilty about the fact that a list of participants hadn't been circulated in advance, which had contributed to the idea of the round of introductions in the first place. My co-leader was rebuked by another group member for taking up the space of the group. This wasn't what we had agreed to do.

But what had we agreed to do and what were the outcomes that we were expected to produce? People vied for influence and tried to negotiate their differences. We were in something of an impasse, with two or three different ideas about how we might proceed, and a certain jockeying for position among two or three vocal people.

People then began to look to me, one of the authority figures, to help them out. Wasn't it a bit of a waste to have me there and not have the benefit of my expertise – perhaps I could just give then another lecture? Perhaps they could abandon this activity altogether and go into small groups and talk about what I had told them yesterday.

I reminded them that we had agreed to stick with this for an hour and a half, I encouraged them not go into small groups and pointed out that we had agreed a task: to talk about, and experience, dealing with uncertainty.

The group descended into silence.

This seemed to me a more measured response to the task we had agreed to undertake, more thoughtful. We sat more or less comfortably in silence for 3 or 4 more minutes and then someone began with an observation about how interesting it had been to experience the first 20 minutes where everyone had got caught up in the rush of the moment. Instead of entering gradually into an exploration of what the task might mean, and how they might undertake it, they had fallen very quickly into routines that they were already familiar with: flip chart pen-grabbing, list-making and introducing each other mechanistically. Even the voting was something which was taken for granted as a way of resolving differences in this particular country. I guess that they would have experienced each of these activities in almost every other workshop they had attended.

For the next hour or so, group members began to engage much more skilfully with the task, talking about uncertain situations within their organizations, commenting on what they had found easy and difficult. At the same time others were able to make links to what we were doing together in the here and now. There were still some moments of crisis. Is this what they were supposed to be doing? Were they likely to achieve their outcomes? What were their outcomes anyway?

The discussion was very animated and involved almost everyone in the group. During the previous day, maybe only six or seven people had spoken. Today, all but three did. People could not help themselves but become involved in the discussion. This is something we remark upon – when things matter to us, it is hard not to get caught up in the game of organizational life.

One participant remarked upon the fact that the hour and a half has gone very quickly, although they viewed the prospect of that length of session together with others with some trepidation. Another observes that although he championed the idea of formal introductions, he was glad that we didn't proceed with it, since he felt that he got to know other people much better through free association.

A number of things occurred to me after the session which we talked through together later on. First, our existing ways of dealing with what we face in organizations don't necessarily serve us well in new situations. We are quite likely to fall back on tried and tested routines, but these may or may not be useful when the challenge is different. Second, the idea that we form intentions first and then act on them was belied in this particular experiment. Mostly, people could not help themselves pitching in, provoked as they were by what was going on around them. They discovered themselves in the act of participation, and sometimes their intervention was a surprise, even to themselves. We found out something that we already knew, that the game of organizational life is very involving. Third, in sustained acts of improvisation and negotiation, people can find their way forward if they can live with the anxiety of being together in a group and not knowing the 'best way' of proceeding. There is no 'best way,' only the way that works for this particular group at the time. Fourth, participants observed that when they were back in their organizations, they often pitched into solving problems as though it were obvious what they should do. They spent very little time sitting with the discomfort of not knowing.

This last observation led them to ponder what they might do differently as managers to create more time and space for talking without any particular end in view.

Power in the organizational literature

There is a rich literature on power written by scholars thinking about how it functions in organizations. For example, Clegg et al.'s (2006) comprehensive volume on power and organizations traces how the subject emerged from the sociology of Weber (1978) and Simmel (1964) to flourish more generally in organization studies. Broadly, a strong critical tradition in organization studies competes with what we might think of as the dominant and orthodox discourse. Where the latter tends to equate power with the establishment of legitimacy, integration and alignment, the former tends to take an interest in power in different forms of domination, much as Bourdieu does. An article reviewing more than 50 years of organizational scholarship on power (Fleming and Spicer, 2014) identifies four cross-cutting themes in the literature. They conclude that there is broad consensus that power in organizations usually operates informally, even though an enormous amount of research tends to focus on the formal exercise of power, particularly in leadership literature. From the perspective that I am trying to develop here drawing on the complexity sciences and process sociology, I make the case that negotiating power relationships is constitutive of being human and operating in groups.

A second cross-cutting theme is the link between power and the management of uncertainty. The twin poles of this certainty/uncertainty are the authors' contention that most literature assumes that organizations abhor uncertainty and power is a way of alleviating it. However, they also note the power that accrues to those organizational agents who can create uncertainty about the allocation of resources like the allocation of resources or promotion, for example, or the criteria for decision-making. For our purposes in thinking about power in the everyday organizational life, the everyday emergence of uncertainty in organizations is a good place to start looking at the fluctuation of power between people trying to negotiate how to take the next step together.

The third cross-cutting assumption the authors find in their review of the literature is that man scholars write as though power operates in the abstract and impersonally, somehow 'through' people not by people. This may be to do with the fact of the enormous influence of the French theoretician Foucault who, as Giddens (1993) observes, writes extensively about the workings of power, but in a way that leaves the concept somehow without a human face. Power becomes something abstract and disembodied. In this book, I try to take a paradoxical perspective, on the one hand acknowledging that broader social patterns, both in society and organizations, may make it seem as though power operates impersonally, but on the other cleaving to the idea that it all arises as a result of what people are doing together. The way that discrimination works might be a helpful example. It is common to talk about 'systemic racism' as though it is a property of a system and as though no one is to blame. Alternatively, employees might be sent on 'unconscious bias' training, as though discrimination is a property of an individual (and second, not fully intended). However, just as the last quotation from Elias indicates, even though large-scale patterns of discrimination may seem as though they operate impersonally, they nonetheless arise as a consequence of what human beings are doing in everyday situations.[3]

And fourth, Fleming and Spicer argue that there is consensus around the idea that power concentrates in questions of indeterminacy and agency. That is, the uncertainty that surrounds the question of the degree to which organizations will cohere, whether employees will do what they are told by managers and whether plans managers make together will result in what is intended. In doing so, the authors allude to Hannah Arendt (1958), whom I think has some interesting things to say about agency, power and indeterminacy in *The Human Condition*, which supports the argument I am trying to make here. She addresses directly why it is we remain uncertain about the outcomes of our plans and intentions, because they concern not only the interweaving of actions and intentions, but also revolve around the negotiation of power constraints. It is through everyday politics that we negotiate our differences and different power chances, an idea which we explore in a variety of different ways in this book (see Chapter 5 on the centrality of persuasion and rhetoric, for example). Politics is most evident when conditions are uncertain.

Hannah Arendt of power, politics and human plurality

Hannah Arendt was interested in this very complexity and uncertainty which we mediate through public political activity. This became a subject of interest to her following her direct experience and scholarly immersion in the opposite: totalitarianism, which is a state where the functioning of politics has broken down. She argues that human beings engage in three kinds of activity, labour, work and action. Briefly, labour is the kind of activity that we all have to undertake to maintain ourselves, keep ourselves fed and all our routine acts of everyday maintenance. Through work, we fabricate things, artefacts which endure in the world and give human life some lasting presence. But through action, we can make things happen in society, we can bring novelty into the world. It allows for the greatest of our achievements. However, we are not in control of exactly what happens when we act: 'action and speech are surrounded by and in constant contact with the web of the acts and words of other men' (1958: 188). It is because our actions intersect with the actions of others that we can have no control over what happens as a consequence (an insight similar to Elias's about the interweaving of intentions). It may also be that our actions and speech leaves nothing tangible in the world in the way that work does, even though it might be aimed at changing objective reality. Yet at the same time, our actions may ripple out indefinitely because they provoke reactions, even beyond our narrow circle of activity. Without using the term 'non-linear,' what I think Arendt is pointing to here is the possibility of the amplification of small actions into large consequences, the equivalent of the butterfly effect which we explored in Chapter 2 on the complexity sciences.

Arendt also speaks into the theme I have been developing above, the idea of our forming society but being formed by it both at the same time. In acting and speaking, we reveal ourselves to each other, and also to ourselves. She has something interesting to say about this indeterminacy of identity, that we don't have full insight into who we are, even in speaking and acting, which I will explore further in the next chapter on the complex self. But she argues that we have a narrative sense of who we are, which we develop in acting and speaking, but we cannot know what we will reveal of ourselves in advance. We also figure in the narratives of others about us, so we are not in total control of our own story. Equally, when people come together to talk about something or to get something done, we might be able to identify the person who got the activity going but will never be able to point to that person as the author of the eventual outcome. This gives extraordinary power to the storyteller. Arendt agrees with Kierkegaard's insight that life must be lived forwards but can only be understood backwards, so the person who gets to narrate 'what really happened' is in a particularly influential position.

Power is at the heart of the ability to get things done, to start something new in the world and to experience freedom. For Arendt, it always arises as a potential when people get together to do something, but it disappears the moment they disperse: it cannot be stored in anyway and is changeable, unmeasurable and contingent. In this sense, power always has a human face and reflects the fact that we are all different, have a different perspective and this needs mediating in some way. This aspect of human plurality is a key concept in Arendt's oeuvre: it's what makes us each unique and uniquely human but is also the engine of making the world anew. The effects of power can be non-linear, just like the effects of action:

> A comparatively small but well-organised group of men can rule almost indefinitely over large and populous countries, and it is not infrequent in history that small and poor countries got the better of great and rich nations.
>
> *1958: 200*

The degree of power created by a group of people coming together to start something new is not proportional to the effect they can have. It remains the most generative way of mediating our differences, our plurality. The alternative to political activity, making ourselves visible to each other and trying to persuade in the public space, in Arendt's eyes, is violence.

I would hazard a guess that most people reading this book will have experienced the use of violence in the organizations where they have worked, where there is no attempt to persuade and negotiate or when negotiation of our differences breaks down. There are a variety of ways of stifling plurality in public and the exercise of power through politics in organizations, some of them superficially benign and quite mundane. You can remove space for discussion in meetings, where managers talk all the time and the managed listen. You can invoke appreciation and positivity, or call for 'constructive feedback' where people become inhibited about whether they are being sufficiently positive or constructive before they speak; you can claim that no one has a right to criticize unless they can come up with an alternative; or you can keep stressing the organization's highly abstract values and underline how important it is for everyone to 'align' with them. At the extreme end is bullying, but each of the examples I have given in its own way is an implicit or explicit shading of the negotiation of power into violence, what Vince and Mazen (2014) have termed 'violent innocence.' In other words, the difficulty of engaging with our plurality is passed from the more powerful to the less, while at the same time there is a denial that things are plural. The representatives of an organization often try to define the limits of what is and isn't thinkable (Bourdieu, 1990: 110), but it is also the job of the employees to engage with those limits actively, and this active engagement, the exploration of difference mediated by power relationships, is what can bring about novelty. Sometimes, this difference is rehearsed first in the shadows of organizational life in the form of gossip, as James C. Scott (1990) points out. Both the more and less powerful gossip together about what they think is going on, and this is another way of maintaining or challenging the figuration of power.

To state unequivocally, it is appropriate that managers have a relationship of power over the people they manage. That's what they are paid to work with, and it is consonant with the ideas that I have been exploring in this chapter that power enables as much as it constrains. We couldn't get things done without power. However, the way that power is exercised, the way we are able or not to talk about how we collaborate, will have a big effect on the extent to which we recognize each other, and the degrees of freedom we experience at work.

Summing up for managers – why the experience of organizing always leads to unexpected outcomes

When it comes to thinking about how we organize, there are a lot of fads and fashions in management, and it would have to be said, sometimes fantasy thinking. As an instrumental discipline, that is, one which is prone to assuming that there are tools and techniques for everything, management discourse can take even something like the concept of complexity and pretend that it is manageable. This takes the form of suggesting that things are complex, but only sometimes, or at times of the manager's choosing. We are sometimes invited to embrace complexity, or even to harness it, as though complexity is something cuddly or is always good, or it can be subject to our will. It is rare for the discussion to hang on to the profound implications of the complexity sciences that human interaction is radically unpredictable over the long term, despite big data, and despite the real and impressive achievements of science, or even experiments in getting better at predicting the future.[4]

In the first two explanations I set out earlier, drawing on Dewey and Bentley, you can see this wishful thinking at work. In the first case, predictable change comes about because of the 'vision' of certain unique individuals, or their charisma or because we are all positive. No further explanation is needed if change happens in and of itself, or because of some mysterious force. To engage critically with this assumption is not the same as claiming that leaders can't make a difference or that our states of mind have no influence on the way we understand the situation we are in, or what we choose to do about it. I also don't deny that a determined group of people can get an enormous amount done, but I am arguing it takes more than believing that we can shape the world according to our will. In the second theory of interaction, you can see rational calculability at work. Interaction focuses on individuals and understands change to come about through the combination and recombination of unchanged particles. There is little focus on the relationship between the particles or any suggestion that the particles might be changed in the interaction.

I spend the longest in this chapter exploring the third of Dewey and Bentley's theories of change, that of transaction, but which they mean the entanglement of agents, human and non-human, time and circumstances. Rather than considering entities which are fixed, this way of understanding the world takes an interest in patterns and relationships. It also assumes a change in the agents which interact, which I understand in social terms as changes in our sense of identity and the way we talk about the world. As an alternative to an entity-based view, I drew on three thinkers in particular, Mead, Elias and Bourdieu, who thought that the idea of a game is a much better analogy for theorizing social life, which is constantly in motion. We play the game, but we are influenced more by it than we are able to influence. Constraints, power relationships and the quality of our interdependence and how this changes the way we think about ourselves are at the heart of understanding this particular view of organizational change. The radical unpredictability of our interactions arises because we cannot fully know ourselves, even in acting, and we cannot know how our actions will reverberate out into the world. By coming together to discuss how we might go on, we embody the ability to start something new, what Arendt calls natality, but there are no guarantees about what we might achieve. I don't mean this to sound like half-heartedness, more like a kind of humility about our place in the world.

In this chapter I have taken up Edgar Morin's invitation to think of complexity in general terms and derive insights from the social sciences as well as the natural sciences to reflect on why human action is always complex. To do so, I have drawn on sociology and political theory to explore why it is that there are no guarantees when we try and act in concert. I make a stronger claim than that: human activity can't be categorized as simple, complicated, complex or chaotic. It is always complex in the sense that, to a degree, it will always have the property of stable instability or predictable unpredictability which has been identified as a characteristic of complex systems in Chapter 2, irrespective of whether it appears simple or chaotic.

One set of questions for managers, then, is how they find themselves caught up in the game of organizational life, how power is exercised and by whom, and to what end. How much is the game playing the manager, rather than the other way round? What can be said out loud and by whom and how do differences get mediated? In paying attention to what is intended, it is also important to notice what is happening as an unintended consequence.

Notes

1 I have chosen three for the purpose of simplification. In their seminal work on the relevance of the complexity sciences for thinking about organizational life, Stacey et al. (2000) outline five theories of what they term teleology, movement towards a final form. These are Natural Law teleology, where there is movement towards the perfect (fashioned by God); rationalist teleology, which is the consequence of human choice; formative teleology, which is the unfolding of a form already given; transformative teleology, a form of self-organization where there is potential for radical transformation; and finally adaptationist teleology, informed by Darwinism and a chance-based competitive selection process adapting to the environment.

  Additionally, in Dewey and Bentley's original work they refer to self-action, interaction and transaction: each is hyphenated. I have kept the hyphen for self-action because it is a neologism, but have removed the hyphen from interaction and transaction because the contemporary meaning is close enough to what Dewey and Bentley intended. I hope that removing the hyphen makes the point less pedantically.

2 In Elias' major work, *The Civilising Process* (2000), he makes no claim that becoming more civilized, i.e., being able to co-ordinate with more and more people more of the time is either an inevitable or a linear process. As a counter to the idea that he might have thought this, it is worth reading his work, *The Germans* (1997), which could be viewed as the antithesis, a sociological account of the evolution of barbarism.

3 In 2005, the film *Crash*, directed by Paul Haggis, won an Oscar for its depiction of everyday racism in Los Angeles. Opinion about the film varies, although it consistently ranks highly among film critics. It uses non-linear narratives to explore the many facets of how the global phenomenon of racism has to manifest in particular, concrete situations between people trying to get things done and navigate the contingency of social life.

4 In the United Kingdom, recently there has been much preoccupation with what are termed 'superforecasters' based on the work of American academic Philip Tetlock (2006). Tetlock's work seems to demonstrate that teams of forecasters can improve their judgement

about the likelihood of certain events transpiring if they improve their understanding of probability, engage in critical discussion and are open-minded. However, the kinds of events they are discussing are framed as binaries, such as whether President Assad of Syria will still be president in a year's time, and are calculable outcomes. This is not the same as predicting longer term, messier and complex change.

References

Arendt, H. (1958) *The Human Condition*, Chicago, IL: University of Chicago Press.

Barad, K. (2007) *Meeting the Universe Half Way: Quantum Physics and the Entanglement of Matter and Meaning*, London and Durham: Duke University Press.

Bass, B.M. (1985) *Leadership and Performance Beyond Expectations*, New York, NY: Free Press.

Bourdieu, P. (1990) *In Other Words*, Stanford, CA: Stanford University Press.

Brinkmann, S. (2013) *John Dewey: Science for a Changing World*, New Brunswick, NJ: Transaction Publishers.

Cabanas, E. and Illouz, E. (2019) *Manufacturing Happy Citizens*, Cambridge: Polity Press.

Clegg, S., Courpasson, D. and Phillips, N. (2006) *Power and Organizations*, London: Sage. Coifman, K.G., Flynn, J.J. and Pinto, L.A. (2016) When context *matters*: negative emotions predict psychological health and adjustment. *Motivation and Emotion*, 40:602–624. https://doi.org/10.1007/s11031-016-9553-y.

Cooperrider, D.L. and Srivastva, S. (1987) Appreciative inquiry in organizational life. In: Woodman, R.W. and Pasmore, W.A. (eds.), *Research in Organizational Change And Development*, Vol. 1, Stamford, CT: JAI Press. pp. 129–169.

Davies, W. (2015) *The Happiness Industry*, London: Verso.

Dewey, J. (1922) *Human Nature and Conduct: An Introduction to Social Psychology*, New York, NY: The Modern Library.

Dewey, J. (1929) *The Quest for Certainty*, New York, NY: Capricorn Books.

Dewey, J. and Bentley, A. (1945) A terminology for knowings and knowns, *The Journal of Philosophy*, 42(9):225–247.

Dewey, J. and Bentley, A. (1949) *Knowing and the Known*, Boston, MA: Beacon Press.

Ehrenreich, B. (2010) *Smile or Die: How Positive Thinking Fooled America and the World*, London: Granta.

Elias, N. (1978) *What Is Sociology?* New York, NY: Columbia University Press.

Elias, N. (1997) *The Germans*, Cambridge: Polity Press.

Elias, N. (2000) *The Civilising Process: Sociogenetic and Psychogenetic Investigations*, Oxford: Oxford University Press.

Elias, N. and Dunning, E. (1986) *Quest for Excitement: Sport and Leisure in the Civilizing Process*, Oxford: Blackwell.

Fineman, S. (2006) On being positive: concerns and counterpoints, *Academy of Management Review*, 31(2):270–291.

Fleming, P. and Spicer, A. (2014). Organizational power in management and organization science. *Academy of Management Annals*, 8(1):237–298.

Friedli, L. and Stearn, R. (2015) Positive affect as coercive strategy: conditionality, activation and the role of psychology in UK government workfare programmes, *Critical Medical Humanities*, 41:40–47.

Giddens, A. (1993) Critique of Foucault. In: Cassell, P. (ed.), *The Giddens Reader*, London: Macmillan. pp. 228–235.

Latour, B. (2005) *Reassembling the Social*, Oxford: Oxford University Press.

Mead, G.H. (1925) The genesis of the self and social control, *International Journal of Ethics*, 35:251–277.

Mead, G.H. (1932/2002) *The Philosophy of the Present*, New York, NY: Prometheus Books.

Mead, G.H. (1934). *Mind, Self and Society from the Standpoint of a Social Behaviourist*, Chicago, IL: University of Chicago Press.

Putnam, R. (2000) *Bowling Alone: The Collapse and Revival of American Community*, New York, NY: Simon & Schuster.

Schein, E. (1999) Empowerment, coercive persuasion and organizational learning: do they connect?, *The Learning Organization*, 6(4):163–172.

Scoot, J.C. (1990) *Domination and the Arts of Resistance: Hidden Transcripts*, New Haven, CT: Yale University Press.

Seligman, M.E.P. and Csikszentmihalyi, M. (2000) Positive psychology: an introduction, *American Psychologist*, 55(1):5–14.

Simmel, G. (1964) *Conflict and the Web of Group Affiliations*, New York, NY: Free Press.

Simpson, B. (2016) Where's the agency in leadership-as-practice? In: Raelin, J.A. (ed.), *Leadership as Practice*, London: Routledge, pp. 159–177.

Smith, R. (2019) Resisting neurosciences and sustaining history, *History of the Human Sciences*, 32(1):9–22.

Spicer, A. and Cederström, C. (2015) *The Wellness Syndrome*, Cambridge: Polity Press.

Stacey, R., Griffin, D. and Shaw, P. (2000) *Complexity and Management: Fad or Radical Challenge to Systems Thinking*, London: Routledge.

Taylor, C. (1989) *Sources of the Self: The Making of Modern Identity*, Cambridge: Cambridge University Press.

Tetlock, P.E. (2006) *Expert Political Judgment: How Good Is It? How Can We Know?*, Princeton, NJ: Princeton University Press.

Thaler, R. and Sunnstein, C. (2008) *Nudge: Improving Decisions about Health, Wealth and Happiness*, London and New Haven, CT: Yale University Press.

Vince, R. and Mazen, A. (2014) Violent innocence: a contradiction at the heart of leadership, *Organization Studies*, 35(2):189–207.

Weber, M. (1978) In: Roth, G. and Wittich, C. (trans.) (eds.), *Economy and Society: An Outline of Interpretive Sociology*, Berkeley, CA: University of California Press. (Original work published 1921).

4

THE COMPLEX SELF

The 'I,' 'me' and 'we'

It may sound strange, but the self has a history. We haven't always thought about self-hood as we do now. The feeling of being a self and the quality of our relationships with others are also dynamic and mutable and are further defined by the culture and time we live in. Inevitably, what we take for granted about the self affects the way we organize and what we pay attention to in the process, and particularly so in a globalized world where there is a great emphasis placed on constant change and adaptability. Organizations which are thought to need constant change and flexibility, in turn, need flexible selves. The way society is, the way organizations are, also affect us and what some philosophers have called our 'lifeworld' since 'I' and 'we' are two sides of the same coin.

The link I make for inquiring into our sense of self, our identity, with the complexity models we explored in Chapter 2, is to ask what changes when the evolutionary complex adaptive systems (CAS) models iterate over time. The short answer by analogy, explored more fully in this chapter, is that we do, our sense of ourselves, and the way we think, talk and act.

In the last chapter, I wrote about three different understandings of how change happens which are based on different interpretations of the relationship between the individual and the group. Broadly speaking, it's about discrete individuals and their states of mind and/or their special powers, self-action and interaction, or it's about group process arising from interdependent social selves, transaction, the latter being a minority point of view. All three perspectives have themselves arisen from people thinking about the world, discussing and arguing together and developing their ideas further. In our highly developed societies, the ideas become institutionalized through education, public policy and everyday ways of speaking and become accepted, perhaps taken for granted. They become ideological: that is, they become natural to us and may obscure other ways of understanding what's going on. Every reader of this book will have their own, perhaps unexplored view

DOI: 10.4324/9781003002840-4

and will consider themselves, whether they know it or not, either Kantians or Hegelians. To be a Kantian is to privilege the autonomous, rational individual, who approaches the world through innate categories of mind, and to be a Hegelian is to take seriously the evolutionary nature of history as it impacts upon us as highly social selves, who develop a sense of self because there are other selves.

But in describing these different interpretations of the same phenomena, I am certainly not claiming that subscribing to the view that the individual is prior means a lack of awareness that people belong to groups and that our interdependencies are unimportant. Nor am I claiming that to adopt the idea that the self is thoroughly social means that there is no such thing as individuality. I do claim though that assuming the individual is prior, or the reverse, assuming that the group is prior has a big effect on the kinds of things we pay attention to and the theories we develop to help us understand what is going on to help us act in the world. But this is not to say that the thoroughly social self is a complex self and the other two perspectives are not. Rather to pursue any perspective is to create complexities of a different quality, and these qualities of complexity of the self are the subject of this chapter. I argue that the priority in contemporary organizational life is for flexible selves who are constantly upgrading and improving themselves, and who consider themselves their only and best resource.

Just to give a current political example of what I mean by saying that to make sense of the world by prioritizing the individual leads to different outcomes than assuming that interdependency as prior. As I write this book, the United Kingdom is in its final round of negotiations with the EU about the shape of the agreement for now. The EU is a project which is based on the idea of a joint undertaking, or interdependence. Yes, it is also a project which is exclusionary for those who fall outside membership, it is elitist and is a difficult club to join (and to leave), but nonetheless it is an institutionalized commitment to mutuality between those countries included. The UK's position is that it the vote to leave the EU was won on the basis of fulfilling a desire for 'sovereignty,' to control the borders, the currency and to choose the country's trading partners. The former, the EU, has 'red lines' concerning any breach of what they think of as the ideology guiding their joint undertaking: mutuality through freedom of movement and trade between their members. The thinking of the politicians who still guide the European project is that the individual nation gains through a commitment to working with other nations: stronger together. Meanwhile, in Britain, the politicians who have planned and won the campaign to leave the EU have red lines to do with the fact that the United Kingdom alone can decide what is in its best interest, rather than extending its sovereignty by co-operating with others, and is somehow diminished by joining in to a joint project. Both are different conceptions of the idea of freedom. For the European project, the freedom of individual states is enhanced by mutuality between states; this view of the world is a personification of the idea of interdependence in action. For the British in favour of leaving the EU, we enhance our freedom by going it alone. John Dewey addressed this question of sovereignty in his book *The Public and Its Problems* (1946) in Chapter 5, arguing, much as I have earlier, that human beings act everywhere in association and that the argument of sovereignty is a denial of political responsibility. By responsibility, he meant our disposition to respond to one another and address our collective difficulties through communication. I suspect that Dewey's reaction to the question of whether Britain should have stayed or left the EU would have been to have recommended different and more fruitful methods of communication.

For me, the European Union example encapsulates two very different responses to the same dilemma, whether one can extend the scope for action by prioritizing one's commitments to others, or whether the best way of achieving this is to strike out alone. The potential benefits of choosing one path rather than another may be summed up by the African proverb: if you want to travel fast, travel alone; if you want to travel far, travel together. So too in organizational life. As a manager, one could go with the flow and place an enormous emphasis on individual achievement and competition, which means focusing on metrics and rating things, which I explore later on, so that everyone can evaluate their individual contribution to the market viability of the joint enterprise. In such an organization, there might be an emphasis on positivity, well-being, resilience and personal responsibility to make good choices. Alternatively, and as a manager, one could still make sure that everyone is contributing in the best way possible, but one would also take an interest in group functioning, provide opportunities for collective deliberation and notice how participating in the group creates both joys and sorrows. A group-oriented manager would keep an eye on 'the bottom line' at the same time as prioritizing the quality of relationships.

In the next section, I want to reprise the notion set out in the last chapter that we are individuals who have been socially formed. More, that this socialization process has, paradoxically, led to our sense of being rational, autonomous and closed individuals, an idea which has been particularly amplified in the last 50 years or so. I do this to demonstrate how our sense of self is evolutionary, is historically formed and go on to argue that a highly individualized sense of self has come to predominate in the late 20th century and early 21st century. It brings with it its own complexities and pathologies, as well as its own freedoms. Although our scope for managing differently is sometimes much more proscribed than we sometimes like to admit, becoming aware of some of the assumptions which underpin current management orthodoxy may give greater scope for action.

The social self – a reprise

To remind the reader of Norbert Elias' theory, who has been our guide for some of the discussion to date, about the way social life evolves, despite and also because of our ability to make plans and organize ourselves:

> It is simple enough: plans and actions, the emotional and rational impulses of individual people, constantly interweave in a friendly or hostile way. This basic tissue resulting from many single plans and actions of people can give

rise to changes and patterns that no individual person has planned or created. From this interdependence of people arises an order *sui generis*, an order more compelling and stronger than the will of the people composing it.

Elias, 2000: 366

I understand Elias to be describing exactly the paradoxical dynamic we were trying to explore in Chapter 2 on the complexity sciences, particularly CAS, where we contribute to society-wide patterns but they constrain us both at the same time. This is not an argument against acting with intention or planning, but it does demonstrate the limitations of doing so because we can never control the outcome. A variety of scholars have drawn attention to the same phenomenon, we mentioned Hannah Arendt in the last chapter, and we could add the moral philosopher Alasdair MacIntyre (1985), noting that our actions are always caught up in a web of others' actions. This makes it impossible to predict all the consequences of what we are doing.

For Elias, the regularities that we can perceive are not identical with the regularities of what we call mind, or the individual or nature, even though all of these factors play a role in creating them: they are mutually constitutive in obvious and less obvious ways. The subtitle of *The Civilising Process, Sociogenetic and Psychogenetic Investigations*, points to Elias' central claim that changes in social development bring about changes in our sense of self and personality structure. He thinks of our sense of self as having an 'I' layer and a 'we' layer, which are inseparable. The 'I' and the 'we' are two sides of the same coin. We become a particular 'I' because of the groups that we belong to:

> The coexistence of people, the intertwining of their intentions and plans, the bonds they place on each other, all these, far from destroying individuality, provide the medium for it to develop … The social fabric, in this sense forms the substratum from which and into which the individual constantly spins and weaves his purposes. But this fabric and its actual course of historical change as a whole, is intended and planned by no one.
>
> *2000: 543*

In other words, the world we live in affects our lifeworld, our subjectivity and makes us who we are. Elias maintains this paradoxical tension of the social self, the intertwined relationship between individuals and the groups they are part of throughout his work. The social 'substratum' in which the individual sense of identity develops he referred to elsewhere as the *habitus*, habituated ways of acting and thinking which shape us just as we shape the *habitus*.

He goes on to say that civilization is neither reasonable nor rational, any more than it is irrational. But for him, it is a perfectly achievable assumption that we could intervene in the pattern of relationships, and with individuals, to make them more reasonable, which is possible on the basis of greater awareness of the unplanned dynamics of groups of individuals trying to pursue their plans. There is a normative assumption in Elias' work too, particularly if you take these observations together with one of the last books he wrote, *The Loneliness of the Dying* (2001), that the natural state for people, particularly when they are at the end of life, is that they should continue to find ourselves in groups. We achieve our satisfactions and our fulfilments, he argues, through our interdependency with others: in highly developed societies, people become dependent on each other for their satisfaction but also for the satisfaction of their needs (1956: 232). For Elias, and for the Canadian philosopher Charles Taylor (1989) whom I mentioned earlier, the sense that we have of ourselves as discrete, closed-off individuals is a relatively recent phenomenon in human history. The feeling of separateness, of autonomy that we have in highly developed Western societies is not shared to the same degree in Eastern societies.

The pragmatic philosophers William James, G.H. Mead and John Dewey, influenced by both Hegel and Darwin, were similarly convinced that becoming a self is a dynamic, evolutionary and social undertaking. Mead in particular argued that our minds, our sense of self and our participation in wider processes of society are all different aspects of the same dynamic phenomenon, which we described in Chapter 2 on the complexity sciences; we are formed by and are forming society both at the same time. We develop a mind because we share attributes with a small handful of other mammals in being able through our physiology to take ourselves as an object to ourselves. This is what Mead means by self-consciousness, which is enhanced through the acquisition of language, when we can think.[1] The private conversation of thinking is simply a silent version of our public capacity for talking to others. We explore the complex phenomenon of talk in the next chapter on complex communication.

Equally our sense of self is dependent on our dealings with other selves through whom we see ourselves reflected. Although we become recognizable to each other and ourselves through our habits and routines, for Mead, there is no fixed self which is 'inside' the individual, and no mind which is cut off from the outside world:

> The self is something which has a development; it is not initially there, at birth, but arises in the process of social experience and activity, that is, develops in the given individual as a result of his relations to that process as a whole and to other individuals in that process.
>
> *Mead, 1934: 135*

The sense of self comprises what Mead refers to as the 'I/me dialectic.' By this rather exotic term, I take him to mean our spontaneous reaction to things, the 'I,' which we can never get on top of and never fully anticipate nor recognize, which becomes mediated and conditioned by our sense of the way that other people who have shared in the same experience view us. Although we can never get hold of the 'I,' we are exposed to a series of 'me's, which is the experience of the 'I' refracted through our understanding of the attitudes of others towards us. Over time, we develop a sense of the 'generalized other' a term used to denote our capacity to anticipate how our actions might be viewed in our wider community. The generalized other is another way of thinking about our *habitus*. The *habitus* is our culture, our accepted patterns of behaving towards each other which we often take up unthinkingly, until something happens to make the invisible visible to us (like going abroad and noticing how people living in different cultures do things differently). Our largely unreflective participation in the *habitus* helps us co-ordinate our actions with others but is also a form of self-control: we might think of our ability to take the attitude of the generalized other as Freud's superego, or conscience.

The importance of these ideas for managers is that we go about our business in a mostly unreflective way taking for granted the way the world works. For the majority of the time, we are unaware of how ideological we are: we think the world is the way we see it and it can come as shock when we are jolted out of our preconceptions we take to be common sense, or obvious. The currency of organizational talk in most organizations is to accept that the individual is prior, which makes the interweaving of intentions less visible.

Making the individual prior

In Chapter 2, I mentioned that I will return again and again to the conundrum of the relationship between the individual and the group, structure and agency. The first part of this chapter reprises the highly social view of the self by drawing on pragmatic philosophy and process sociology. I have referenced thinkers who believe that the social is prior: culture, the *habitus*, forms our sense of self. This is not to deny our individuality but is an explanation of how we become individuals. To make the strong link between 'outside' and 'inside' and to understand the relationship of the self to the social as two sides of the same coin leads to thinking that whatever we consider social life is amenable to human intervention, even if that intervention is unlikely to go according to plan. The pragmatists were interested in what they termed 'intelligent conduct', drawn from our capacity to take ourselves as an object to ourselves, we can reflect on our interactions and think about how we conduct ourselves more reasonably. The pragmatists set great store by democracy as a mechanism by which societies could become more just, more reasonable.

Elias too thought it was possible to become more familiar with how our attempts to co-operate with each other can provoke strong feelings in us, and so to reflect upon our own feelings may help us gain greater purchase over them. Elias was a troubled friend and collaborator with S.H. Foulkes (1975), the founder of the group analytic tradition in the United Kingdom, which was premised on the insight that the best place to learn about oneself and one's own motivations is in a group. In the last chapter, and drawing on Elias and Arendt, I wrote about how power and politics are themes through which we can understand the constant negotiation that takes place between motivated individuals trying to collaborate and compete to get things done. Politics brings the workings of power into view.

Accepting that the relationship between individuals and society is complex, paradoxical has not resulted in any sense of fatalism from those thinkers I have quoted. They do not conclude that the world is complex and radically unpredictable and so there is nothing to be done. I think this is relevant to those of us who are involved in organizations and organizing, where sometimes the idea of complexity is adduced to evade responsibility or to claim a kind of helplessness in the face of social evolution which is not controlled even by the most powerful.[2] The passages in this book where I appear to be deflating the concept of the heroic individual, or heroic groups, who bend the world to their will is not the same as claiming that we are all powerless. This book is not anti-management or anti-leadership. Rather, it encourages turning to the group and group process as an underutilized resource in considering how we might go on together. However, it is possible to consider the same complex ordering of society and draw the opposite conclusion that the individual is prior and primary and that efforts to get the best outcome for social process is best focused there. For me, this can lead to a kind of fatalism, at least about the collective: there is a reduced role for the group, be it those groups governments, or senior management teams, because the greatest resource for society is the individual and their private motivations.

Although we live in an era where the focus on individuals has become acute, as I have argued throughout this book that there is a long history to the process of becoming the individuals we consider ourselves. There are a variety of reasons why there is premium placed on individuals, particularly in the Western tradition of thought. For example, Nesbitt (2005) argues that both culture and geography contribute to the way we understand the world, and the course of individualism was forged in the rugged landscapes of Ancient Greece partly because it was less hospitable to collective undertakings like agriculture. For pragmatic philosophy, and particularly for C.S. Peirce, it was Descartes who in the Enlightenment began the radically subjective intellectual break with the idea of our interdependence. If all that we can be certain of in understanding the world is our own thinking, then this is the beginning of a series of separations from which we are still recovering: mind is thought to be separate from body, thinking from acting and one self from another self. Both Elias and Charles Taylor have written about how this individualization process has been a long, inexorable, although not a linear process, along with currents and traditions of privileging the group rather than the individual (no social process is ever monolithic). Elias argues that in highly differentiated societies, particularly in large cities, more and more people are dependent on more and more others, more of the time. The chains of interdependence are very long and mostly opaque to us. It is only in times of crisis, such as during the time of the pandemic, that we realize just how long the chains are, and what takes place in the background to maintain our sense of living in a modern society. This largely hidden hinterland of interdependent activity may obscure the reality of our need for one another and may have amplified the idea that we are autonomous individuals cut off from one another.

German sociologist Hartmut Rosa (2015) argues the transition from pre-modern to modern times has marked an increasing transfer of responsibility to the individual to shape their own lives. Increased individualization has been accompanied by social acceleration, a speeding up of the number of types and numbers of experiences which we are caught up in, intensified by technology and increased competition. Instead of the more settled trajectories of both private lives and careers that older generations may have expected, our work and lived experience has become more fragmentary. I claim along with others that further impetus has been leant to the idea what Elias termed 'homo clausus,' man closed off against others, by the prevailing orthodoxy, the habitus particularly in Western/Northern countries, where priority is given to market relations and the idea of the autonomous, calculating self.

Although the individual/group dilemma has a history dating way back, the first four decades of the 20th century were very turbulent with competing notions of freedom and the kinds of society that would deliver it, including the role of the state. In our multipolar world, it may seem a distant memory that at the beginning of the 20th century, it may have felt as though there was a binary choice between communism on the one hand and capitalism on the other, state control in the former and degrees of laissez faire in the latter. Taking a position in the discussion required taking a view about what causes social stability and change, the relationship between the individual and the group and the role of rational planning, much as we have been trying to do in this volume with respect to organizations.

Another major thinker of the 20th century, one who, with his thought collective,[3] has come to have a huge influence on our daily lives in the 21st century, the Nobel Prize–winner Friedrich Hayek. Although Hayek graduated in law and political science, his ideas (and those of his collaborators) about economics and the role of the market in ensuring individual freedom have now come to dominate in many developed societies, predominantly in the West but not exclusively there. I argue that the growing dominance of market thinking over the last 30 years has profoundly affected how we think about the world, how we try to organize it and how we have come to think about ourselves. In many ways, Hayek is an ally in the task of this book, which is to elaborate a more complex understanding of social life and to point to the limitations of restricted ways of comprehending it:

> Yet the confidence in the unlimited power of science is only too often based on a false belief that the scientific method consists in the application of a ready-made technique, or in imitating the form rather than the substance of scientific procedure, as if one needed only to follow some cooking recipes to solve all social problems. It sometimes almost seems as if the techniques of science were more easily learnt than the thinking that shows us what the problems are and how to approach them.
>
> *Hayek, 1974*

Hayek shares some of Elias' concerns about the reductiveness of some scientific methods when they are applied to making dynamic and complex social phenomena intelligible. They are often more suited to making divisions and analysing atomistically than for thinking about processes in flux. Of course, neither Elias nor Hayek were aware of the sophisticated CAS modelling which I wrote about in relation to the pandemic, and in Chapter 2, where I tried to discuss both their strengths and limitations.

Hayek's view about the evolution of society is similar to Elias' in the sense that he thinks that the actions and plans of individuals pursuing their interests contribute to the spontaneous ordering of society:

> Since a spontaneous order results from the individual elements adapting themselves to circumstances which directly affect only some of them, and which in their totality need not be known by anyone, it may extend to circumstances so complex that no mind can comprehend them all. Consequently, the concept becomes particularly important when we turn from mechanical to such 'more highly organized' or essentially complex phenomena as we encounter in the realms of life, mind and society. Here we have to deal with 'grown' structures with a degree of complexity which they have assumed, and could assume only because they were produced by spontaneous ordering forces.
>
> *Hayek, 1973/2013: 39–40*

But where he agrees with Elias ontologically, that is, they share a view about how social reality becomes, they disagree epistemologically, the degree to which we can know much about what is happening. In Hayek's case, he was convinced that markets were the highest form of human achievement. The market activity of large numbers of people contained knowledge beyond the reach of individuals, or any collection of individuals, such as governments. The central role of governments, then, was to ensure the proper functioning of the market and property rights – nothing more. Hayek's position assumes a radical individualism, which he made clear in in his most famous book *The Road to Serfdom* where he contemplates the individualism of the Judeo-Christian tradition:

> But the essential features of that individualism ... are the respect for the individual man *qua* man, that is, the recognition of his own views and tastes as supreme in his own sphere, however narrowly that may be circumscribed, and the belief that it is desirable that men should develop their own individual gifts and bents.
>
> *1944: 14*

Hayek's self is a socially constructed individual, and becomes a self because of his experience: 'Experience is not a function of mind or consciousness, but mind and consciousness are rather a product of experience' (1984: 226), as is Elias' self. But there is little indication that Hayek takes experience to mean the self-interacting with other selves. Hayek writes into the conservative liberal tradition where he assumes that going down the collectivist path can only inhibit individual freedom (Stedman Jones, 2012: 59), so the market is made by individuals making constant means–ends calculations and evaluating risk. The needs of the sovereign individual must never be subsumed under the collectivist ideal, and individuals best realize themselves by using market rationality to engage with each other. Hayek even had a suspicion of the word 'social' which he considered a construct of intellectuals to impose their ideas of the collective (Davies, 2015: 50). The principal mechanism for achieving individual liberty is the competitive dynamic between risk-calculating individuals, and market relations can be extended into every area of social life.

There is a rich literature exploring the provenance of the history and philosophy of economic individualism which has been termed 'neoliberalism' in its most recent manifestation, which I don't intend to explore here (Peck, 2010; Stedman Jones, 2012; Davies, 2014, 2015; Streeck, 2014; Chandler and Reid, 2016), along with scholars who argue that when the term is taken up by a wide range of sociologists and political scientists rather than economists, it becomes too vague and contradictory a term to be useful (Venugopal, 2015). The critique is that it can become a catch-all term for everything in contemporary life which one opposes. I don't intend to get hung up on whether the word neoliberalism is or isn't helpful: we could say instead that we are describing instead the characteristics of late modernity. What interests me most here in this chapter about the complex self is how we might think about our amplified sense of individualization and what it produces in terms of focusing our attention. It may help explain why the theories I have drawn attention to in the last chapter, based on ideas of self-action or interaction, have gained purchase, or more, have come to dominate. If we think that the individual is prior and preeminent, and that the way society best advances is through market relations, then we might focus on the individual's states of mind, their resilience, their positivity, their 'skillsets' and how they might enhance their 'human capital' to trade in the market. We come to think about individuals as businesses operating according to contractual relationships. It is interesting to think about the kinds of pathologies and opportunities that present in a highly individualized, competitive world, where we strive to remake ourselves constantly, dependent upon 'likes,' clicks and appreciation, what the French scholar Michael Feher (2018) terms 'rated agency.'

The entrepreneurial self – the current phase of individualization

One of the first scholars to think through the consequences of extending market relations to every area of social life including our sense of identity was Michel Foucault. Foucault's central intellectual project was to consider how power and what he termed discourse, systematic and institutionalized ways of talking about the world produce selves and what he termed 'regimes of truth.' One of the insights which the complexity thinking I set out in this book shares with Foucault is the idea that whatever we think of as 'structure,' or global patterning or the 'system' as people sometimes call it arises simply and only because of how people are interacting locally, how they relate, how they talk to one another and how they practice: the *habitus*. A way of talking about the world which becomes widely taken up and then taken for granted through policy, academic study and practices becomes what Elias refers to as the social substratum from which we derive our sense of self.

In one of his last series of lectures at the College de France, Foucault (2008) reflected on the development of economic thinking since the 17th century and how it impacted upon practices. He noted the way that the Austrian/German concept of ordoliberalism, where markets are privileged but there is still a strong role for the state, transformed into neoliberalism, particularly in the United States, which still emphasized the importance of markets but developed a deep suspicion about the role of governments, the collective, as we have discussed, placing the autonomous, calculating individual at the heart of their thinking. What Foucault noticed about the work of Nobel Prize–winner Gary Becker, an economist at Chicago University, where a strong school of neoliberal thought developed, was that it called for:

> extending the economic model of supply and demand and of investment – costs – profits, so as to make it a model of social relations and of existence itself, a form of relationship of the individual to himself, to those around him, the group and the family.
>
> *2008: 242*

These economic ideas would not just affect the way the economy was run but would come to affect the way we think of ourselves:

> The stake in all neoliberal analyses is the replacement of *homo oeconomicus* as partner of exchange with a *homo oeconomicus* as entrepreneur of himself.
>
> *2008: 226*

If, as the first woman Prime Minister in the United Kingdom claimed, 'there is no such thing as society, only individuals their families'[4] then the mediation of social risk and uncertainty falls to the individual themselves. To survive in the social marketplace, the individual has to invest in herself (Feher, 2018), to keep herself upgraded and adaptable, to make the right choices. Rather than focusing on power relationships, inequalities and analyses of how groups come to dominate over other groups, attention is focused instead on the individual and their states of mind and market-readiness.

Here are some examples of the consequences of considering ourselves entrepreneurs of the self. Christina Scharff (2015), a feminist scholar at King's College London, interviewed 60 self-employed women musicians and noted how their sense of self was highly individualized along with their work predicaments. She noted how they had internalized the pressures that they experienced in finding work, were unable to notice structural inequalities such as gender bias in job selection but rather blamed themselves for not being good enough. Meanwhile, they were constantly involved in optimizing, trying to improve themselves, trying to 'stay positive' and blamed others for not trying as hard as they did. This is an example of how treating the self as an entrepreneurial project can lead to anxiety, self-doubt and insecurity. In turn, atomized and anxious individuals may turn and be encouraged to turn to self-help remedies, well-being courses, resilience training or life coaches to develop an improved self. There is a good deal of research demonstrating that women are more likely to be prone to self-criticism than men, so the experience of modernity is likely to be highly gendered. Nonetheless, I think Scharff's respondents demonstrate in extreme form the kinds of pressures that employees experience both inside and outside organizations, where they are invited to locate the difficulties they experience with themselves, rather than with structural conditions.

Coaching to improve performance has become a ubiquitous preoccupation in the 21st century. Sam Binkley (2011), an American sociologist, interviewed a number of life coaches to think about how the focus on the optimized, market-oriented individual affects our psychological life. He noted the way that life coaches were deeply sceptical of the talking therapies because they caused clients to dwell on their troubled pasts. He records the techniques that one life coach uses with his/her clients. One is called 'A perfect world' where the client is asked to imagine how she would be different in a year's time, how she would hold herself, what she would wear, what sort of relationships she would have and what her 'energy' would be. Then she needs to take the steps to achieve this in logical fashion. Scholars of strategy will note the resemblance between this and Ackoff's idealized design strategy methodology where employees are invited to imagine an idealized future and then work backwards from there in logical steps. Instead, this method focuses on the individual rather than the firm. In this particular formulation, we can see shades of Dewey and Bentley's self-action, where through some quasi-mystical focus of will and 'energy' the individual bends the world to their own ends.

Just as Foucault predicted, there would be a broad trend towards the development of discourse, techniques and consultancy aimed at optimizing the self for a competitive world: we are encouraged to develop ourselves continuously, make ourselves flexible for the globalized economy, measure and digitize ourselves with fitbits, perform to metrics and objectives we set ourselves and claim that we are taking personal responsibility. Notice, we do this to ourselves: it is not just 'they' who make us do it. We have personal goals just as we have performance goals at work. As we discussed in the chapter on the complexity sciences, there is nowhere to stand outside the *habitus* of accelerated individualization but we find ourselves co-opted and reproducing the dynamic ourselves.

There is nothing wrong with people wanting to reflect on their lives, to get fitter and to change things which distress them, but in the cases that Binkley draws to our attention, the emphasis is on an idealized future, the responsibility is with the individual to make good choices and positivity is the norm. There is also the sense that the rich variety of experience gets reduced to a series of metrics and goals and they are therefore flattened in terms of their human significance. The principal goal of the individual is to make themselves more tradable in the marketplace, to upgrade themselves constantly.

For a third example, there has been a lot written about the neoliberal university and how the values of the marketplace have come to dominate, Parker (2014) and Alvesson and Spicer (2016) are examples. As with the project of the self, so the neoliberal university individualizes academic achievement with metrics for publishing, demands for income from research funding and expectations that even doctoral programmes will 'wash their faces' financially. One way of thinking about the university is as the institutionalization of curiosity. Another is that it is a place where we produce future employees with the competences to adapt and be constantly flexible, to meet the needs of the corporation they join.

Investment in the university sector in the United Kingdom has come to mean an investment in human capital, as summarized by Milton Friedman's paper, an eminent neoliberal economist at Chicago University, *The Role of Government in Education* (1955):

> [Education is] a form of investment in human capital precisely analogous to investment in machinery, buildings, or other forms of non-human capital. Its function is to raise the economic *productivity* of the human being. If it does so, the individual is rewarded in a free enterprise society by receiving a higher return for his services.

A degree is worth having in relation to the amount of money a graduate can earn as a consequence of completing it (and thus pay off their student loan).[5] Here, for example, is the vision and mission statement of an anonymous business school in a university:

- Vision – *Empowering students through transformational education and research*
- Mission – *Transforming students from learners to professionals ready to succeed in the global economy, by challenging them with teaching, learning and research that delivers tomorrow's business ideas today*

Notice the emphasis on functionality of education for producing successful professionals in an ideal future: their education is only as good as their relevance to the global economy and the 'value' that they bring. It seems to be taken for granted now in the United Kingdom that students are principally customers who are buying an asset to trade. It is part of their personal entrepreneurial development. This will affect their relationships in their institution, their fellow students and their teachers as education becomes commodified. This is very different to the idea of an education as a good in and of itself.

In my own university, I facilitated a meeting when senior colleagues remarked up on the increasing incidence of psychological distress among undergraduates. This of course is directly related to the larger number of young people studying for a degree, and for some of them, it is the first time to live away from home. Nonetheless, burdened by debt and seemingly less able to communicate and work together in groups, the broader pattern of social isolation and atomization also shows up at my own university with consequences for teaching students and managing their engagement with others. Rather than frequenting communal spaces to meet each other, undergrads are just as likely be alone in their rooms communicating with each via social media or dating apps. Meanwhile, employers complain that graduates do not have the basic social skills to work in groups.

More broadly, in the United Kingdom, there is an emerging pattern of psychological distress among the young in general and students in particular, and especially among young women. A national study reported in the *Guardian* newspaper stated that:

- A record 1,180 students experienced mental ill health and left university courses early in 2014–2015, up 210% from 2009 to 2010.
- 87,914 Students requested counselling in 2015–2016, compared with 68,614 in 2013–2014, a rise of 28%.
- Most young people asked for help because of anxiety; the numbers doing so rose by 43% over three years. There was a 39% rise in students seeking counselling for depression over the same period.[6]

Meanwhile a report from the Office of National Statistics noted the way that these rising tides of depression and anxiety are gendered:

- A quarter of young women in the United Kingdom have suffered from anxiety and depression.
- Young women were 'significantly more likely' than their male counterparts to recognize and admit being anxious or depressed, with less than one in six young men reporting similar symptoms.
- The study also reveals that in the four years from 2009–2010 to 2013–2014, the number of young people saying their mental health had 'deteriorated' rose from 18% to 21%.[7]

Here are some accounts of what young people say about their mental distress at university:

- 'It's hard being a modern student, everything relies on money.'
- 'The taxpayer is subsidizing my presence here … how can I let people down?'
- 'As a mature student I felt a huge amount of pressure to be successful.'
- 'On results day Facebook is full of posts celebrating firsts and 2:1s, but I have never seen a post celebrating or even just admitting a 2:2.'
- 'For this modern student, there's no room for self-exploration or indulgence; excellence has to come first.'[8]

These young people's thinking is dominated by a sense of increased competition with other students, coupled with a pressure to succeed, which is then potentially laid bare by the confessional of social media. Students may be beset by highly abstract and idealized notions of 'excellence' and success. These feelings are similar to the ones described by the young women freelance musicians I described in the research carried out by Scharff earlier – they all felt individually responsible for whatever happens to them and considered themselves entrepreneurs of the self, just as Foucault suggested. In a neoliberal, or market-based perspective of the world, our social predicaments are thought to arise simply from our own individual choices. The journalist Barbara Ehrenreich (2010) carried out research for a book on employment in the United States. She pretended to be unemployed and paid for a number of re-employment training programmes where she was assured that if she wanted a job badly enough, then she would find one. She was told that it was only her own attitude which got in the way of her success. The book critiques the pervasiveness in public of what we might think of as two dominating theories of social order, that it arises from the mysterious force of the individual or that it arises from closed off individuals interacting with each other.

Complex selves in organizations

In this chapter, I have written about the long, slow process of individualization, amplified by the Enlightenment and more recently by modernity and the increasing influence of technology. I have argued that individualization is a social process, yet paradoxically, it has resulted in the dominance of an ideology which prioritizes the individual. In times of huge technological change and upheaval, we are encouraged to be competitive, isolated selves closed off from one another and looking to no one but ourselves as a resource. I have shown how two major thinkers of the 20th century, Norbert Elias and Friedrich Hayek, shared a similar analysis about the stable instability of social life, how it arises from the interweaving of intentions of myriads of people pursuing their plans but came to different conclusions about what this means for the way we engage with the world. For the former, our sense of being an independent individual is misleading, and our recourse is to learn more about groups and how they function and the kinds of strong feelings they evoke in us, particularly when we risk exclusion; for the latter, turning to the collective presages a kind of tyranny which stifles individual autonomy and freedom. It is the second point of view which has come to predominate, equally so in organizations.

There is nothing monolithic in the privileging of the individual, nor is it all-embracing, and the extent to which we are exposed to it will partly depend upon where we find ourselves in the world. The grip of market-based individualistic ideology appears greater in Anglo countries than in other, particularly Eastern societies. But even then, during the pandemic, many countries have rediscovered the importance of the state intervening to shore up economies and keep citizens safe. In Western/Northern societies, the ideology of individualism competes with collective traditions: there have been very many examples during the pandemic of communities reigniting their sense of collective purpose, or looking out for each other and understanding their predicaments as best being dealt with collectively. The race to find a vaccine has involved many different communities of scientists co-operating together for the common good. Equally, though much diminished, collective undertakings like trades unions and social movements continue to flourish. Although I have set out some of the pathologies of a dominating perspective such as increased anxiety, feelings of isolation and burn out (Chabot, 2019), and a high incidence of depression in the West, there are also those who consider the ideology of individualism to be liberating. The invitation to morph and change, to be constantly on the front foot exploring different possibilities, is enticing to some. As the eminent German sociologists Hartmann and Honneth (2006) have noted, the new individualism along with increased incomes post–World War II:

> allow a growing part of the population to interpret their lives no longer as fixed and linear processes of sequentially assuming professional and familial roles, but as opportunities for the experimental realization of their own personalities.
>
> *43*

The invitation to think of oneself as an inventor of oneself and as an entrepreneur of the self has been embraced with enthusiasm by many as a particular understanding of freedom. Nonetheless, where the last 30–40 years might be seen as a triumph of individualization allowing for larger variety of lives to be led, it has at the same time eroded other social norms such as social solidarity and long-term identification with employers (and vice versa), as well as blurring the boundaries between lifeworld and professional world. Hartmann and Honneth note that employees are expected to bring increased 'subjective action capacities' to the workplace, that is, they are expected to bring their heart and soul to work as human capital, and at the same time subjective aspects of private life find themselves colonized by organizational and economic thinking.

This blurring of boundaries, the importation of corporate thinking into the individual, and the entrepreneurial self into the corporation is one clear effect of individualized and marketized thinking. The second, it seems to me, is the erosion of deliberation and contestation, organizational politics, in favour of a focus on optimizing individual performance. I remarked in the last chapter that politics in organizational terms is the way we make ourselves visible to each other and negotiate how to go on together. Starting from the premise that there are a variety of points of view which are possible when engaging with the complex problems which present in any organizational environment, so by means of politics, we may mediate our differences and lay ourselves open to be changed in the exchange. This is by no means an easy process, and nor do I claim that politics works well in most organizations. But when organizations are increasingly marketized and individualized, a premium is placed on measurement as a substitute for the more messy process of deliberation. This has the effect of forming a hierarchy but is supposed also to create a means of choosing for 'consumers' in a manufactured market. These metrics are ubiquitous and are often proxy measures for other, less tangible qualities, such as good teaching, which are hard to define, let alone count. The move from quality to quantity, from intangible human processes to tangible numbers to create a commensurable way of comparing and to create a market is what the British sociologist Will Davies' terms the disenchantment of politics by economics (2014), and the political scientist Wendy Brown (2015) terms 'undoing the demos.' What I think they mean by this is that the human back and forth of discussion, argument, negotiation and making judgments is replaced by pseudo-facts, numbers which claim to be objective but are often just proxy measures. These, in turn, are used to justify marketization, and if this produces unintended consequences, then further marketization is called for.

The third area of concern for employees in organizations is what a number of sociologists in their studies of the phenomenology of the self in the modern organization refer to as indeterminacy (Honneth, 1999), or lack of rootedness. We might understand indeterminacy as an inability to find the self in the back and forth of dialectic between self and others. We are either lost in the requirements of the group to which we belong, or we are lost to ourselves in narcissistic preoccupation. It is a relation of relationlessness, according to Hannah Arendt. For example, Richard Sennett the contemporary pragmatist argues that the increasing flexible workplace erodes relationships of solidarity and trust and destabilizes the work identity which leads to what he terms the 'corrosion of character' (1998). By this, I think he means an undermining of group identification, and an over commitment to the project of the self. Meanwhile, Hartmut Rosa notes that in the frenetic standstill that we experience in contemporary society:

> self-projects which are oriented toward stability appear to be anachronistic and condemned to failure in a highly dynamic environment, while forms of identity based on flexibility and readiness to change are systematically favoured.
>
> *2015: 243*

Brinkmann (2017), too, sees the invitation to be constantly flexible, self-improving and adaptable as something to be resisted. The narrative of self-improvement and continuous development militates against ever being rooted, of reflecting and staying put. His injunction was that we should say no to self-development, no to the life coach and no to endless flexibility and fitting in.

Summing up for managers – why our sense of self is complex and sometimes indeterminate

To take a highly social view of the self and identity formation is to acknowledge much broader and historical forces which shape us and our senses of self, and which play out in everyday organizational life. These broader social and historical trends are difficult to resist, both for individuals and for organizations, but that does not mean we cannot pay attention to the particular dilemmas that they throw up for us at work, or that we have no agency. Mead identified these dynamics very clearly:

Thus the relations between social reconstruction and self or personality reconstruction are reciprocal and internal or organic; social reconstruction by the individual members of any organized human society entails self or personality reconstruction in some degree or other by each of the individuals, and vice versa, for since their selves or personalities are constituted by their organized social relations to one another, they cannot reconstruct those selves or personalities without also reconstructing, to some extent the given social order, which is, of course, likewise constituted by their organized social relations to one another.

1934: 309

We shape the society of which we are part, and, in turn, it shapes us powerfully. Management practices which are taken up simply as 'the way we do things around here' and unquestioningly are underpinned by all kinds of assumptions about the role of individuals and groups, and what we choose to value. As we proceed through the book, I argue that paying attention, noticing and deliberating on these processes in organizations may make a difference to how groups can deal with some of the consequences of the pressures that arise when the individual is privileged with the responsibility, and the group recedes in importance. Employees in organizations feel the weight of individual responsibility keenly, and it shows up in surveys of mental distress at work.

Here are three ways of thinking about the pressures of modernity on the self that I take from reading Byung-Chul Han's *The Burnout Society* (2015) in relation to what interests me in complex social processes of identity formation, some of which we have covered earlier. I think Han covers the ground of this chapter very well, so I will draw on his arguments to sum up what I think I have said in this chapter about the complex self.

The first is his idea that we live in an achievement society and there is no limit to the extent to which we are encouraged to be flexible, accommodating and self-improving. We commit to stretch targets and key performance indicator (KPIs), more for less, smart working, efficiency savings and we make ourselves lifelong learners. We focus on our own health and the habitual improvement of the body. Byung-Chul Han argues that freedom and constraint now combine in the same individual, so we are both the exploiter and the exploited as we endeavour to achieve more and more. As a result, he argues, we risk depression and burnout. We are encouraged to commit to the dictum that 'nothing is impossible,' but as a consequence, the opposite is also true, that nothing is possible. We can go on improving ourselves, fitting in, meeting new and more exacting targets and getting more for less without end, until we hollow ourselves out. There is no one else to look to for help or guidance if we are all to be self-starting entrepreneurs. We are entirely responsible for our own futures; we must depend on ourselves rather than others. As I have mentioned, there are some people who thrive in these circumstances: it is not experienced as oppressive by everybody.

I think it behoves managers to pay attention to these processes and to bring them into view for those they manage. There may be no bucking the trend of demanding more and more flexibility from employees but it might feel like a political act to draw attention to what's happening potentially to find greater scope for action.

The second argument I take from Byung-Chul Han, which I think I have made in my own terms earlier, is the pressure we are under not to reflect on our current situation of self-exploitation: that contemporary multitasking which arises from the bombardment of new technology and the pattern of work does not lead to freedom but to fragmented attention. Hyperactivity potentially makes us passive, where we are always responding and never initiating. In contrast, Byung-Chul Han agrees with Walter Benjamin on the importance of being bored, of languishing undistracted to be with one's own thoughts. And he turns Hannah Arendt (1971) on her head by pointing out that although she ultimately valorizes action over contemplation, in the end for Arendt, it is contemplation, thinking, which is most help to us 'when the chips are down.' It is a great skill to learn not to act immediately to a stimulus but to reflect, resist or say no. Only through continuous attention can we recognize what is important about a lived life.

For managers, this would mean a challenge to a relentless action-orientation at work. Some managers in organizations talk about the importance of 'delivery.' Previous governments in the United Kingdom were so enamoured with the idea that they set up a Delivery Unit. There is a time for action, but there also needs to be time for reflection on what's going on. Sometimes it is worth meeting together to think about what we're doing together, with no particular end in view.

The third argument which interests me in Byung-Chul Han's book is that contemporary society suffers from an excess of positivity, an absence of negative constraint. I have referred to this tendency in this chapter. He understands constraint in Hegelian terms, that we are defined as subjects through the negation of others in the back-and-forth dialectic between the self and other selves: to fully recognize ourselves, we negate the negation of others, and in doing so become ourselves through and with the other. We are plagued with narcissistic disorders where we are unable to find ourselves and each other. As entrepreneurs of the self, as achievers, we are supposed to define ourselves. However, my claim in this book is that we are incapable of pulling ourselves up by our own bootstraps but need the otherness of others, the exploration of difference in a group to find ourselves. Meanwhile, computers for Byung-Chul Han, are symptomatic of the age, since they are the epitome of autistic self-referentiality requiring no otherness to perform, even in the age of Zoom meetings. And in a sense, we come to mimic them, endlessly performing, exploiting ourselves, in a self-referencing loop.

Complex, social selves are at the heart of understanding complex organizations and why questions of 'authenticity' and the constant invitation to 'look inside' to find ourselves will always be problematic. We might think of one of the responsibilities of contemporary managers as being the custodian of the idea of interdependence, becoming entrepreneurial in finding ways of bringing people into relation with one another.

Notes

1 Mead distinguishes between consciousness and self-consciousness with the idea of reason. Consciousness is the awareness of bodily states such as pain or pleasure. Self-consciousness is the awareness of a self in relation to other selves. Through language we are able to reason, which is the ability to consider ourselves dispassionately, to treat ourselves as an object to ourselves and thus to have the potential to follow an intelligent path of action.

2 In a speech to the Labour Party Conference in 2005, Prime Minister Tony Blair said: 'I hear people say we have to stop and debate globalisation. You might as well debate whether autumn should follow summer.'

3 Hayek invited a number of economists, philosophers and businessmen to join with him in setting up the Mont Pelerin Society in 1947. The original founders included the philosopher Karl Popper, and the economists Ludwig von Mises, Frank Knight and Milton Friedman. Their principle intellectual targets were bureaucracy, collectivism and Keynesian economics where it foresaw a role for the state in intervening in the economy. The Mont Pelerin Society was modelled on the Fabian Society, its socialist equivalent, and its founders intended to develop a coherent body of ideas to influence society when the opportunities arose (Bergin, 2013).

4 Mrs Thatcher talking to *Woman's Own Magazine*, 31 October 1987. Some commentators have pointed out some degree of confusion in the neoliberal social project as to whether the individual is the primary unit of analysis, or the family is, as encapsulated in this famous quote. Nonetheless Mrs Thatcher herself was convinced that her intentions went beyond mere economic policy:

> What's irritated me about the whole direction of politics in the last 30 years is that it's always been towards the collectivist society. People have forgotten about the personal society. And they say: do I count, do I matter? To which the short answer is, yes. And, therefore, it isn't that I set out on economic policies; it's that I set out really to change the approach, and changing the economics is the means of changing that approach. If you change the approach, you really are after the heart and soul of the nation. Economics are the method; the object is to change the heart and soul.
>
> *Interview in the Sunday Times, 3 May 1981*

5 One of the key metrics for universities in the United Kingdom in what is called the Teaching Excellence Framework, or TEF, is the percentage of graduates of a particular university who go on to secure a job. Although the framework is focused on teaching, no teaching is ever observed. The award is granted on proxy measures, such as employability, continuation in study and student (consumer) satisfaction.

6 Higher Education Statistics Agency, quoted in the Guardian 23 May 2017.

7 Office for National Statistics, quoted in the Guardian 14 April 2017.

8 www.theguardian.com/education/2016/sep/23/mental-health-isnt-addressed-properly-students-on-the-pressures-of-university.

References

Alvesson, M. and Spicer, A. (2016) (Un)Conditional surrender? Why do professionals willingly comply with managerialism?, *Journal of Organizational Change Management*, 29(1):29–45.

Arendt, H. (1971) Thinking and moral considerations, *Social Research*, 38(3):417–446.

Bergin, A. (2013) *The Great Persuasion: Reinventing the Case for Markets since the Great Depression*, Cambridge, MA: Harvard University Press.

Binkley, S. (2011) Psychological life as enterprise: social practice and the government of neo-liberal interiority, *History of the Human Sciences*, 24(3):83–102.

Brinkmann, S. (2017) *Stand Firm: Resisting the Self-Improvement Craze*, London: Wiley.

Brown, W. (2015) *Undoing the Demos: Neoliberalism's Stealth Revolution*, New York, NY: Zone Books.

Chabot, P. (2019) *Global Burnout*, London: Bloomsbury Academic.

Chandler, D. and Reid, J. (2016) *The Neoliberal Subject: Resilience, Adaptation and Vulnerability*, London: Rowland and Littlefield International.

Davies, W. (2014) *The Limits of Neoliberalism: Authority, Sovereignty and the Logic of Competition*, London: Sage.

Davies, W. (2015) The chronic social: relations of control within and without neoliberalism, *New Formations*, 84:40–57. Winter 2014/Summer 2015.

Dewey, J. (1946) *The Public and Its Problems*, New York, NY: Gateway Books.

Ehrenreich, B. (2010) *Nickel and Dimed: Undercover in Low Wage America*, London: Granta.

Elias, N. (1956) Problems of involvement and detachment, *The British Journal of Sociology*, 7:226–252.

Elias, N. (2000) *The Civilising Process: Sociogenetic and Psychogenetic Investigations*, Oxford: Oxford University Press.

Elias, N. (2001) *The Loneliness of the Dying*, London: Continuum Books.

Feher, M. (2018) *Rated Agency: Investee Politics in a Speculative Age*, New York, NY: Zone Books.

Foucault, M. (2008) *The Birth of Biopolitics: Lectures at the Collège de France, 1978–1979*, New York, NY: Palgrave Macmillan.

Foulkes, S.H. (1975) *Group Analytic Psychotherapy: Method and Principles*, London: Karnac Books.

Friedman, M. (1955) The role of government in education. In: Solo, R.A. (ed.), *Economics and the Public Interest*, New Brunswick, NJ: Rutgers University Press. pp. 123–144.

Han, B. (2015) *The Burnout Society*, Stanford, CA: Stanford University Press.

Hartmann, M. and Honneth, A. (2006) Paradoxes of capitalism, *Constellations*, 13(1):41–58.

Hayek, F. (1944) *The Road to Serfdom*, London: Routledge.

Hayek, F.A. (1973/2013) *Law, Legislation and Liberty*, London: Routledge. pp. 39–40.

Hayek, F.A. (1974) *The Pretence of Knowledge*, Lecture to the memory of Alfred Nobel, 11 December 1974. Retrieved from: Nobelprize.org

Hayek, F.A. (1984) *The Essence of Hayek*, Stanford, CA: Stanford University Press.

Honneth, A. (1999) *Suffering from Indeterminacy: An Attempt at a Reactualization of Hegel's Philosophy of Right*, Amsterdam: Van Gorcum.

MacIntyre, A. (1985) *After Virtue*, London: Gerald Duckworth and Co.

Mead, G.H. (1934) *Mind, Self and Society from the Standpoint of a Social Behaviourist*, Chicago, IL: Chicago University Press.

Nesbitt, R.E. (2005) *The Geography of Thought: How Asians and Westerners Think Differently – And Why*, Boston, MA: Nicholas Brealey Publishing.

Parker, M. (2014) University Inc: Changing a Business School, *Organization*, 21(2):281–292.

Peck, J. (2010) *Constructions of Neoliberal Reason,* Oxford: Oxford University Press.

Rosa, H. (2015) *Social Acceleration: A New Theory of Modernity*, New York, NY: Columbia University Press.

Scharff, C. (2015) The psychic life of neoliberalism: mapping the contours of entrepreneurial subjectivity, *Theory, Culture & Society*, 33(6):1–16.

Sennett, R. (1998) *The Corrosion of Character*, London: WW Norton and Co.

Stedman Jones, D. (2012) *Masters of the Universe: Hayek, Friedman, and the Birth of Neoliberal Politics*, Princeton, NJ: Princeton University Press.

Streeck, W. (2014) *Buying Time: The Delayed Crisis of Democratic Capitalism*, London: Verso.

Taylor, C. (1989) *Sources of the Self: The Making of Modern Identity*, Cambridge: Cambridge University Press.

Venugopal, R. (2015) Neoliberalism as concept, *Economy and Society*, 44(2):165–187.

5

COMPLEX COMMUNICATION

Persuading and being persuaded

The following quotation encapsulates for me what it's like joining an organization, as a consultant, or as a new employee. It's a quotation that contemporary pragmatic philosopher Richard Bernstein (1992) uses in his book *The New Constellation* to illustrate how important conversation, discussion and debate are to being part of a group, any group:

> Imagine that you enter a parlor. You come late. When you arrive, others have long preceded you, and they are engaged in a heated discussion, a discussion too heated for them to pause and tell you exactly what it is about. In fact, the discussion has already begun long before any of them got there, so that no one present is qualified to retrace for you all the steps which have gone before. You listen for a while until you decide that you have caught the tenor of the argument, then you put in your oar. Someone answers; you answer him; another comes to your defense; another aligns himself against you, to either the embarrassment or the gratification of your opponent, depending on the quality of your ally's assistance. However, the discussion is interminable. The hour grows late. You must depart. And you do depart with the discussion still vigorously in progress.
>
> *Burke, 1941: 110–111*

I also think it's helpful for us in considering the central role of conversation in helping us try to stabilize the predictable-unpredictability of organizational life enough for us to negotiate how to go on together. Conversation, deliberation, also produces knowledge, which is another insight derived from the pragmatic tradition. Charles Sanders Peirce (1984), the first pragmatist, argued that knowledge arises in communities of inquiry, groups of scientists or researchers who share an interest in common, who carry out their research, then debate and leaven their inquiry by

DOI: 10.4324/9781003002840-5

contesting each other's methods and findings. Through the movement of debate knowledge also moves, something we look into further in this chapter.

Although this might appear to apply particularly to social science, I understand the philosopher of science Stephen French to make a similar claim in his book *There Are no Such Things as Theories* (2020), even for natural science, which we would usually consider to have a more orthodox attitude to 'truth' or 'facts.' French argues that there is no simple correspondence between a scientific theory and what it purports to describe. Using the example of quantum theory, he demonstrates how, both at the time and subsequently, different variations of quantum theory arose in the 1920s and 1930s, which led to contestation, debate and sometimes fierce rivalry between adherents of particular schools of thought. The key protagonists, Dirac, von Neumann, Weyl, all developed Schrödinger and Heisenberg's work and critiqued and disagreed with each other, and in the process moved thinking on. The debate continues still as new discoveries allow quantum physicists to reinterpret older work:

> The point, then, is that we need to abandon the idea that the history of the field, or the relevant practice of the scientists in general, supports the claim that this is 'a,' or 'the' theory of quantum mechanics, as a limited and well delineated entity, with definite identity conditions. This was clearly not the case of the so-called quantum revolution, nor in the immediate aftermath, nor subsequently, if we understand a theory, qua entity, as incorporating some claim as to how the world is, or could be.
>
> *2020: 209*

According to French, we cannot entirely trust the scientists' own accounts of how they 'discovered' their theories. What we take to be knowledge, or truth or theory arises in patterns of practices, discussion of those practices and different contested interpretations of the same which arise in groups of committed practitioners. This is Peirce's idea of the community of inquiry. The analogy which French uses is that the social process of knowledge development is like the layering of barnacles on the hull of a ship, only to find that when you scrape away the barnacles there is no longer a ship there. Although science has its particular standards and norms, it is nonetheless, and in the words of the title of historian of science Steven Shapin's book on scientific development (2010); *Never Pure*. I think Shapin's subtitle is a good rendering of the idea of social nature of knowledge which I am trying to convey here: *historical studies of science as if it was produced by people with bodies, situated in time and space, culture and society, and struggling for credibility and authority.*

In the same vein as Burke's parlor which began this chapter, when you enter an organization, you pitch into a discussion which is already going on and in which there are several threads and contested opinions. There is a history to each one of these threads, and one which we will never fully discover: everyone will have their own interpretation of what has 'really been going on' in the organization. As a newcomer, or as a consultant, sometimes it's a struggle to join in, to understand what is being said and what it might mean for what we do next because we don't yet have enough history with this particular group. We take up a role and try to become part of the action, influencing and being influenced. Once in the organization, not to participate is as significant as participating, because people have already noticed you. Do you have anything to say, and if you do say something, will it be recognized and/or accepted? There's no 'safe space' that people sometimes crave in team awaydays, and nor is there a view from outside of what is going on where you can make sense independently, somehow uninfluenced by the discussion you find ourselves in the middle of. As a newcomer, you may have less stake in the game than others who have been there longer. However, the moment we speak our 'truth' we have become part of the discussion; we have taken sides in organizational politics.

This is the aspect of the ongoing organizational conversation, or rather conversations, which doesn't come through so clearly in the quotation, that of organizational politics and power. In Burke's analogy, people do make alliances with each other, sometimes unfortunate ones, or ones we would rather not be part of. In organizations, some people's voices count more than others, and some ways of speaking count more than others. Status, power and accepted ways of speaking all make a difference; what Bourdieu refers to as symbolic power, or symbolic capital (Bourdieu, 1991: 180), can mediate whose voices get heard and whose opinion counts. What I think Bourdieu means by this is that who is speaking is sometimes as important as what they say.

In this chapter, I explore why speech is complex and unpredictable, reflect upon the connection between ways of speaking and the production of our social reality and consider a variety of responses to try and stabilize this inherent unpredictability, some of them more or less helpful. I explain why conversation is at the heart of what we are exploring here, the practical, everyday ways we talk our organizations into being and make them work by adapting and responding to each other. Speaking, thinking and acting, then, are all manifestations of the same process of creating our social worlds and are inseparable. To make better sense of our organizational reality, we have to pay attention to what people say about what they are doing. Linking back to the complexity models which we explored in Chapter 2, the back and forth of conversation framed by power relationships produce what Norbert Elias referred to as the structured flux of everyday organizational life.

The unpredictability of communicating

In Chapter 3, on complex action, we explored G.H. Mead's ideas about how we learn to participate in the social world through the playing of games and adjusting our behaviour according to our growing sense of a 'generalized other.' To play the game of hide and seek, we have to understand the role of everyone else in the game including our own, and as we learn to widen the idea of a game to comprise what Mead terms a social object, the tendency of large numbers of people to act in particular ways in societal routines, we learn how to attend school, participate in the workplace and engage with social rituals. Our increasing capacity for generalizing and comprehending the social game we are participating in enables us to imagine how other people would respond to our actions. This allows us both to participate and anticipate. Adopting a sense of the generalized other is also a form of reflexive social control: we are able to imagine what other people would think of what we say and do. We instantiate these generalizations in everyday conversation with others in our daily activities. This is what I have been trying to explain with what I have termed my elisionist position: structure and agency are present both at the same time in our dealings with each other. It's what we explore when we negotiate with one another on how to go on together.

To continue with Mead, central to the emergence of a sense of mind and self in Mead's terms is language. Language is a social phenomenon par excellence. To learn our own language is at the same time to be inducted into all kinds of shared social practices, beliefs and values: it is how we imbibe our culture and have the means to recreate it. Mead argues that we communicate in significant symbols. A symbol, a gesture which is likely to be made in speech but may also be bodily, is significant if it carries a similar meaning for all parties in communication. In other words, as individuals we are using generalized symbols to communicate: population-wide signification, a language in common, which is available to us locally as we engage in conversation with each other. For Mead, significant symbols are also the primary means through which we develop a mind and a sense of self. If mind is the activity of a body towards itself, then language, speaking to ourselves in private conversation or speaking out loud, which is the public manifestation of the same phenomenon, is the most obvious activity through which mind and self-develop. We could also understand this formulation as Mead's response to the structure/agency problem which we have discussed above. The fact that the symbol is significant, i.e., shared by other social beings, means both particular and general social phenomena are co-present. The Russian psychologist Lev Vygotsky (1982), whose ideas about children's intellectual development have been very influential in the field of education, had the same insight that the internalization of speech, what we call thinking, is central to the development of mind and self of young children.

It's worth dwelling on Mead's (1934) ideas about conversation because it may help us understand all those occasions when we have communicated with someone else expecting them to have understood exactly what we intended to convey, only to find ourselves misunderstood. It may also explain the naivety of managers who claim that they want to 'send out a clear message' to those they manage. This kind of thinking tends to rely on the idea that the message sent is exactly the one received.

One way of understanding Mead's explanation of both thinking and talking is that they are two sides of the same coin. Thinking is simply the private conversation we have with ourselves, while talking is public expression of our thoughts mediated by the context and company we keep. We don't simply say what we are thinking out loud, although we might do so by accident with sometimes uncomfortable social consequences. As we explored previously, our sense of the 'generalized other,' a generalized sense of what other people would think of what we say and do, constrains us and is a form of social control. But when we communicate with others, we also use our own bodies as a sounding board, according to Mead. What we say calls out in us a similar response that we expect to call out in those we are conversing with. That's how we can anticipate not only how they might react by feeling the effect of our words on ourselves, but also how we might find ourselves changing our minds about what we are saying even as we are saying it. We may find ourselves listening to what we say as we say it and adapting in the full flood of speaking. At the heart of the act of communication, then, is the potential for spontaneity, surprising ourselves and surprising others.

There is one further insight into Mead's ideas about human exchange which may help us understand why there is nothing inevitable or deterministic about communicating with one another, no matter how clear the message we think we are conveying. Mead argues that when we communicate, no one party has the monopoly over meaning; meaning lies in the gesture and the response taken together. We may be more or less in control, or clear about the meaning we want to convey, but we won't be sure about what has been communicated until we experience the response. We all have different life histories and the same message can call out a variety of different responses in us, according to that experience. For example, a senior manager inviting her staff to unite around a positive and bright future for the company could call out cynicism from every employee who has experienced similar events before, or enthusiasm from those who haven't. The meaning of the gesture, to invite staff to cohere around an idealized representation of the future will be multiple according to how staff have previously experienced her, the context, their previous experience of 'visioning,' etc. There is no one meaning. The manager, in turn, responds to the gestures she experiences from the staff she is dealing with, which will play out over time. An emergent pattern of meaning-making arises between all those engaged in making sense of what the joint activity signifies which is never at rest and is never concluded. One way of thinking about organization is as an endless chain of gesture and response.

The ethnomethodologist Deidre Boden (1994) demonstrates how the organization is created moment by moment in conversational activity in her book *The Business of Talk*. At the same time, she takes a similar position on the structure–agency debate that we have been exploring here. Since Chapter 2, on complexity models, I have been suggesting that structure/agency, individual/group is a paradox. It's not that interacting agents give rise to social structure at a separate level of social reality, nor that social structures act in a determinate way to condition what individual agents are doing, but rather people reproduce and potentially transform social reality in their everyday working contexts. Similarly, Boden argues that there is no such thing as separate action and structure, rather 'structure' is instantiated moment by moment in conversational activities between people who create and recreate the organization:

> As people talk organizations into being they simultaneously pick out the particular strands of abstract order that can relevantly instantiate the moment. In so doing, they significantly support, shape and occasionally subvert the

organization, which will then move forward into the next moments through other actions with other actors.

1994: 202

In studying people taking turns and talking the organization into existence, Boden makes a number of other points which I think are salient for our argument here. First of all, she makes a strong case for paying attention to what people actually say and do in their micro-interactions with each other, just as we are doing in this book. In other words, if we want to understand what's happening at work, it is easy to get lost in abstractions which cover over what we most need to notice: it feels very familiar for people to say something like 'the organization is going in a different direction' or 'we need to align our values,' but what does this really mean? A lot of literature on organizations more commonly deals in abstractions, and the quotidian is more likely to be considered a messy distraction. But for Boden, it is in studying the particular that we can find out the granularity of how the organization becomes.

Second, she notes that work only works because reflexive beings are constantly adapting and responding to each other to get things done. They deliberate and work out together 'what's happening,' which allows then to take the next steps together in a fluid and flexible way. Boden claims that organizational reality is produced from 'within' rather than in relation to some external set of abstractions such as organizational rules or policies and procedures. What I think she means by that is that what we might take to be the 'smooth and reasonable surface' (ibid.: 198) of the organization is sustained by staff operating according to the logic of practice in their local situation. People try and collaborate together in the present, making sense of past events and in anticipation of the future, negotiating how to go on together.

Our sense of self depends on our relations with others (Chapter 4), our actions are caught up in a web of other people's actions (Chapter 3) and so we have to talk our way into making sense of what we are doing and what we might do next. This is particularly the case in situations of uncertainty, where we find ourselves immersed in trying to influence, and being influenced, in the struggle over deciding what's best for 'us.'

Imposing a view to settle the uncertainty

In the introduction to this chapter, I made a connection between ways of speaking and the production of knowledge, what is and isn't acceptable to say about the situation we might find ourselves in. The connection between ways of speaking, discourse, power relations and the production of knowledge is one of the key themes in Foucault's oeuvre. Next, I explored how Peirce's idea of a community of inquiry where knowledge develops as a result of the back and forth of debate and noted that power relations are one quality of relating, affecting how the discussion unfolds. Who speaks and what they say also counts. I explore this in more detail in Chapter 6 on complex knowledge.

I now investigate two ways of imposing one kind of order rather than another on the predictable unpredictability of organizational life through speaking. The first is to create dominant ways of speaking about what's important in the organization, and the other, no less tied to the first, are tools and techniques of management and organizational development (OD), which are intended to clear up the messiness and the political jeopardy, the uncertainty of communicating with each other. Both are more or less ideological in the sense that they try to cover over existing power relations as though they are natural and to be taken for granted or claim that we can do away with power relations. They create, in the words of the early 20th century historian of science Ludwik Fleck's words, a 'thought collective' (1935/1981). We might understand a thought collective in similar terms to Peirce's idea of a community of inquiry: it requires a kind of discipline and focus, a shared vocabulary among a group of scholars or practitioners interested in a set of ideas to take the work forward. What Fleck brings to the term, however, is the paradoxical quality of being a member of a thought collective: it both enables and constrains in the sense that you have to enter into the 'thought style' to continue with the discipline, but at the same time it becomes difficult to realize that one is hemmed in by it:

> Although the thought collective consists of individuals, it is not simply the aggregate sum of them. The individual within the collective is never, or hardly ever, conscious of the prevailing thought style, which almost always exerts an absolutely compulsive influence upon his thinking and with which it is not possible to be at variance.
>
> *1935/1981: 41*

In a way, we are all ideological most of the time, assuming that the world is the way we see it. It is very hard to inquire into our own taken-for-granted assumptions. Fleck documents how novelty arises in thought collectives, even when they seem to challenge the existing thought style, and shows the effort the collective will make to accommodate contradictory facts into existing ways of thinking. But the social cost can be quite high. Anyone speaking out against the prevailing orthodoxy in contemporary organizations will similarly have found that the potential consequence of doing so is to risk exclusion from the group.

Managerialist ways of imposing order

To give another example of ways of speaking and acting in organizations creates a thought collective, which raises the stakes about being included or excluded from a group, I went to hear Prof Colin Crouch promote his book *The Knowledge Corrupters: Hidden Consequences of the Financial Takeover of Public Life* (2016) at the Institute for Government in London.

Crouch's thesis is that the financialization of public institutions reduces the meaning of what they do to a limited number of numerical targets and performance indicators often of a financial kind. This has the effect of also reducing the spectrum of knowledge we need fully to be employees, citizens and customers and constrains expert judgement. It has the effect of trumping all other valuations of particular organizational or social problems with one supposed truth, that of the bottom line or a financial target. I explored a similar argument in my previous book (2015) by drawing on Gadamer (1993), how the demands of technology and administration which are oriented towards standardization threaten to rob the experienced practitioner of their practical judgement along with their fulfilment at work. Gadamer argued that bureaucratic demands, 'feeding the beast,' can often produce social irrationality.

One example Crouch gives of the consequences of financialization from the United Kingdom is the monetary incentive offered to General Practitioners (GPs) to refer more patients with suspected Alzheimer's disease for further medical tests. The incentive is problematic on a number of fronts: although it is offered on the basis of encouraging behaviour which politicians deem to beneficial to the public as a whole, it nonetheless implies that GPs would not refer patients without such a financial reward. It enacts a theory of motivation at odds with the medical profession's own values: the overwhelming majority of doctors would not consider it either necessary or desirable to be offered money to refer someone for tests who needs them. Additionally, in Crouch's terms, it has the potential for corrupting expert knowledge as well as creating perverse incentives. Crouch is not implying that professionals need no scrutiny or don't need managing, but he does argue that financial targets, and numerical targets, more generally, are a crude measure of what is really important in specific situations when the work is complex. It is a very crude, mistrustful intervention to bring about a greater focus on potential Alzheimer's sufferers.

When the discussion started after Crouch's presentation, it became clear that there were a number of senior professionals present who complained about the gradual erosion of their scope for action over a number of years and following 'reforms' of public services by governments of all hues. The government has created artificial markets where none have previously existed, even by setting up 'purchasers' and 'providers' in the same service. The same is true of the higher education sector in the United Kingdom: in the 12 years since I have been an academic, the number of forms I need to fill to do anything has proliferated, and I am hedged around by risk assessments, often of a financial kind because of the uncertainties which markets create. And the higher education sector is certainly considered a market place now.

Anyone who works in a managerial organization has probably also experienced the crisis of confidence that managers seem to have in employees exercising their practical judgement, or contesting and deliberating on what is to be done. Privileging targets and financial outcomes can also demonstrate a distrust of negotiation of what we take to be the good in any given situation. In contemporary managerial organizations, all goods are often subsumed within the dominant way of thinking of the financialized organization. In doing so, managerialism both suppresses particular kinds of speaking and particular kinds of knowledge, especially *phronesis* or practical judgement, the 'what to do' in any given situation, and particular forms of engagement about what is important knowledge, i.e., politics with a small 'p,' the 'how we might decide.' I explore the ramifications of this general social trend again in Chapter 8 on complex ethics.

Managerialism privileges measurement, which we might understand as a new form of Taylorism, aimed at placing management methods on a 'scientific' basis, and thus rendering decisions less contestable (although here I have been arguing a completely opposite view of the sociology of knowledge that scientific insight is produced in communities of engaged inquirers who argue with each other). In contemporary organizations, it can be a way of cutting short discussion by appealing to the 'facts': this is not inevitable, depending on the institution, because quantification can also be used as a way of starting a conversation rather than closing it down. Another way of thinking about it is that it is a way of creating the kind of uncertainty that advantages managers, with everyone on the back foot anxious about whether they are meeting their targets or not. So the struggle is not over stability or uncertainty, but over the quality of uncertainty and who this puts at an advantage.

In many orthodox organizations, other ways of narrowing the range of what is discussable is to emphasize particular ways of speaking to each other, such as the injunction to accentuate the positive, or at least avoid negative and critical engagement with what's going on. This may be accompanied by strong invitations to align, perhaps with the vision or with other symbols of organizational unity. Other methods involve proceduralizing the way we engage with each other at work. Anyone who has been on an organizational awayday is probably familiar with having to agree the rules of engagement in advance at the start of the day. We might, for example, be enjoined to offer only 'constructive feedback' as though we can know beforehand what the other person will experience as constructive, a notion which Mead's theory of communication makes problematic.

Alternatively, managers might be sent on communication courses to improve the way they communicate with their staff. I have nothing against people trying to enhance the way they communicate, but the discourse analyst Elizabeth Stokoe (2018), who considers herself a highly social psychologist, warns against the kinds of manual-based communication courses which proceduralize, say, 'active listening' and 'building rapport' so that, ironically, they become unnatural. Stokoe argues that conversation is both simple, it follows particular patterns and is analysable, and complex in the sense that context counts: it's important to think about who is in the conversation and what they are trying to achieve together. Stokoe thinks that we should, of course, listen to each other, but this isn't about following the rules to demonstrate the required competence but paying attention to what the context demands. Abstracting from conversation to train people in 'best practice' can have exactly the opposite effect that it intends, rendering people thoughtless in their interactions with each other rather than improvising together in conversation, adapting and responding to what the situation demands.

Eva Illouz (2007) reflects in a similar way on the effects of neoliberal modernity on our sense of self in a study she conducted into lonely hearts advertisements. She argues that in the 20th and 21st centuries, the language of therapy and self-help has joined with the language of economic productivity to make our emotions 'domains of action submitted to the public gaze' (2007: 37). Particular ways of speaking about our lifeworld have become standardized: it's as if there are accepted templates for speaking about our inner life. This, she contends, puts our emotions and intimate relationships at the centre of a model of economic bargaining and exchange. In this way, our emotions become disentangled from the concrete particulars of our relationships with others and are conveyed as a 'model of communication' as though we are taking the position of an abstract other. It's important to stress that Illouz doesn't claim that this has come about through anyone's design. Much as Elias describes, the patterns of our relationships emerge in way that is of no one, or no particular group's choosing. Rather, we are all subject to longer terms trends which shape us and our *habitus*.

Organizational development interventions

At the other end of the ideological spectrum from managerialism and target culture are OD interventions, ways of 'designing organizations,' which purport to increase collaboration and transparency. They claim to be a counterweight to the emphasis on hierarchy and magical thinking about leadership. But in doing so, and for me, they produce magical thinking about human relationships and the uncertainty surrounding talk.

For example, sociocracy and holacracy are two methods for structuring organizations and proceduralizing work and claim to make organizations more rational. Sociocracy locates its intellectual heritage in the thinking of Comte, one of the first proponents of the discipline of sociology, aspiring to think more scientifically about the social. Sociocracy takes up principles of engineering and cybernetics applied to 'human systems.' In the 20th century, Dutch electrical engineer Gerard Endenburg put his workers in teams, or 'circles,' organized hierarchically, where all decisions within the circle are reached by common consent. While sociocracy suggests a gradualist approach to organizational change, holacracy, on the other hand, offers a more comprehensive programme, a 'complete package,' for transitioning wholesale to a holacratic organization based on a 'constitution' which covers the way to design your organizational structure (circles and sub-circles), efficient ways to run your meetings and problem-solve 'without bureaucracy.' Holacracy draws on the parts/whole thinking said to originate with both Arthur Koestler and Ken Wilbur, where the part is both autonomous and contributory to the whole at the same time.

Both perspectives claim to be egalitarian in their intent. Sociocracy and holacracy maintain that applying their methods means that decisions are not made autocratically or on the basis of prejudice or politics, but rather on reasoned argument. When a team member senses a gap or tension between what is and what could be and makes a recommendation to the team as to why a change should be made, an elected facilitator holds the ring while the team member's ideas are tested by questioning from other team members. The holacracy constitution has a very detailed account of how this might be done which currently stretches to more than 20 pages. Both design methods assume that human beings are somehow prevented from reaching their full collaborative potential because of restricted ways of working and organizational structures which get in the way. They argue that they enhance value alignment, trust, co-operation and harmonious working and create greater organizational resilience and distribute power throughout the organization. Organizational politics are largely considered an impediment to effective organizational working, as are managers and leaders; they are part of an 'old mentality.' Staff in organizations are said to be self-organizing, or self-managing, because they operate according to clear rules of engagement which enhance transparency.

So there is a clear thread of rationalist/positivist thought in each of these perspectives which dates back to Kant, continuing through Comte to Habermas. Habermas' theory of communicative action (1984, 1987) imagines the abstract conditions under which human beings can communicate and be understood, untrammelled by unequal social relations and power. Equally, but from a critical and emancipatory perspective, in these OD methods, it is held that there are more rational, procedural ways of conducting ourselves, so that we can set aside our differences and the messy ambiguity of staying in relation with each other. Through the application of reason, we can overcome our fear of tradition, religion and authority and release ourselves from our need to dominate each other.

These examples could be understood as attempts to cover over everyday politics and contestation and to create order out of uncertainty. They are also based on emancipatory intent to replace the uncertainties of power relationships and politics with an ideal of harmony and rationality.

All organizations have to struggle with questions of authority and control: and they must do so if they are to coordinate the activities of many employees to achieve what it is they are constituted to achieve. But for some reason, we seem frightened by what might happen if we encourage people simply to speak to each other and learn to deliberate together, taking account of a variety of partial points of view. Because of a number of tendencies in contemporary organizational life, the financialization of organizations, a dependence on abstract targets, the discourse on leadership, the idea that every meeting needs a concrete outcome and that talking might threaten to 'open a can of worms,' we may become alienated from what matters to us, from our experience and from our ability to exercise judgement.

Dwelling in uncertain speech – rhetoric and judgement

Having outlined what I consider the orthodox appeal to the abstract, either the abstractions of quantification realized as metrics, targets or financialization or the idea that we can create procedures, rule-based abstractions for doing away with hierarchy, power and politics, I want to turn to arguments in favour of remaining messily engaged with each other and leaving ourselves open to persuading and being persuaded. So rather than assuming a universal position, in the tradition of

Plato, Kant and Habermas, instead I am going to argue in favour of partiality, prejudice, in the sense of inevitably bringing prejudgements and rhetoric in navigating uncertainty. The case I make is that the conversational work that we engage in, in organizations, involves a lot of persuading, coaxing and appealing to each other's judgement and that this is a legitimate, even helpful way of recognizing each other in the midst of complexity. My assumption here is that power always manifests itself one way or another because we are interdependent. And the attempt to cover it over or wish it away with appeals to rationality, to quantification and to the 'vision' of the organization is also an ideological appeal. Additionally, involving each other in deliberation about the particular uncertain situation we find ourselves in together is, in my view, more likely to be helpful in a specific context, rather than ideas taken from 'best practice' or aspiring to a view from nowhere.

As in the rest of the book, and in further making my assumptions clear, I take a position along with Gigerenzer (2008) and Mercier and Sperber (2017) that human reason arises in social and specific contexts and works well to help people function in groups. Reason often produces knowledge useful beyond the group, given particular conditions which we explore below, drawing on Elias. That the group is central for the functioning of reason is a view which is contrary to perhaps the dominant discourse on reason rooted in cognitive psychology, which is likely to hold that reason is both our greatest, but most flawed asset, understood to arise from an individual thinking by themselves. From a cognitive perspective, as individuals, we are prone to struggle with probability, and we are lazy and look for arguments which confirm our own biases (what's known as confirmation bias). Gigerenzer, Emeritus Director at the Max Planck Institute of Human Development, builds on the idea of 'bounded rationality' developed by Herbert Simon. Both he and Mercier and Sperber take aim at Kahneman (2012) and Taversky, whose ideas have become very popular after the former psychologist won the Nobel Prize. Reason is not as flawed as we have come to believe, measured against abstract standards of logic and consistency viewed from an individual perspective, Mercier and Sperber argue. This is because human beings are very adept at rule-of-thumb heuristics that make much greater sense in context (Gigerenzer), and are 'interactionist' (Mercier and Sperber): in other words, humans are group animals reasoning with and through others. Looking for other information which bolsters your viewpoint might be a good social strategy if your focus is on convincing other members of your group:

> According to the interactionist approach, reason didn't evolve to enhance thinking on one's own but as a tool for social interaction. We produce reasons to justify ourselves and to convince others ... Why not envisage, then, the exchange of reasons and the mechanism of reason could have evolved for the benefit of the group, rather than for the benefit of individuals?
>
> *2017: 333*

Mercier and Sperber in particular reintroduce the social quality of reasoning in a group, which may take longer and may produce twists and turns and dead-ends.

But in the end, it may also produce agreement, or knowledge or trust that enables a group to go on together.

There are traditions of scholarship in sociology and philosophy that also try to cleave to the social and conversational view of reason. Nearly 80 years ago, the sociologist Karl Mannheim, who was Norbert Elias' supervisor, argued that politics and argumentation is particularly evident when an area of social life is not yet settled and routine: when we experience 'tendencies and strivings in a constant state of flux' to try and settle the matter. He noticed the way that bureaucracies try to cover over questions of politics and value with an appeal to administrative rationality and assume that all political problems lend themselves to administrative remedies, oblivious to the fact that current bureaucratic procedures are also the product of previous struggles over value. Our modern-day appeal to metrics is not new, then. In the present disposition, and in many domains of organizational life, the emphasis of targets and financial reporting reflects the dominance of a particular understanding of administrative rationality resulting from a particular power figuration, and in this sense is ideological.

For Mannheim, there is no abstract, independent view on situations in flux: in other words, all points of view on the situation are partial and informed by particular social positions. In Mannheim's terms, our point of view is informed by social background, a perception which we might critique as overly relativistic. But to better to resolve complex social situations, Mannheim argued that we need to bring all the partial points of view into play, including our own, rather than denying them. One of the reasons that Mannheim gives for his argument against abstracting is that the kind of knowledge we need for resolving problems arising from particular concrete situations is that it is impossible to separate the knowledge we need from the specific context in which it arises. Abstracting and systematizing of course has its value, but not, he argues, for developing insight into situations which develop from a particular set of circumstances and are a product of them. To separate the two out is to do violence to our understanding, he argues.

Elias takes Mannheim's thinking one step further; in two papers, he writes about the sociology of knowledge (Elias, 1971a,b) to mitigate against what he thinks of as two fallacies. He is keen to navigate between what he considers the twin and unhelpful poles of assuming that absolute truth is timeless and thought up by individuals cogitating on their own, the position of unnuanced philosophy. The alternative is that truth arises in groups and can only be relative to that group, which he considers the position of unnuanced sociology. The idea that knowledge arises in groups of scholars who deliberate together seems to him to be relatively settled, and the idea of the autonomous cognizing individual as inadequate as an explanation. However, there is more to say about the functioning of groups. First, he argues that, and contra Weber, scientific knowledge is never completely value-free. For example, groups of scientists embrace disinterestedness as a public value: they have values about not letting their values interfere with their work. Second, groups of scholars, in whatever discipline, are able to produce knowledge that is relatively autonomous of the groups which produced them. Elias also extends this definition of relative autonomy to works of art, or music, which may be popular for hundreds of years. Shakespeare's works are not only a product of a particular time and place, but have also endured in their ability to say something about the human condition to future generations. This pertains to Elias' other criterion of 'object adequacy,' the ability of the insight produced to be more adequate to the 'object' described than to the subjectivities of the groups trying to describe them. All knowledge, he argues, is produced in groups but sits on a spectrum of relative autonomy from the group which produces it and object adequacy. For Elias, there is no such thing as absolute objectivity and absolute detachment, and sometimes the subject adequacy of the knowledge produced is privileged.

For Mannheim and Boden and those who take a highly social view of human activity, the grappling isn't just over truth, or facts or what counts as knowledge but is also about who gets to call the shots and impose some order on the disorder. For Elias, knowledge can be relatively autonomous from the groups producing it and relatively object adequate, but this may come with a consequence for its subject adequacy, when groups ask the question, who are we and what do we think we are doing?

The importance of rhetoric

This idea that our partial points of view, our prejudices if you like, are vital for navigating the flux and change of social life, particularly in highly fluid situations where judgement is required, has a long history in philosophy dating back in particular to Aristotle through to Gadamer in the 20th century. Contemporary philosophers Danielle Allen (2004), Adam Sandel (2014), Bryan Garsten (2009) and organizational scholar Robin Holt (2006) take this thinking further. Sandel explores the philosophical basis for our prejudice against prejudice, Garsten explores the history of the rhetoric against rhetoric and Allen thinks about what is required to improve a sense of citizenship when society is fractured by polarized thinking about race. Holt encourages to think about why rhetoric is helpful in re-moralizing management, particularly is it has become overly dependent on instrumental thinking, in the ways I have described earlier. All make a case for the importance of trying to convince each other through politics and persuasion of the strength of relative value claims, just as we found Hannah Arendt doing in Chapter 3.

In doing so, they try to rehabilitate the importance of practical judgement, exactly the kind of practical knowledge which is, in my view, most under threat in contemporary organizations where there is a strong appeal to the abstract. We need to take the time to talk to each other and share our partial views of the world and find space for exercising our practical judgement about things which matter to us as groups. This is a more active form of engagement with each other because it requires all of us to participate. I take up the theme of rhetoric in this section and return to the importance of practical judgement in the next chapter on complex knowledge. In Chapter 8, I explore more fully the ethical implications of engaging in everyday politics.

Those interested in rhetoric set out why we need to be wary of it; its critics remind us that, at its worst, rhetoric can be used by people to manipulate or to pander to groups. In an organizational context, Holt notes that:

> rhetoric can become an end in itself, exposing the managerial exponents to accusations of superficiality, fabrication and a preoccupation with self-serving gratification.

2006: 1667

where the outcome can be cynicism and disappointment on the part of staff. Suspicion of rhetoric and practical judgement has a long philosophical history. In brief, and to pursue Garsten's argument, the case against distrusting our judgement started in the early modern period with Hobbes. Garsten argues that from the perspective of a philosopher writing amid the English civil war, the imperative was to find ways of binding human beings together in a social contract where they didn't resolve their difficulties by fighting each other to the death. The solution, Hobbes suggested, was to put our faith in the sovereign: to submit to the king so that paradoxically we could all enjoy freedom. Meanwhile, Rousseau was also concerned to find ways of preventing mankind's natural fanaticism by appealing to what binds us together, our place in nature, rather than the authority of men. According to Garsten, Rousseau's project was to convince without persuading, to bring about an internalized and naturalized 'shared authoritative perspective on controversial issues' (2009: 83), a shared agreement which is thought to be a manifestation of the natural or the divine. Garsten sees contemporary manifestations of this form of rhetoric in contemporary nation states which shows up as prophetic nationalism. In Garsten's account, both Hobbes and Rousseau took seriously the history of their times which produced fanaticism and killing on the grand scale. In trying to find ways of binding people together, however, they potentially generated ways of oppressing people in other ways.

Kant, according to Garsten, also had a suspicion of prudential wisdom, or *phronesis*, because it was messy and contextual. Citizens could participate in the polity, but only once they had become enlightened autonomous individuals disciplining themselves not to follow their common sense or ordinary opinions but the sovereign dictates of critical reason. (It is also true that this involved taking into account the opinions of other reasoners.) The idea was that a group of enlightened individuals could develop together one authoritative perspective with which every reasonable person would agree. This last idea is manifested in contemporary liberal politics, when political discussion can revolve around a concept of what most 'reasonable people' believe, the danger of which is that minority views, or passionate views, are discounted. In the United Kingdom, our recent experience of the Brexit discussion makes clear the weakness of the argument that reasonable people can necessarily agree, or that the views of expert reasoners are enough to persuade others that their views are acceptable.

These ideas put me in mind of contemporary organizational life which I have set out earlier in this chapter. The link I make with Hobbes, for example, is connected to the modern discourse on leadership (which we explore in Chapter 7 on complex authority) particularly the idea of transformational charismatic leadership. One way of understanding the popularity of the charismatic leader is as an appeal to sacrifice our judgement to the omnipotent sovereign. Similarly, I see vestiges of Rousseau's thinking in many humanist writers whose appeal is that we give up our bad (partial) selves and submit to the natural order of the organization: we are invited to 'align' with the organization understood as a whole, because it is the nature of things which we should not oppose. This theme is very prominent in what we might think of as 'New Age' writing about organizations understood as 'living, breathing wholes' with purposes of their own. Meanwhile, in facilitated meetings, or appraisals or many manifestations of action learning theory, there is often an appeal to abstract Kantian reasoning: we stick to pre-agreed rules of engagement, that we will be constructive in our feedback, or that we will follow prescribed ways of interacting, asking only questions, not offering solutions or only speaking when we are allowed by the facilitator to do so just in case politics or prejudice break out.

Exercising judgement, taking a position, involves drawing on both emotion and reason, because it is based on our lived experience. In complex situations, emotions are relevant to what is going on and may be good 'data' for indicating what matters to us. Additionally, emotions can shock us out of habitual ways of responding to what is going on; they are, in Martha Nussbaum's (2001) terms, 'upheavals of thought.' If we are to deliberate together about the complex and ambiguous situations in which we find ourselves, then this involves drawing on our practical judgement with all its partiality, messiness and contingency, rather than searching for or appealing to an abstract and often idealized position. The point of rhetoric, as Allen reminds us, is to provoke our audience into using their judgement:

> Rhetoric is the art of not rousing people to immediate or unthinking action, but of putting as persuasive an argument as possible to an audience, and then leaving actual choices of action to them.
>
> *2004: 141*

The flux and change of social life is ceaseless, and resolving one set of difficulties often results in producing others.

For Holt, the judicious use of rhetoric is a way of achieving a 'smart compromise' when there are competing points of view and valuations of the good. Rhetoric is:

> the ability to persuade others of the apposite nature of specific purposes and interests, whilst maintaining regard for the interests of others and the conversational conditions by which others are able to express their own interests. I have described this ability as phronesis; the sagacity to recognize that interests

can only be understood as arising under one particular aspect or another, and none of which are a-historical, universal and unchanging.

2006: 1677

Valuing practical judgement and understanding what we are doing as a necessary political process which tries to bring as many partial truths into view as possible, then appealing to our colleagues' critical faculties may be one way of humanizing the workplace. In Aristotle's terms, rhetoric is understood as an ethical means of persuading a plurality of others to act for the good of the community. Understanding the role of rhetoric may help us more fully recognize ourselves and each other in what we do. This involves appreciating our context and history and the unique qualities of the group we are addressing. It also involves a more active engagement of the community addressed by the rhetor, and so a different kind of power relationship between those trying to convince and those who are to be convinced.

Summing up – why speech will always be complex: implications for managers

In this chapter, I have highlighted the inherently improvisational nature of speaking to each other which contributes to, and yet also mediates, the predictable unpredictability of organizational life. How we speak, act and reason depends upon our relationships with others in groups. There are good reasons and bad for trying to cut through the messiness of speech: we don't have time to deliberate over everything, particularly in an accelerating world, and there is value in the appeal to standards, metrics and abstractions. We cannot navigate the world without using abstractions, but being able to functionalize, to understand their importance for 'us' in the here and now is also a necessary step. The appeal to numbers, to the vision and to a universal position cannot sidestep our experience and judgement about what our current situation needs.

Dwelling in the messiness of everyday conversational life of the organization and noticing who is speaking, what they are saying and how this prompts us to respond is central to taking each other seriously. We may never get on top of exactly what is being said for the reasons that Mead supplies: conversation is an endless cycle of gesture and response and we can only grasp for meaning in the gesture and response taken together. In the spontaneous improvisational gesture-response lies the potential for maintaining, or perhaps transforming the work we do together. To return to the book I quoted at the very beginning of this chapter, Richard Bernstein's *The New Constellation* (1992), the kind of reasoning together that we require he describes as 'engaged, fallibilistic pluralism.' What I think he means by this is that when the going gets tough in our relationships, and what we should do next is far from obvious, we have no option to aspire to detachment: we cannot help but be engaged because what is going on matters to us. However, we need to be open to the contingency and fallibility of our own position as well as radically open to the positions of others. We need to be plural in our considerations. I return to these themes in Chapter 8 on complex ethics. A skill worth cultivating for managers, then, is the ability to pay attention to what a group requires to go on together, and to be able to speak into that need. This requires developing good skills of persuasion which involve recognizing the audience and what's important for them.

I worked with a group of senior managers in a higher education establishment to help them think about their ways of working while they discussed strategy. A pattern emerged in the discussion about current difficulties and in anticipation of future changes that drew on ideas of an education marketplace, and which called forth economic language. Managers were concerned about 'buy in' to plans and strategies, they worried about brand, they were anxious about their students' customer experience and they wondered how they would act if their institution were a supermarket, a supermarket like John Lewis, for example. They were anxious about competitive threats from the Chinese, they wanted to make business cases for change and they were concerned about their products. Education needed to be as flexible as possible so that students could consume whatever, whenever they wanted. They were worried about student satisfaction. These notes of market vocabulary were the clearest melody, although there were also contrapuntal themes opposing them – some argued that being businesslike isn't the same as being a business.

I wondered what might be going on in the group, and what else was being communicated with all this market language. Perhaps it is one way of reducing uncertainty and anxiety by developing a discourse shared in common, and by identifying with the currently dominant and perhaps reductive way of thinking about strategy dilemmas. Young economists Joe Earle, Cahal Moran and Zac Ward-Perkins (2017) have pointed to how this phenomenon I experienced in this particular group of managers has been amplified more generally in society. They refer to it as an Econocracy, where all social problems and questions of policy become reduced to questions of economics, and economics of a particular and abstract neoclassical kind. So one explanation would be that the adoption of the language of the marketplace is a response to the marketization of higher education, and not just education but also an identification with a dominant power figuration. It has become a common sense and taken-for-granted way of thinking about the world. Members of this particular group were signalling to each other that they understood, and perhaps even agreed with, the current orthodoxy.

In doing so, group members communicated to each other that they think they belong to an elite group: they are an in-group which really understands the particular and contemporary difficulties they all face. Elsewhere, Norbert Elias has referred to this as a 'heroic we identity' (1994). A minority of members of the group had recently been on management courses where they had been taught to think and talk this way. One might, then, understand this phenomenon as an example of MBA-thinking considered appropriate to a cadre of managers/leaders operating at this level of the hierarchy: there is cachet in being fluent in business-speak. Perhaps there is an assumption that other senior management teams in a similar cohort of higher education establishments talk about their strategy dilemmas in similar ways. It's what senior managers do.

In creating an in-group through the now common-sense ideology that all social problems can be reduced to questions of economics, it became quite difficult to explore different ways of thinking, and particularly arguments to the contrary. If the dominant way of talking is to draw on business terms, then it may sounds unbusinesslike, naïve even, to make a different kind of argument. Framing strategy dilemmas in terms of economics is beguiling and reduces complexity. But it also produces an enhanced sense of risk – there was a good deal of anxiety in the room about competitors, about 'loss of market share,' about technology and about 'the Chinese.'

Patricia Shaw (2002) made the case that changes in organizations are changes in conversations: people talk about what they are doing differently, which at the same time makes them think and act differently. In another piece of research I carried out in different Higher Education Institution, a senior member of the management team described how some years ago he had participated in a workshop facilitated by an outside consultant to help his team think through processes of change:

> Oh, it was all you know, sort of get the monkey off your back and all those kinds of management book clichés really, it was all of that stuff, Americanisms and yeah, it wasn't the language we were used to using at all. It would be really interesting to have done a study on to what extent now amongst those people who sat in those rooms and found his terminology a bit alien and confusing and hilarious at times; are they actually now using some of those terms? I think they probably would be.

What starts out as alien and incongruous becomes ubiquitous and taken for granted. It is hard not to talk into a conversation using different vocabulary from everyone else.

Some of the other voices in the group I was working with tried to raise the following questions, potentially disrupting the university-as-business discourse: to what extent should students be satisfied? Isn't there something inherently disturbing and unsettling about the educational experience, which doesn't lead immediately to feelings of satisfaction? (This doesn't dismiss the idea that the institution should provide the best possible education for students who pay a lot of money for it.) And what about the university's responsibility to the academic disciplines which make up a higher education establishment? Is there a trade-off between flexibility and academic rigour? How important are the relationships within which learning takes place, and which are particularly important for developing learners – do we have a tendency to over-glamourize technology as the answer to everything? To what extent does the university turn on the idea of transmission rather than transaction, more-experienced learners struggling with less-experienced learners in a community of inquiry, the notion that learning takes place between human bodies trying to stay in relation? Is education an end in and of itself, rather than being a passport to a job in an organization?

References

Allen, D. (2004) *Talking to Strangers: Anxieties of Citizenship Since Brown vs Board of Education*, Chicago, IL: University of Chicago Press.

Bernstein, R.J. (1992) *The New Constellation: Ethical/Political Horizons of Modernity/Post Modernity*, Ann Arbor, MI: MIT Press.

Boden, D. (1994) *The Business of Talk*, Cambridge: Polity Press.

Bourdieu, P. (1991) *Language and Symbolic Power*, Cambridge: Polity Press.

Burke, K. (1941) *The Philosophy of Literary Form: Studies in Symbolic Action*, Los Angeles, CA: UCLA Press.

Crouch, C. (2016) *The Knowledge Corrupters: Hidden Consequences of the Financial Takeover of Public Life*, Cambridge: Polity Press.

Earle, J., Moran, C. and Ward-Perkins, Z. (2017) *The Econocracy: The Perils of Leaving Economics to the Experts*, London: Penguin.

Elias, N. (1971a) Sociology of knowledge: new perspectives: Part One, *Sociology*, 5(2):149–168.

Elias, N. (1971b) Sociology of knowledge: new perspectives: Part Two, *Sociology*, 5(3):355–370.

Elias, N. and Scotson, J. (1994) *The Established and the Outsiders: A Sociological Inquiry into Community Problems*, London: Sage.

Fleck, L. (1935/1981) *Genesis and Origin of a Scientific Fact*, Chicago, IL: Chicago University Press.

French, S. (2020) *There Are No Such Things as Theories*, Oxford: Oxford University Press.

Gadamer, H.-G. (1993) *Reason in the Age of Science*, Cambridge, MA: MIT Press.

Garsten, B. (2009) *Saving Persuasion: A Defense of Rhetoric and Judgment*, Cambridge, MA: Harvard University Press.

Gigerenzer, K. (2008) *Rationality for Mortals: How People Cope with Uncertainty*, Oxford: Oxford University Press.

Habermas, J. (1984) *Theory of Communicative Action, Volume One: Reason and the Rationalization of Society*. Translated by McCarthy, T.A. Boston, MA: Beacon Press.

Habermas, J. (1987) *Theory of Communicative Action, Volume Two: Lifeworld and System: A Critique of Functionalist Reason*. Translated by McCarthy, T.A. Boston, MA: Beacon Press.

Holt, R. (2006) Principals and practice: rhetoric and the moral character of managers, *Human Relations*, 59(12):1659–1680.

Illouz, E. (2007) *Cold intimacies: the making of emotional capitalism*, Cambridge: Polity Press.

Kahneman, D. (2012) *Thinking Fast and Slow*, London: Penguin.

Mead, G.H. (1934) *Mind, Self and Society from the Standpoint of a Social Behaviourist*, Chicago, IL: Chicago University Press.

Mercier, H. and Sperber, D. (2017) *The Enigma of Reason; a New Understanding of Human Reason*, London: Allen Lane.

Mowles, C. (2015) *Managing in Uncertainty: Complexity and the Paradoxes of Everyday Organisational Life*, London: Routledge.

Nussbaum, M. (2001) *Upheavals of Thought: The Intelligence of Emotions*, Cambridge: Cambridge University Press.

Peirce, C.S. (1984) *Writings of Charles Sanders Peirce: A Chronological Edition*, Vol. 1, Bloomington, IN: Indiana University Press.

Sandel, A. (2014) *The Place of Prejudice: A Case for Reasoning in the World*, Cambridge, MA: Harvard University Press.

Shapin, S. (2010) *Never Pure: Historical Studies of Science As If It Was Produced by People with Bodies, Situated in Time and Space, Culture and Society, and Struggling for Credibility and Authority*, Baltimore, MD: Johns Hopkins University Press.

Shaw, P. (2002) *Changing Conversations in Organizations: A Complexity Approach to Change*, London: Routledge.

Stokoe, E. (2018) *Talk, the Science of Conversation*, London: Robinson Press.

Vygotsky, L. (1982) *Speech and Language*, Ann Arbor, MI: MIT Press.

6

COMPLEX KNOWLEDGE, COMPLEX KNOWING

In *Flights*, written by the Nobel Prize–winning Polish novelist Olga Tokarczuk (2007), one of the unnamed protagonists reflects upon why she found it difficult to study psychology at university. All the questionnaires were confusing:

> I'd wind up with the strangest personality profiles – curves on a coordinate axis. 'Do you believe that the best decision is also the decision that is easiest to change?' Do I believe? What kind of decision? Change? When? Easiest how? 'When you walk into a room, do you tend to head for the middle or the edges?' What room? And when? Is the room empty, or are there plush red couches in it? What about the windows? What kind of views do they have? The book question: would I rather read one than go to a party, or does it depend on what kind of book it is and what kind of party?
>
> What a methodology! It tacitly assumed that people don't know themselves, but that if you furnish them with questions which are smart enough, they'll be able to figure themselves out. They pose themselves an answer. And they'll inadvertently reveal to themselves that secret they knew nothing of till now.
>
> And there is that other assumption, which is terribly dangerous – that we are constant, and that our reactions can be predicted.
>
> *2007: 21*

I think Tokarczuk's character puts her finger on the difficulty presented by the assumptions in personality tests, and general findings about managing and leading organizations, which assume that we are constant, predictable and discrete, and that abstract knowledge is enough for us to know how to go on. The personality profiles she reacts against are ones which set out to show what is essential and immutable about her character: they are context-free and relation-free. Thinking back to the

DOI: 10.4324/9781003002840-6

chapter on the complex self, the theories of self we are working with in this book understand the self as relational, fluid and interdependent. I am not arguing that we have no habits of thought and action which make us identifiable one to another. To a degree, and according to the pragmatists, we are our habits, and any reader who has reached a particular age will probably have struggled against becoming overly habit-driven, where we resist the lure of the novel.

But the confusion Tokarczuk's character experiences will be similar to that experienced by managers presented with management knowledge of an abstract kind: general insights which sum up 'best practice,' or industry standards or truisms that we know in theory but have great difficulty in applying in practice. These are often insights of an idealized kind, for example, that 'high performing' teams have high levels of trust, communicate well and cohere around a shared set of values. This makes sense instinctively, but says nothing about the fact that this ideal state is impossible to achieve that individuals in a team compete as well as cooperate, that communication is often imperfect and involves misunderstanding one another with all the good will in the world, as we explored in the last chapter on communication and that values can conflict around particular cases. What kind of knowledge is needed for this particular team, with this particular history of getting along and not, and facing these particular circumstances? As Gadamer has explained, drawing on Aristotle, resolving questions of ethics, what is good for us as a community, will never have the precision of mathematics because they can't be answered in the abstract (1975: 312). A manager or leader is confronted with something s/he has to do in very specific circumstances. Management is a lot about acting in the blooming, buzzing confusion of everyday organizational life where our knowledge about what's going on is always going to be imperfect and where we can't predict the outcomes of our actions.

If we are interdependent, if communication is imperfect, if our relationships with each other are in 'structured flux' as Elias would term it and if the future is unknowable, what kinds of ways of knowing, of knowledge, are useful to us in our pursuit of trying to take the next step together? It's worth dwelling a while on knowledge and ways of knowing to think more about what our complex social reality requires, what's possible in our reflections together about how to go on.

Hierarchies of knowledge

Recently, in the final viva of one of my doctoral students, an eminent professor of organization studies asked the candidate, with his tongue firmly in his cheek: 'you draw on both Foucault and Bourdieu in your thesis. What is it that they have in common apart from the fact that they both spoke French?' I think it behoves me similarly to explain further, even if briefly, what it is that connects the majority of thinkers I bring into this book, and why they are helpful in uncovering complex social reality, particularly as it pertains to organizations. Given the scope of the task I have given myself, it can never be a satisfying explanation, but I hope to show, at least in very general terms, how the creation of knowledge by the traditions of thought I draw on share some things in common, at least as family resemblances. Of course, the different traditions are by no means saying the same thing, but they are in their own terms trying to make sense of similar phenomena, emergent social processes which are never in equilibrium, and for which there is no outside evaluative view.

As this book has unfolded, I have returned again and again to some of the ideas sketched out in Chapter 2 in the discussion of the complexity models which demonstrate radical unpredictability. There is a lively discussion in the critical organizational literature, some of it drawing on the complexity sciences, much of it not, problematizing ways of knowing which are developed from natural sciences methods based on assumptions of making accurate predictions and universal generalizations and thus having greater control over nature. In other words, in aspiring to be critical, it raises questions about the extent to which human behaviour can be predicted and controlled, in the same way that the complexity models challenge the dominant orthodoxy of science. Natural scientific methods are highly successful as much for what they exclude as what they include (if we can even make such a generalization that the methods are all of a piece given that a variety of scholars, Baert (2005), for example, have pointed out the differences between natural science disciplines). Some schools of thought in organizational theory aspire to management adopting the prestige and authority of the natural sciences in its methods and want it to become 'evidence-based,' to achieve the same status as science. They assume that producing evidence would put management research at the top of the research hierarchy. The evidence base is intended to provide those interested in management the grounds to recommend 'what works' with a reasonable degree of assurance that it does. But to what extent is this perspective useful if the future is unpredictable and if there is a great deal of the world beyond our control?

I dealt with some of these questions in my last book (Mowles, 2015), particularly the discussion which raged in the Academy of Management between the adherents of an evidence-based approach (Rousseau, 2006; Briner and Rousseau, 2011) and those who argued that a narrow definition of evidence, if understood in relation to the gold standard of evidence, the randomized control trial, would never be adequate to the domain of inquiry being explored (Learnmonth and Harding, 2006). The debate still continues between perhaps a majority of organizational scholars still digging away to produce knowledge which they assume is more or less generalizable and applicable irrespective of time and context, all things being equal, and a substantial minority of scholars who assume that things are never equal and that no human experience repeats itself in exactly the same way. In a famous observation by philosopher Alasdair MacIntyre, social science's weakness is that 'we cannot say of them in any precise way under what conditions they (generalisations) hold' (MacIntyre, 1985: 91). This doesn't prevent us from saying some generalizable things about human beings trying to get things done together, but just that they are sometimes so general means that they are necessary but insufficient to help us know with certainty how to go on together. This is exactly the point of the unnamed character in Tokarczuk's novel which I quote at the beginning of the chapter: what room are we talking about, and are there plush red couches in it?

The emphasis I place on context, history, power relations, interdependence and dynamic process is shared more or less by a number of other schools of thought who make up the substantial but still minority tradition which we might broadly think of as critical management studies (CMS). There is a different quality to the degree of criticality of each tradition, and I am using the term in the widest sense. As a broad church of perspectives, it comprises critical theory, feminist perspectives, postcolonial and subaltern studies, post-structuralism, critical realism, process perspectives and pragmatism. This is a lot of 'isms,' which says a lot about the plurality of perspectives. What they share in common is that they take both the subject/object of inquiry and the process of inquiring into it into account. In concentrating on the perspectives, which I have found useful in my own research in what follows, I don't mean to create another hierarchy nor to suggest that other perspectives are not helpful. But one thing they all have in common is that in inquiring into the conditions of knowledge creation, each of these perspectives is inherently reflexive. Critical reflexivity is not the preserve of organizational studies and the critical scholars who write into these traditions. Anthropologists and sociologists also have traditions of criticality and reflexivity which I explore later in this chapter as a way of demonstrating transdisciplinarity.

Those scholars who might think of themselves as explicitly writing in the critical tradition informed by the Frankfurt School take interdisciplinarity seriously, as much as the original founders of the Institute for Social Research in Frankfurt did (Jeffries, 2016). Morin's (2005) injunction to broaden the focus of complexity science from a restricted to a general sense is an echo of perspective of the founders of the Frankfurt School, who were keen to develop an inter- and transdisciplinary perspective on social research, bringing together philosophy, sociology and psychoanalysis. Next, critical theory is based in dialectical thinking (Jay, 1996) arising from both Hegel and Marx, which works against the separation of subject and object, particular and general, which is a taken-for-granted assumption in the Western philosophical canon since Descartes (although there is an equally strong case to argue that the separation started with the Ancient Greeks). In the chapter on the complex self earlier, I note how the pragmatists shared this perspective, rejecting the splitting out of subject and object in favour of paradox. Those writing in the tradition of the Frankfurt School express in common the desire to unite theory and practice, another insight shared with pragmatic philosophy.[1] Seeing theory and practice as two sides of the same coin is another manifestation of dialectical thinking. For CMS scholars who are informed directly by the Frankfurt School, history is very important which comes with the insight that we can never fully understand ourselves as historical beings or the social reality in which we participate. There is no originary position.

CMS scholars share the Frankfurt School's critique of capitalism and undertake their research with emancipatory intent: in other words, for critical scholars (echoing Marx), it is not enough just to describe social reality, the point is to change it in favour of those who are systematically oppressed by the pathologies of capitalism. This explains their scepticism towards natural science alone as the requisite discipline for understanding social life. If it is used simply to describe what's going on in society, it may just keep things stable, preserving inequalities and injustices, whereas they theorize to emancipate. The danger of valorizing just the natural sciences and their methods is that they transform qualities into quantities through mathematics and offer explanation but no understanding. According to Jay (1996), critical theorists draw on Kant and Hegel's distinction between Verstand (understanding) and Vernunft (reason) – the former is 'common sense' realism, an uncritical acceptance of 'the facts,' the status quo, and the latter is critical inquiry which relies on the importance of the negative, seeing one thing and its opposite. The intent is not just to understand things as they are but to inquire into how they became as they are on the assumption that things could have been different. If understanding is unable to consider what it takes for granted, reasoned reflection allows the inquirer to question and to examine further. Dialectical thinking is integral to this way of trying to comprehend the world, and the power of the negative is particularly evident in Adorno's work (1966/1973):

> Thought as such, before all particular contents, is an act of negation, of resistance to that which is being forced upon it.
>
> *ibid.: 19*

Again and again, Adorno stresses the importance of reflective reason, and the negative in puncturing technocratic positivity which covers overthinking. The reason for citing Adorno in particular is that he provides a strong antidote to the contemporary preoccupation with positivity and points out its limitations.

In its contemporary manifestation as CMS, scholars broadly take a view of organizations which 'denaturalizes' (Fournier and Grey, 2000), that is to say, it attempts to make the familiar unfamiliar. They are 'anti-performative,' meaning that they don't assume that organizational scholarship should just be aimed at optimization or improving performance, and they encourage reflexivity, i.e., they want us to inquire into how we come to know what we know, including questioning our own assumptions. In a keynote seminar to our annual conference,[2] Mats Alvesson argued that CMS scholars take an interest in the four 'I's: ideology, institutions, interests and identities, particularly when they are dominant, harmful and underchallenged. CMS scholars are critical in the sense that they focus their inquiry on our current grounds for making sense of the world: nothing may be taken for granted including our own points of view. To a degree, then, the critical perspective can be very destabilizing and may sometimes have to consciously reconstruct the world after systematically deconstructing it.

Some similarities and differences between critical theory, pragmatism and process theories

If the founding scholars of the Frankfurt School gave little public attention to pragmatic ideas in the early part of the 20th century, this changed with the second and third generation of critical scholars, such as Habermas (1984, 1987) and Honneth (1996), who revisited the work of the pragmatists, in particular Mead's theories of communication, mind, self and society. Contemporary German social theorist Hans Joas (1996, 2000) considers himself to be writing in the pragmatic tradition having explored the work of both Mead and Dewey in developing his theories of action and values.

Just to dwell on similarities and differences between the pragmatists and critical theorists briefly, as an insight into why I regard both their perspectives on the world relevant to study of the predictable unpredictability of organizational life. In making a comparison, I also accept that pragmatism too is a broad church but I strive to point out some of the key themes that both traditions share in common.

In previous chapters, I have written about Mead's theory of the co-emergence of mind, self and society, and how the sense of being an individual arises intersubject-ively, and through language. I also wrote about Dewey and Bentley's idea of trans-action, which is a theory of action involving a complex of time, human agency and objects. In exploring these ideas, I have tried to show how the pragmatist project contends with complex social reality comprising complex selves. Dewey's major work *The Quest for Certainty* (1929/2008) is a good starting point for thinking about how the pragmatists thought about knowing and knowledge. The work speaks to a number of common pragmatic themes. It is a treatise on the inadequacy of importing natural scientific methods simplistically into understanding human experience (he doesn't specifically make a comparison between natural science and social science but is interested in what is generalizable about scientific method per se). The idea that we can ever stand on solid ground, he argues, is a hangover from a much older metaphysics which privileges the eternal and the unchanging. In its way, and long before complexity theory, *The Quest for Certainty* is a radical statement of an epistemology that is appropriate for an emergent and changing universe. What interests Dewey about scientific method is that it mobilizes doubt. This is not the kind of radical, subjectivist doubt manifested by Descartes, where the only thing he could be certain of was his own thinking: on that both Dewey and Peirce were agreed. Rather, it is doubt and curiosity about a specific problem which inhibits us from taking the next step:

> Attainment of the relatively secure and settled takes place, however, only with respect to *specified* problematic situations; quest for certainty that is uni-versal, applying to everything, is a compensatory perversion. One question if disposed of; another offers itself and thought is kept alive.
>
> *ibid.: 182*

We can be relatively settled, develop a good enough understanding for now, per-haps to take the next step together. This is fallibilist knowing, sometimes referred to as post-foundationalism; not scepticism, not relativism, but a unity of observer and observed, where the controlled inquiry of the former transforms both at the same time: 'the mind is in the world as part of its ongoing process' (ibid.: 232). There is no knowing from an outside, spectator position, Dewey argues, but only a knowing from within:

> From knowing as an outside beholding to knowing as an active participant in the drama of an on-moving world is the historical transition whose record we have been following.
>
> *ibid.*

So, Peirce, Mead and Dewey followed scientific progress closely (and the last lived long enough to reflect on the findings of quantum physics). Perhaps as North Americans they had less cause to be pessimistic than had the members of the Frankfurt School about what the latter considered to be the failures of the Enlightenment project, which they held responsible for the emergence of totalitarianism in Europe. But they shared with critical theorists the insight that there is no separating the knower from the known, subject and object, and that experience cannot just be quantified. Both schools of thought take a highly social view of the self, and a historical and emergent view of human development; both think that reflective human intelligence can improve the human condition, but only if the methods are appropriate for the domain of inquiry. For both, there are no transmuting qualities into quantities. Mead and Dewey were active in their support of the labour movement and were alive to social inequalities. However, their work does not explicitly deal with the pathologies of capitalism as directly as does critical theory, and it is much less explicit in its treatment of power.

The last of the traditions of organizational scholarship I wanted to touch on, no matter how briefly, is the process school of organizational theory, because it too is preoccupied with emergence and the world in its becoming. I dealt with the process school in more depth previously (Mowles, 2015; Stacey and Mowles, 2016), noting that there are weak and strong schools of process philosophy. Sandberg et al. (2015) identify five categories of process scholar between those who think that the world is mostly stable but endures periods of instability, through to scholars who think that process is all there is. This latter perspective of 'hyper-process' Sandberg et al. critique for making human agency all but disappear. But generally process theories draw on philosophy that was written around the time of the early pragmatist writings, and in particular on Alfred Whitehead's process interpretations of science (here on electromagnetism, 1934):

> The fundamental concepts are activity and process … The notion of self-sufficient isolation is not exemplified in modern physics. There are no essentially self-contained activities within limited regions … Nature is a theatre for the interrelations of activities. All things change, the activities and their interrelations.
>
> *Whitehead, 1934 [2011]: 35–36*

In addition, process organization studies scholars refer to Bergson's (1859–1941) theory of time, and William James' writings. So time, emergence and process are very much to the fore in process metaphysics, but less clear are the roles of interdependence, power and human activity.

To sum up, there are broad categories of scholars whom I draw on in this book, and some who don't fit neatly into any category, like Norbert Elias, Hannah Arendt or Pierre Bourdieu, to try and understand complex social reality. Later in this chapter, I call on social anthropologists and sociologists to show that the concerns of organizational scholars inquiring into complex social reality in organizations are shared by other disciplines whose objects of interest may not be organizations. They don't map over each other directly and nor are they saying the same thing. However, they share in common an interest in emergence and process, ways of seeing which are concerned with flux and flow, not stable entities studied at rest. In general, they do not think of human beings as discrete and fully formed but caught up in relationships with others, and with a history which can never be fully accessed, and still becoming. Broadly, the thinkers are interested in interdisciplinarity and doubt that human experience can be reduced to quantification: as effective as natural science methods and mathematics are for exploring nature, there are qualities in social life which need other methods to reveal them, including the reflective and reflexive ability of the inquirer. Becoming reflexive may also require us to become more aware of our unconscious and how it affects our behaviour in groups. Each of the scholars I adduce in this book is interested in the interdependence between human beings, which figures more or less as power relationships.

Having attempted a brief categorization of schools of intellectual tradition, I now turn to the kind of contextual knowledge which is most useful for thinking about managing and leading organizations, and the paradoxes upon which it depends.

Knowing involves dialogue, dialectic, politics and ethics

Dialogic knowledge

In the last chapter, I argued that knowledge and reasoning are social, dialogic phenomena which arise in groups of people. In the sense that group process involves investigating what is going on for 'us,' it also concerns questions of valuations of the good, or ethics (which we explore more fully in Chapter 8). Groups dedicated to exploring the same themes over an extended period of time were described as a community of inquiry by pragmatic philosopher Charles Sanders Peirce. The deliberative back and forth of ideas through critique and argumentation produces a movement in thinking. We might think of this as an extensive explanation of how scientific thinking develops: a recent biography of the American geneticist Jennifer Doudna (Isaacson, 2021), who won the Nobel Prize in 2020 for her work in gene editing, portrays a good example of this, demonstrating how her research developed out of many other researchers' prior findings, some of whom realized the importance of what they had discovered, some of whom didn't. The biography shows clearly how scientific discovery is governed by chance, rivalry, personality and intense engagement with other scientists' ideas. And the discipline of inquiring together both enables and constrains community members in how they are able to think about what they are most interested in: they can be described as a thought collective, after Ludwig Fleck. We might think of this as a convergent explanation of how scientific thinking develops. There can be no expertise unless inquirers follow a particular discipline, but the strength of the discipline can make it difficult for novel ideas to challenge the orthodoxy. Discipline in thinking and talking imposes a particular kind of order, where there is a risk of exclusion from the group if group members become too unorthodox in their thinking.[3]

Organizational life is no different to academic communities, with the added complications of the politics of allocating resources, hiring and firing, promoting or not and encouraging very diverse people to cohere to fulfil organizational purpose. In organizational life too, it can be risky to speak out against the orthodoxy, not least in the very organizations which claim that their staff are their biggest asset and that they value their points of view. I claimed in the last chapter that the organization arises from conversational activity, that conversation is inherently unpredictable and so it leaves the problem of how to stabilize the 'structured flux' of being together in ways that benefit the organization. I argued that in many contemporary organizations, the appeal is to idealizations, the vision or to 'the facts' in the form of metrics and targets or to other abstract ways of knowing. The appeal to an abstraction is one way of achieving coherence by referencing a universal outside the group. Reference to 'the facts' is not the same as saying that this move necessarily alleviates organizational uncertainty: rather it can be a way of establishing a particular kind of order which tilts power towards managers and keeps staff uncertain and anxious about continuing to belong to the group. Conversation may be prefaced by appeals to Golden Rule–like principles such as being 'constructive' or being positive, where it is hard to gauge in advance of speaking what this might mean in practice, just as it is hard to know what generalized prescriptions for leadership and management might mean in the absence of particularities. It is easier, then, to self-silence. Consistently calling for positivity in the workforce may bring about an anxious and hypervigilant order.

As an alternative, I argued that deliberating with each other, using persuasive and rhetorical arguments that draw on and draw out partial points of view, including those of the speaker, appeal to ethics, what's good for 'us.' Against a background of general ideas about the good, or even about 'best practice,' deliberation and persuasion are aimed at establishing what is needed in the here and now with this group to go on together. Arguments involving rhetoric sometimes provoke strong emotions but may be more apposite for producing the kind of contextual, concrete knowledge that is required to take the next step by a particular group of people facing a specific set of difficulties and in uncertain times. In various places throughout the book, so far, I have referred to practical judgement, *phronesis*, which I think needs more exploration, and the kinds of practices which might make it more evident.

Dialectical knowledge

What is interesting about practical judgement is that it has a paradoxical quality noted by Eikeland (2008): it is practical knowledge of context and history required in a specific community at a particular time, but at the same time it draws on a background of more general, abstract knowledge, *episteme*. Eikeland denies that you can split the particular and the general and that it is possible to disentangle the relationship of the two forms of knowledge *episteme* and *phronesis* (and he takes Flyvbjerg (2001) to task for doing exactly that). The link that I make to the complexity models which we explored in Chapter 2, is that they too have paradoxical quality where global patterns arise from local interaction, but at the same time the global patterns constrain and inform local interaction.

I want to explore the importance of the paradox of the particular and the general, the individual and the group, subjective and objective and demonstrate how it recurs as a theme throughout discussions of ways of knowing in the social sciences, just as it does in complexity models.

Let's take a popular cultural example to illustrate why the twin poles of the paradox are important for understanding the nexus between our individual lives and the societies we find ourselves living in, the structure/agency and individual/group question which we have been returning to again and again. In *The Scientific American*,[4] sociologist Zeynep Tufekci (2019) explores why it is that devotees had such a strong adverse reaction to the ending of the *Game of Thrones* TV series. Fans of the series will know that that author of the books, George R.R. Martin, hadn't finished the last of the novels the series was based on, but the TV showing had built up a huge following (17 million viewers watched the opening show of the series) who wanted to know how things were going to turn out. So the series producers hired two Hollywood scriptwriters, Benioff and Weiss, to work with the plotlines but to craft the final series, which turned out to be a disappointment to many. What had gone wrong?

Tufekci argues that the finale felt unsatisfying because the scriptwriters had switched from a sociological mode of writing, where characters acted against a background of history, culture, institutions and group expectations, to a psychological mode of writing, where the principal motivations are to do with the inner state and agency of the key characters. In previous series of the show, characters whom the audience may have identified with were often killed off to the extent that plot always trumped character. This is not to say that the characters and what they did were unimportant. Rather, what happened in *Game of Thrones* up to the last series personified exactly the way that Norbert Elias describes the warp and weft of social emergence, which involves the interweaving of everyone's intentions (2000: 366). Of course, there are individuals and their intentions and plans, but the way they intersect and cut across each other produces outcomes of which no one is in control. Tufekci, like Elias, encourages us to view local action in a historical perspective, to look at the role of institutions, technologies and broader social trends and to take what Elias elsewhere refers to as the perspective of both the airman and the swimmer (2001: 12). Individual choices are enabled and constrained by the context and history in which they act:

> Every large and complex society has, in fact, both qualities: it is very firm and very elastic. Within it scope for individual decision constantly appears. Opportunities present themselves that can either be seized or missed. Crossroads appear at which people must choose, and on their choices, depending on their social position, may depend either their immediate personal fate or that of a whole family, or, in certain situations, of entire nations and groups within them … And whichever opportunity he seizes, his deed becomes interwoven with those of others; it unleashes further chains of actions the direction and provisional outcome of which depend not on him but on the distribution of power and the structure of tensions within this whole mobile human network.
>
> *Elias, 2001: 49–50*

To take a fuller account of what's happening and what it means, it's important to take the paradoxical perspective. Reflecting on the disappointment experienced by fans of *Game of Thrones*, Tufekci makes a point both about good storytelling and good sociology: only when we understand the deeper social and well as psychological pressures are we able to make a full connection with the characters as they try to make sense of their lives. In other words, we need to pay attention to the individual perspective but also strive to understand the historical context and the broader social trends in which our activities take place.

Political knowledge

There is a long tradition of trying to investigate the generative tension of experience understood from the individual's point of view, but set against a background of broader social trends. A seminal text in sociology is C. Wright Mills (1959/2000) *The Sociological Imagination* in which he speaks to the paradox of the particular and the general in a similar way to Elias and Tufekci. Information overwhelms us in the modern age,[5] he argues (and he wrote this book in 1959) so what a variety of people need, including journalists, scholars, artists, editors and scientists is:

> a quality of mind that will help them use the information and to develop reason in order to achieve lucid summations of what is going on in the world and of what may be happening with themselves.
>
> *1959/2000: 10*

Warning sociology scholars against the emptiness of grand theory and abstracted empiricism, Wright Mills argues that there is no avoiding politics and value judgements in engaging with the social world, because we are born into a particular society at a particular time. There is already a play going on and we are invited to take up a part:

> We have come to know that every individual lives from one generation to the next, in some society; that he lives out a biography, and that he lives within some historical sequence. By the fact of his living he contributes, however minutely, to the shaping of this society and to the course of its history, even as his made by the society and by its historical push and shove.
>
> *ibid.: 11*

The way to make good sense of what is going on, then, is to put together 'the personal troubles of milieu' and the 'public issues of social structure,' the particular and the general and the individual and the group. Just as I observed earlier at the beginning of the chapter, we all know in theory what a high-performing team should be like: it is quite another thing to bring one about with our own particular team. As Wright Mills observes in the appendix to the book, 'the most admirable thinkers within the scholarly community you have chosen to join do not split their work from their lives.' Abstract knowledge uninflected by personal experience only takes us so far, and that personal experience is likely to tell us something about the stresses and strains of trying to work with particular sociological constraints which tell us about broader social trends with which we are trying to deal.

This is a sentiment echoed by Edward Said, who was both an historian and a literary scholar. Giving the BBC Reith Lectures in 1993, he reflected on being a public intellectual:

> Politics is everywhere; there can be no escape into the realms of pure art and thought or, for that matter, into the realm of disinterested objectivity or transcendental theory.
>
> This involves a steady realism and almost athletic rational energy; and a complicated struggle to balance the problem of one's own selfhood against the demands of publishing and speaking out in the public sphere is what makes it an everlasting effort - constitutively unfinished and necessarily imperfect.

The struggle is to combine the personal and the abstract: to be able to say something about the human condition but always spoken in a voice which has a particular context and history, shaped by one's position in the social network. Inevitably this will involve saying something about power inequalities.

Ethical knowledge

Just to give one last example of the paradox of knowledge and knowing from the field of social anthropology to demonstrate that there are scholars beyond the domain of organizational studies who have found themselves wrestling with similar paradoxical themes. In a famous essay, *Thinking as a Moral Act*, Clifford Geertz (1968) reflects upon the moral as well as the epistemological implications of studying human beings while at the same time as taking a scientific attitude. In other words, trying to reveal the particularity of real people's lives at the same time as abstracting from them as unique individuals to analyse and generalize to make claims about wider social processes:

> The methods and theories of social science are not being produced by computers but by men; and, for the most part, by men operating not in laboratories but in the same social world to which the methods apply and the theories pertain.
>
> *1968: 140*

Geertz argues that when it comes to social science you can never separate the personal from the professional, the moral from the technical and the particular from the general. In walking the talk on this insight, Geertz claims that he has bumped up against this realization in his own research work and that it pertains for everyone involved in similar work. But maintaining the generative tension between the particular and the general, the personal and the professional, involves work on the part of the inquirer. It is not something which we necessarily know how to do:

> in anthropological fieldwork, detachment is neither a natural gift nor a manufactured talent. It is a partial achievement laboriously earned and precariously maintained.
>
> *ibid.: 156*

Geertz warns against the twin poles of what he considers scientism or subjectivism: on the one hand, simply 'collecting data' in an unconcerned way from respondents and not recognizing their particularity as moral beings, or becoming lost in one's own subjectivity, or the subjectivities of the people one is concerned to study. Particularly with sciences which are predicated on people and their functioning,

> A professional commitment to view human affairs analytically is not in opposition to a personal commitment to view them in terms of a particular moral perspective. The professional ethic rests on the personal and draws its strength from it; we force ourselves to see out of a conviction that blindness- or illusion-cripples virtue as it cripples men. Detachment comes not from a failure to care, but from a kind of caring resilient enough to between moral reaction and scientific only grows as moral perception deepens and scientific knowledge advances.
>
> *ibid.: 157–158*

Human experience is complex, Geertz argues, and demands the full panoply of skills to render some kind of sense of it if the knowledge is going to prove to be of some help for 'us.' One approach is to develop the ability to look at people, and events, and he adds oneself, with an eye which is both 'cold and concerned,' perhaps both involved and detached. For human studies, there are is no separating the subjective and the objective, whatever we take these to mean.

In Chapter 4, on the complex self, we started exploring the body's paradoxical ability to take itself as an object to itself, drawing on Mead, and noted that this is the basis for consciousness and self-consciousness. In terms of complex knowledge, Elias works at Geertz' dilemma of being both 'cold and concerned' with the idea of involvement and detachment as a more helpful way of thinking about studying the social than assuming that we can be objective. Subjectivity is often considered the poor relation of objectivity, even if social life where there is no avoiding or standing outside our subjectivity. He argues that only very young children are completely subjectively caught up in what they are doing, and complete detachment implies some kind of social pathology, but to more or less a degree we are both involved and detached in social life. The principal question, he argues, is the extent to which we can become more detached about our involvement, so that we can develop more knowledge about the social world in the way that we have about the natural world. He suggests that our ability to be detached about our relationships with each other lags behind our interventions in nature:

> Success and failure of any attempt to change from a more involved to a more detached view of social phenomena is bound up with the capacity of men to revise the picture they have of themselves in accordance with the results of more methodical studies, and often enough in a way which runs counter to deeply felt beliefs and ideals. In that respect the problem of increasing detachment in the social sciences is hardly different from that which plays its part in the development of the natural sciences.
>
> *1956: 234*

One of the 'deeply felt beliefs and ideals' that we hold, and which according to Elias is an impediment to becoming more knowledgeable about ourselves and the societies we co-create, is the idea that we are individuals closed off from one another:

> men are being brought up to experience themselves, more perhaps than ever before, as beings set apart from each other by very strong walls. There can be little doubt that the picture of self which is thus built up in the growing person makes it rather difficult to envisage oneself in a more detached manner as forming patterns with others and to study the nature and structure of these patterns as such.
>
> *ibid.*

Elias thinks of our individualism as a contemporary blindness which inhibits our ability to notice and describe the patterns that we make in our dealings with each other. More, he argues that that adopting an overly simplistic understanding of 'scientific method' from the natural sciences and assuming that it applies equally to the stable instability of human interaction is also a familiar pattern in human history, when we borrow from the prestige and authority of existing standards until new ones can be found.

Developing reflexive criticality – the importance of groups

In this chapter, we have been exploring the kinds of knowledge and ways of knowing which are appropriate for better understanding our predictably unpredictable lives, lives which are both stable and unstable at the same time. We live in a particular society at a particular time in history which are subject to the tensions, strains and possibilities of broader social trends: yet at the same time our lives are indisputably and individually unique and ours. We have been inquiring into the forms of knowledge and ways of knowing which might help us practically in knowing how to go on together, and perhaps not repeat what might be unhelpful ways of trying to cooperate with one another.

I have given a very brief overview of critical traditions of thinking about organizations, which I draw on extensively in this book as a demonstration of interdisciplinarity. These more or less critical traditions try to overcome the taken-for-granted dualisms in more orthodox scholarship about organizations which assume that we can split things out into objective and subjective, leader and follower, mind and body, theory and action, where the former is preferred in all cases. Instead, and borrowing the arguments of the scholars I adduce, I have tried to recast them as a paradox. As I explained in a previous book (Mowles, 2015), paradox is the coexistence of one thing and its opposite, where the contradiction is preserved but brought together in a higher state (*aufgehoben*, in Hegelian terms). The body's ability to take itself as an object to itself, which we explored in the chapter on the complex self, is *aufgehoben* as self-consciousness. Our capacity to think about how we are thinking, in Elias' terms becoming more detached from our involvement, is *aufgehoben* as reflexivity. Reflexivity is the antithesis of context-free, abstract knowledge which is produced by rational, cognizing discrete individuals.

There is a good deal of organizational literature on reflexivity which links it to *phronesis*, or practical judgement, and emphasizes the context of the group in which dilemmas occur, the ethical and the embodied. For example, Antonacopoulou (2010) argues that reflexivity needs to be critical, i.e., provoke *krisis* or judgement, particularly in those moments of practical activity which require sifting competing priorities in organizational life. To do so means to enrich experience by problematizing it, and making it more complex, and thus to help the choices we make be more consonant with the kinds of dilemmas we face. Shotter and Tsoukas (2014a,b) also hold that practical judgement is necessary to make sense of confusing situations where we can feel our way into novel problems based on our moral sensibilities and using language to explore possibilities with others. The kind of insight which is required is not based largely on rationalization, but on emotions, feeling our way and, drawing on Aristotle, being the kind of person who has developed good judgement about how best to take our community forward. In other words, to act virtuously requires being a virtuous person. Reflexivity may mean making many positions and many voices more explicit, as Alvesson et al. (2008) explain, including, and perhaps especially, that of the person wishing to provoke critical reflexivity in others. Thomas (2010, 2012) argues that *phronesis* has a self-referencing quality, being drawn from practice for practice, and in this sense has a different kind of generalizability to what might be expected in the natural sciences. The ability to draw practical insights out of a particular problematic context using anecdote and narrative exemplifying *phronesis*, in turn, calls out the practical judgement of the reader to make use of it. Echoing Gadamer, Thomas argues that practical wisdom is offered against a particular shared horizon of meaning: that is, if we work in a similar context as someone who is able to describe the dilemmas they faced and how they managed to make sense of their situation, then we will recognize both what is similar and different about what is being described from our own situation. We will resonate with the description, but in relation to our own experience.

While the literature I have quoted in this chapter says a lot about the quality of reflection which is required of us to better understand our complex social world and points to how critical reflexivity can provoke us into understanding it in a more plural way, it does little to help us know how to develop it. Encouragement to be critically reflexive only takes us so far. There are a variety of educators who have thought about this in terms of students they have on doctoral or MBA programmes (Heron, 1974; Reynolds, 2009; Vince, 2010) and from the perspective of the doctoral programme I run with my colleagues at the university of Hertfordshire. Much of what I have written in this book has emphasized the importance of the thoroughly social self who becomes a self because of the groups s/he has been part of. Perhaps it comes as no surprise then that there is a discipline that we draw on at the university which starts with the assumption that the best place to find out about the social self and the stable instability of groups is in a group. And there are ways of working in a group which seem to me to enhance the reflexivity of its members. Reflexivity, then, is a practice which can be developed.

The Institute of Group Analysis was founded by S.H. Foulkes, a psychiatrist and member of the broad network of scholars involved in founding the Institute for Social Research in Frankfurt, where he attended the early meetings. He fled as a German Jewish refugee to the United Kingdom along with Norbert Elias, with whom he had a long term but problematic friendship. There are three principal traditions of thought which informed the development of Foulkes' group analytic methods. The first is an insight he gained from the work of the biologist Goldstein (1939), and from conversations with Elias, that whatever we think of as the 'whole' is not reducible to the sum of the parts studied separately. Rather what should concern us are the dynamic patterns emerging from the interaction between the parts. The second emerges from this training as a psychiatrist based on Freud's teachings, which is concerned with the way that defensive unconscious drives prevent us from fully engaging with and understanding each other and may provoke unhelpful behaviours in groups. And lastly, he was influenced by the insight promoted by the sociology of the Frankfurt School, and shared by Elias, that we are social through and through. He held that the combination of disciplines allowed for an understanding of both the individual and the group. Foulkes took an interdisciplinary approach to group analytic practice and thought that we are products of our social, economic and psychological environments.

To work in the group analytic tradition is to sit in a circle facing each other, usually for an hour and half, and to meet without an agenda. The task given to the group is to talk about what is going on in the minds of its members, and in free-flowing association, to try to make sense together of what it means to be participating in the group together. Group members are encouraged to try and make sense of the patterns of feeling and meaning that arise when participants take their experience seriously, being included and excluded, feeling engaged and detached and provoked into feelings of rivalry or affiliation. Usually, the group is convened by a conductor, a term Foulkes chose to imply that this person's role is not to lead or direct but to facilitate and encourage group members to more fully communicate with each other: to help clear away obstacles to communication. The conductor may offer tentative interpretations of what is happening, but these can be challenged by the group: there is an obvious power relationship, but unlike in the Tavistock tradition, the conductor is also considered a full member of the group and can be challenged.

The point of convening such a group, which pays attention to discussing its own purpose and in doing so notices the ebb and flow of emotions and the pattern of interactions this creates, is that it acts, in Foulkes' terms (Foulkes, 1984 [1957]), like a 'hall of mirrors' where we see ourselves and our reactions reflected back to us. This is not just a cognitive noticing but a full, embodied experience of being oneself through and with others. There are three major capacities which I think the group-analytic experiential group helps develop. The first is that, over time, it helps enhance the individual's ability to cope with uncertainty. We have explored previously the imperfections and predictable unpredictability of communicating with each other, and groups can be very uncertain places where we can experience both great joy and great suffering. This is particularly the case in this free-flowing mode of meeting, quite unlike most meetings in organizations which are often concreted over with agendas and action points. The group-analytic-informed experiential group meets with no particular end in view and thus takes uncertainty as its object of study.

Second, and over time, participants often enhance their ability to notice how they are participating and are sometimes better able to exercise practical judgement, *phronesis*, in terms of when to speak and what to say to make a contribution to the meeting. Contribution, here, is understood as enhancing the group's ability to function as a group made up of highly social individuals. The third capacity that participation in this kind of group enhances is the ability to understand experience as infinitely complex. One interpretation by a participant of what just happened may be contradicted by another, or a partial point of view can be rounded out by someone else. Then the group finds itself talking about the process of interpretation that, in turn, provokes the conversation to move onto something else. The dynamic never stands still. There is an endless cycle of gesture and response and yet largely and in general, particularly when it is practised at this way of meeting together, copes well with the changes. In other words, the endless complexity of being together does not paralyse the group into inaction as group members realize that they can themselves participate in small and large ways to affect the course of the conversation. Rather than experiencing complexity as being overwhelming, more skilled group members may begin to realize an enhanced sense of agency.

My claim is that participation in a group such as this over time may help both individuals and groups and become wiser about some unhelpful patterns they may fall into when confronted with complex and uncertain conditions, which make us anxious. We don't lack examples of the kinds of behaviours that groups demonstrate when the world is uncertain, from panic-buying during a pandemic to simplified and binary politics which may support demagoguery and increase racism and discrimination. We explore some of these processes of unhelpful group identification in the next chapter on complex authority. Complex global trends, and indeed the pandemic itself, have widened inequality and it can be reassuring for groups who are suffering and who have felt excluded to believe that one particular politician has the answer, and that answer is to build a wall excluding other groups. There are more mundane patterns of unhelpful behaviour in organizations if targets are not met, or an achievement has been missed, which can result in blaming and scapegoating. The dynamic process of trying to cohere with colleagues is a restless improvisation, which doesn't always bring out the best in us. And learning a group practice, based in groups to think about groups, is another contribution to producing the kinds of knowledge we may find helpful in better understanding the webs we weave together.

Summing up for managers – why finding out about our lives is a complex undertaking

This chapter has been a review of the traditions of thinking which have contributed a body ideas and methods which take dynamic process seriously and are more suited to studying the patterns that human beings perpetually create as they try to get things done together than quantification. The patterns may be recognizable and may last for a long time: patriarchy, for example, is a pattern of relationship between men and women which has lasted for millennia. But it shifts and changes and never appears quite the same, dependent on history and context. These perspectives on knowing and knowledge never separate the knower from the known: in articulating a point of view, we strive to be as detached as we can from the broader structural trends we are part of, but our particular inflection and interpretation of what they mean for us may help others make similar sense of their experience. The methods are dialectical and historical and raise political and moral questions which invite the community we are working with to exercise their practical judgement about how to take the next step. In the critical organizational literature, the kind of attitude which is encouraged in research is critical reflexivity and I have argued in this chapter that there are methods for developing this capacity through taking the experience of being together in a group seriously.

In everyday parlance being critical can mean being negative. I hope I have demonstrated in this chapter that being critical, in its gentlest form, can simply mean being provoked to make judgements about what a particular situation demands for people to go on together and to provoke judgement in others. If social reality is in constant flux and change, then we may never identify a secure and stable place from which to proceed, but rather, we might develop an understanding which is good enough for now to go on together. The challenge for managers in contemporary organizations is how they might take into account their own assumptions. This may not result in a change of mind but may reveal more about how our minds are made up. A good resource for finding out is deliberation in a group, as messy and incomplete as that may be sometimes.

Notes

1 Even though they were contemporaneous, and a number of critical theorists fled to America to escape the Nazis, there is little evidence that the pragmatist and scholars from the Frankfurt school were actively informed by each other's work. Both take their inspiration from earlier German philosophy, however.
2 Roffey Park Management Institute, 2010.
3 There are a number of scientists whose findings have been so revolutionary that they were ostracized by their peers until their experiments were replicated elsewhere. In my last book I mentioned Nobel Prize–winning chemist Daniel Shechtman as a more recent example of this, whose theory of quasi-crystals was at first denied, then accepted by other leading chemists.
4 Zeynep Tufekci: The Real Reason Fans Hate the Last Season of *Game of Thrones*. It's not just bad storytelling – it's because the storytelling *style* changed from sociological to psychological, *Scientific American*, 17 May 2019.
5 Wright Mills' echoes the poet T.S. Eliot's (1934) questions in the opening stanzas of Choruses from the Rock: where is the wisdom we have lost in knowledge? Where is the knowledge we have lost in information?

References

Adorno, T. (1966/1973) *Negative Dialectics*, London: Routledge.
Alvesson, M., Hardy, C. and Harley, W. (2008) Reflecting on reflexivity: reflexive textual practices in organization and management theory, *Journal of Management Studies*, 45:3.
Antonacopoulou, E. (2010) Making the business school more 'critical': reflexive critique based on phronesis as a foundation for impact, *British Journal of Management*, 21:S6–S25.
Baert, P. (2005) *Philosophy of the Social Sciences*, Cambridge: Polity Press.
Briner, R.B. and Rousseau, D.M. (2011) Evidence-based I-O psychology: not there yet, *Industrial and Organizational Psychology: Perspectives on Science and Practice*, 4:3–22.
Dewey, J. (1929/2008) *The Quest for Certainty: The Later Works 1925–1953*, Vol. 4, Carbondale, IL: Southern Illinois University Press.

Eikeland, O. (2008) *The Ways of Aristotle: Aristotelian Phronesis, Aristotelian Philosophy of Dialogue and Action Research*, Bern: Peter Lang.

Elias, N. (1956) Problems of involvement and detachment, *The British Journal of Sociology*, 7:226–252.

Elias, N. (2000) *The Civilising Process: Sociogenetic and Psychogenetic Investigations*, Oxford: Blackwell.

Elias, N. (2001) *The Society of Individuals*, Oxford: Blackwell.

Eliot, T.S. (1934) *The Rock*, London: Faber and Faber.

Flyvbjerg, B. (2001) *Making Social Science Matter: Why Social Inquiry Fails, and How It Can Succeed Again*, Cambridge: Cambridge University Press.

Foulkes, S.H. and Anthony, E.J. (1984 [1957]) *Group Psychotherapy: The Psychoanalytic Approach*, London: Karnac Books.

Fournier, V. and Grey, C. (2000) At the critical moment: conditions and prospects for critical management studies, *Human Relations*, 53(1):7–32.

Gadamer, H.G. (1975) *Truth and Method*, London: Continuum Books.

Geertz, C. (1968) Thinking as a moral act: ethical dimensions of anthropological fieldwork in the new states author(s), *The Antioch Review*, Summer, 28(2):139–158.

Goldstein, K. (1939) *The Organism: A Holistic Approach to Biology*, New York, NY: American Book Company.

Habermas, J. (1984) *Theory of Communicative Action, Volume One: Reason and the Rationalization of Society*. Translated by McCarthy, T.A. Boston, MA: Beacon Press.

Habermas, J. (1987) *Theory of Communicative Action, Volume Two: Lifeworld and System: A Critique of Functionalist Reason*. Translated by McCarthy, T.A. Boston, MA: Beacon Press.

Heron, J. (1974) *The Concept of a Peer Learning Community (Human Potential Research Project)*. Guildford: University of Surrey.

Honneth, A. (1996) *The Struggle for Recognition: The Moral Grammar of Social Conflicts*, Cambridge: Polity Press.

Isaacson, W. (2021) *The Code-Breaker: Jennifer Doudna, Gene Editing and the Future of the Human Race*, New York, NY: Simon and Schuster.

Jay, M. (1996) *The Dialectical Imagination: A History of the Frankfurt School and Institute for Social Research 1923–1950*, Berkeley, CA: University of California Press.

Jeffries, S. (2016) *Grand Hotel Abyss: The Lives of the Frankfurt School*, London: Verso.

Joas, H. (1996) *The Creativity of Action*, Chicago, IL: University of Chicago Press.

Joas, H. (2000) *The Genesis of Values*, Chicago, IL: University of Chicago.

Learnmonth, M. and Harding, N. (2006) Evidence-based management: the very idea, *Public Administration*, 84(2):245–266.

MacIntyre, A. (1985) *After virtue: a study in moral theory*, London: Duckworth.

Morin, E. (2005) Restricted complexity, general complexity. In: *Presented at the Colloquium "Intelligence de la complexite: "epistemologie et pragmatique", Cerisy-La-Salle, France, June 26th, 2005"*. Translated from French by Carlos Gershenson.

Mowles, C. (2015) The paradox of stability and change: Elias' Processual Sociology. In: Garud, R., Simpson, B., Langley, A. and Tsoukas, H. (eds.), *The Emergence of Novelty in Organizations*, Oxford: Oxford University Press. pp. 245–271.

Reynolds, M. (2009) Wild frontiers: reflections on experiential learning, *Management Learning*, 40(4):387–392.

Rousseau, D. (2006) Is there such a thing as 'evidence based management'?, *Academy of Management Review*, 31(2):256–269.

Sandberg, J., Loacker, B. and Alvesson, M. (2015) Conceptions of process in organisation and management: the case of identity studies. In: Garud, R., Simpson, B., Langley, A. and

Tsoukas, H. (eds.), *The Emergence of Novelty in Organizations*, Oxford: Oxford University Press. pp. 318–343 (Perspectives on Process Organization Studies).

Shotter, J. and Tsoukas, H. (2014a) In search of phronesis: leadership and the art of judgement, *Management Learning and Education*, 13(2):224–243.

Shotter, J. and Tsoukas, H. (2014b) Performing phronesis: on the way to engaged judgment, *Management Learning*, 45(4) 377–396.

Stacey, R.D. and Mowles, C. (2016) *Strategic Management and Organisational Dynamics: The Challenge of Complexity to Ways of Thinking about Organizations*, 7th Edition, London: Pearson Education.

Thomas, G. (2010) Doing case study: abduction not induction, phronesis not theory, *Qualitative Inquiry*, 16(7):575–582.

Thomas, G. (2012) Changing our landscape of inquiry for a new science of education, *Harvard Educational Review*, 82(1):26–51.

Tokarczuk, O. (2007) *Flights*, London: Fitzcarraldo Editions.

Tufekci, Z. (2019) Scientific American blog, May 17. https://blogs.scientificamerican.com/observations/the-real-reason-fans-hate-the-last-season-of-game-of-thrones/ , accessed 20/8/2021. I did reference this in note 4.

Vince, R. (2010) Anxiety, politics and critical management education, *British Journal of Management*, 21(s1):S26–S39.

Whitehead, A.N. (1934 [2011]), *Nature and Life*, Chicago, IL: University of Chicago Press. Reprinted Cambridge: Cambridge University Press.

Wright Mills, C. (1959/2000) *The Sociological Imagination*, Oxford: Oxford University Press.

7

COMPLEX AUTHORITY

The leader in the group and the group in the leader

I was recently invited to fill out a questionnaire for a colleague who was being assessed for a 360-degree appraisal concerning her leadership abilities, although I did not work for her organization. I was being invited to offer an 'outsider's' perspective. To the best of my knowledge, this colleague does not lead a large team, although she has a very senior position. I understand this questionnaire to be a reflection of many organizations' preoccupation with leadership and their need to quantify and assess the leadership potential of their employees, whether they are in leadership positions or not. It is part of a much wider discourse about leadership and a widely accepted supposition that it is a critical determinant of organizational success.

This particular questionnaire comprised 40 or so Likert scale questions with 4 discursive questions at the end asking about the colleague's principal strengths and weaknesses. The questions divided roughly into eight main themes.

Theme one asked for my assessment of my colleague's ability to promote collaboration and team working and to encourage team contributions. Theme two concerned the colleague's ability to embrace/encourage/generate change and innovation – was my colleague able to take risks and stand by them? Theme three, was my colleague confident and positive? Four, did she have an aspiring, compelling vision which she could communicate to enthuse colleagues? Five, could she communicate positively, stating clearly what she believes and able to convey complex ideas with brevity? Six, was she able to create the right culture where people were motivated and enjoyed high morale? Seven, was she able to acknowledge different positions and find ways of reconciling them? And finally, was my colleague able to concentrate on performance and develop metrics to measure it?

Thematically the questionnaire covered what one might expect from an orthodox perspective on what good leadership might be, including that these are skills or abilities which a member of staff 'has' for all time irrespective of context

DOI: 10.4324/9781003002840-7

or who she would be working with. There are a number of other assumptions implicit in the questionnaire which seem to me to be questionable, not least the idea that there is a difference between leadership and management; many of the areas of enquiry would seem to be suitable for either discipline, if they are separate disciplines.

The tenor of questionnaire conjures up an orderly organizational world with the leader in rational control, proposing and disposing, choosing and identifying, analysing and solving. This leader is aware that there might be differences of opinion, even conflict (although there were only 2 questions from the 40 acknowledging this), but this does not faze them, since they are able to point out the differences, accept, soothe and reconcile. The leader has positional power and can use it to convince colleagues of change, which is good for them and which they are likely to oppose. Change is always good, and so is innovation: this leader is always innovative, knowing in advance what will turn out well for the organization. The leader is able to tell the difference between a risky risk and one that is reasonable: they are just on the right side of edgy. This leader is authentic, possessing an authenticity aligned with organizational objectives and can speak clearly about who they are and what they stand for, but not in a way that uses words and phrases which are too highfalutin. S/he is committed to good performance and can develop systems to measure it. Moreover, the leader has powers to create a culture, if teams could be deemed to have such a thing, where staff work with high morale and motivation. Not least of the leader's skills is the ability to see into the future and to convey their foresight in compelling and exciting terms.

The staff this leader inspires are bit part players, adjuncts to the leader's will, a cast of actors to be directed, moulded, aroused and measured, all for the good of the organization.

This rendition of what a leader should be doing and is assumed to be capable of is close to the theory of action I set out in Chapter 3 and termed self-action. It presumes a range of abilities and insights in the leader which are somehow self-generated. It also has all the tropes about positivity, vision and the importance of metrics which we have explored elsewhere in this book in a critical fashion.

Thinking about leadership as a longer term social trend

Let's stay with a number of the assumptions underpinning the questionnaire and think about how we come to have such a completely overinflated and ubiquitous discourse on leadership. As I argued in the last chapter on complex knowledge, it's important to take the object of study and the conditions of its emergence into account, to be critical, if we are to understand the phenomenon we are interested in, in more detail.

If we return for a moment to the computer-based models we explored in Chapter 2 on the complexity sciences. One of the central insights I claimed particularly about the complex adaptive systems models, which are populated with large numbers of interacting agents, is that the stable instability of the fluctuating pattern that emerges does so as a result of all the agents engaging locally. There is no one central site of control, or group of controlling agents. Equally so, in the flock of starlings, there is no chief executive starling with a vision, or executive team with a strategy. The ordered disorder arises simply and only because of the activity of the whole population of agents. If we use this model of stability and change to understand how societies work by analogy, then the idea that organizations, or even countries, are dependent on leaders having a degree of control over how people interact is hard to sustain (unless you live in North Korea, and then the control over how people behave only shows outwardly). Whatever we mean by 'culture,' whether we think of it as *habitus* after Bourdieu and Elias, or simply as the habituated pattern of co-operating and competing together in a particular context and at a particular time, no leader can control the way people are interacting locally with each other. Nor is it possible that they can see into the future and chose one which is ideal for the functioning of the team and the organization, simply because they cannot know what the future might hold. And nor can they adopt a position outside the dynamic which they co-create and judge what is 'appropriate' for the exact calibration of their team.

In short, the questionnaire contains just about every cliché about leadership and the management of organizations. Although we might acknowledge that there is a substantial minority critical tradition in organizational scholarship, it doesn't appear as though much of this has seeped out into organizations in terms of what they take for granted day to day in managing. The leader imagined by the questionnaire is expected to have a unique insight into the human condition because of some magical quality that enables them both to see into the future, to see into human souls and to have just the right touch of intervening which brings about the optimum results.

In making this critique, I am not claiming leaders and senior teams have no influence. We all have experience of workplaces which were delightful places to be, because of the kinds of relationships which those in authority positions encouraged, and perhaps modelled, and more commonly we have experience where this not the case: there are lots of instances of suffering at work. The way senior people behave can make a difference and leaders can have a big impact on our experience at work, through active or passive encouragement of particular ways of working. But not to the degree presumed in the questionnaire I had to fill out. Equally, I am not trying to suggest that human beings are like starlings, ants or fish because we have complicated relationships with authority, not least because of our early experiences in the family group, which I explore further later. To an extent, the inflated discourse on leadership is self-amplifying: it takes on the quality of the double hermeneutic that the sociologist Giddens once described (1993). In other words, a term which is developed to make sense of some social phenomenon is then adopted by the groups so described to make sense for themselves. The description takes on a life of its own. There is so much of it that it becomes taken for granted, and in being so, we come to expect leaders to have the kinds of idealized qualities that the discourse suggests.

I think we have become addicted to the one-armed bandit machine of leadership, permanently expecting miracles at the same time as anticipating the inevitable disappointment. It can mean that every aspect of power relating or the exercise of authority in organizations can be reduced to questions of leadership. And leadership becomes associated with everything good that's happening in an organization (Alvesson et al., 2017: 8).

But it has not always been the case that leaders have had such prominence in thinking about what's going on in organizations and it is worth reviewing some of the reasons why there is such an avalanche of leadership talk and whom it benefits. It also merits locating the discourse in the central preoccupation of this book, which is to think about social complexity and how organizational scholarship helps us orient ourselves or not in conditions of uncertainty. What do the ubiquitous tropes about leadership have to say about how we might go on together when we can't know what the future holds?

When I teach much younger people on postgraduate management courses, it comes as a surprise to them that there hasn't always been such a focus on leadership in organizations. Indeed, when I was a young employee in the not-for-profit and public sectors we hardly used the word. I mention in the introduction that when I did a management course in the early 1990s there was no leadership module to speak of. Of course, we had directors, as they were called then, and what they did and said mattered, but we were much less preoccupied with the leadership aura. Martin and Learmonth (2012) make a related observation about the way that the term administrator gave way to the word manager, which, in turn, gave way to the preference for leader in the National Health Service (NHS) in the United Kingdom. The term has now become so ubiquitous that everyone involved in the health service is encouraged to be a leader, even patients. A similar experience has been encountered by other academics (Ford and Harding, 2007) who have found themselves obliged to run modules on leadership rather than look at the exercise of authority in organizations in the round – move over management, we're all leaders now, as the authors title their article. Given that the way we talk about leaders is couched in such portentous language, it may be no surprise that people aspire to being leaders. However, in my own experience of being asked to run leadership modules because it is expected, or because there is always money available to offer leadership development, we end up by talking about a lot else concerning the exercise of power in organizations, and what leaders are doing is only one aspect of this (Masua et al., 2019).

The critical tradition focuses on leadership as a phenomenon of history and the political economy, claiming that the rise in the discourse on leadership is coterminous with the rise of the influence of neoliberalism as political economy. These include scholars like Khurana (2007) who argue that the emergence of the amplifying split between leadership and management in the 1980s arose at time of another crisis in capitalism (Harvey, 2011), where the economy failed to make sufficient returns to the holders of capital. According to Khurana the early 1980s saw the ascendancy of the idea of agency theory, a concept developed by the Chicago school of economics, where it was posited that the principal responsibility of a head of a company was to act as an agent for the owners of the company, who were deemed to be exclusively the shareholders. The idea that the leader should be a steward of the company's future on behalf of a variety of stakeholders, including the workers and the local community, was too vague and distracting, according to this perspective, and indeed was unmeasurable. Rather than being transactional, trying to balance competing interests, the leader needed to be transformational, radically changing the fortunes of the company and thus the return to shareholders. Khurana notices that it was around this time that the remuneration of the leader of the company became linked to the performance of the company: if the company did well, the leader was in turn amply rewarded. He charts the way that business schools, particularly in the United States, but now everywhere, became part of a symbiotic relationship of both promoting and benefitting from the leadership turn in organizational scholarship.

Leadership studies became a lucrative self-reinforcing industry where business schools could charge large amounts of money for producing leaders who would then earn large amounts of money, encouraging new generations of managers to attend business schools to become leaders. In the welter of scholarship on leadership, which has been produced since the early 1980s, we have come to accept as given a number of dualisms that leadership is distinct from management, that transformation is required rather than transaction, that there are leaders and followers and that being a leader requires a particular magical property that only certain individuals have. The idea of magical individuals is consonant with the age in which we live, when individuality is lionized.

It has become a given that leaders should be charismatic and transformational, even if they sometimes leave a trail of destruction, as any number of corporate episodes in the last decades show, and as Tourish (2013) has documented.[1] I explore what might be some of the unconscious processes which might be in play when we are caught up in idealizing a leader later, but politically Davies (2014) understands the phenomenon in terms of the entrepreneurial individualism which neoliberalism encourages and is seen as a direct response to managing in conditions of uncertainty. Drawing on the work of Boltanski and Thévenot (2006), he compares and contrasts what we might understand as liberal democratic order where we are required to offer each other justifications, and we expect to be listened to and challenged, with a neoliberal order where justifications are withheld and the public space to challenge is closed down. The explanation for this is that leaders are exceptional individuals who are able to act outside the rules.[2] Set against an existential threat of extreme competition, what I have referred to elsewhere as an anxiety narrative, the charismatic leader ascribes to themselves the authority of acting without justification, which sometimes involves the use of violence:

> One advantage that business leaders have in operating without justification and purely on the basis of decision, is the capacity to transform the

enterprise, alter its market productive functions, downsize its employees, such that it evades critique. Managers retain the option to simply eradicate certain employees as an alternative to morally engaging with them.

Davies, 2014: 145

The environment of competition, which the neoliberal perspective itself encourages, creates a feeling of existential threat, which the transformational leader with their exceptional abilities is considered best equipped to deal with unconstrained by existing routines and regulations.[3] However, studies of what transformational leadership might actually mean in the everyday environment of organizational life reveal that the concept is much talked about, but very little experienced (Alvesson and Sveningsson, 2003a,b). Leadership activity is mostly very mundane but takes on an added significance simply because it is undertaken by leaders.

A more recent critique of the whole panoply of leadership discourse and scholarship is offered by Learmonth and Morrell (2019), which turns on the role of language. For Learmonth and Morrell, language doesn't just reflect social reality, it creates it, much as I argue in Chapter 5. They point to the numerous ways in which the language of leadership has colonized us and the way we think about organizational landscapes. For them, the discourse adds to the creation and flattering of elites and flatters those who flatter them. But because it is everywhere, it becomes impossible talk about leadership without getting corralled into offering alternative forms of the very phenomenon we are trying to problematize, because we are already pulled onto the leadership ground in doing so. I noticed the same thing when undertaking a piece of research for a leadership institution. Their commission was to research the phenomenon of 'transformational' change in the higher education sector, which involved talking to senior teams in six different UK universities. I was sceptical about the commission because I share the same doubts as other critical scholars both about leadership and about transformation. Having experienced at first hand in an higher education (HE) context what passes for transformation, I wondered how much I could keep an open mind. I found that some respondents adopted the language of leadership and transformation unproblematically, others were much more conscious of the ways in which they found themselves being taken over by it.

I have been making the case throughout this book, drawing on the pragmatists, that thinking and speaking are also forms of action. Equally I have argued that there is no standing outside social reality which shapes us. The all-encompassing nature of the language and concepts of leadership make it hard to avoid and reduce every expression of power or authority, sometimes every social problem, to questions of leadership or the lack of it.

Learmonth and Morrell remind us that the leadership leviathan has served leaders and elites very well, but not so much the rest of us. Seemingly indestructible leaders who often flit from one highly paid job to another have massively increased their remuneration in proportion to the rest of the workforce who have either seen their incomes stagnate or reduce. The same socio-economic forces that have turned all managers into aspiring leaders, all senior management teams into senior leadership teams and all leaders into CEOs have led to the casualization of work and the deterioration of living standards. They point to the double bind of critical engagement with the discourse that even to reflect and take seriously what is said and how is partially to accept some of the assumptions. Critical scholars get drawn onto the ground of leadership even as they try to critique it, offering an alternative view of what they could or should be doing.

I am conscious of this but equally keen to say something about leadership from a complexity perspective that challenges the assumption of individuality and deflates the notion that it is the catch-all for describing all of our social ills.

Uncertainty, authority and group dynamics

We live in a hyper-individualized age and one which is hypercompetitive and increasingly dynamic. The German sociologist Hartmut Rosa (2013) makes the connection between all three phenomena and argues that each of these is mutually reinforcing. In such circumstances, he argues, our deliberative processes of liberal democracy, which we used to consider responsive to our social concerns, is no longer timely enough to make decisions about what most presses. Group processes appear to be too slow for what we need: because we don't have the time, the problems pile up and as the problems pile up, we have even less time to tackle them. Rather than accelerating towards an improved future, Rosa, argues, we are caught up in condition of frenetic standstill, treading water faster and faster just to keep afloat. In terms of how we deal with our problems, Rosa concurs with Davies that instead of making claims and justifying them to each other as we have been used to in a liberal democratic order, we revert instead to a struggle instead over images and symbols. The vacuum of more centralized authority is filled by executive decisions, constitutional courts, deregulation of the economy and the individualization of personal responsibility (Rosa, 2013: 267).

If ever there was a feeling that even our national and organizational leaders are not in charge, then the current accelerating competitive dynamic amplifies this. When societies and organizations seem to be in a state of continuous reforming, Marris (1996) has observed that the burden of uncertainty falls disproportionately on the already marginalized and poor. It is in circumstances like these that the role of the unfettered and heroic leader perhaps has most appeal, when they claim the authority to 'move fast and break things.'[4] That large numbers of the disenfranchised should start to choose leaders who are authoritarian and have little regard for democracy and the deliberative process shouldn't surprise us if the promise of these leaders is to put right decades of widening inequality. Equally in organizations, we have seen the rise of charismatic leaders who may act in highly cavalier, sometimes destructive ways, and then claim credit for doing so, or even deny that they have acted destructively. Highly dynamic circumstances create the conditions where a particular kind of leader may come to the fore because at the same time they create expectations in groups.

Perhaps we can think about what might be going on when a group is anxious and what this might lead to in their expectations of people in authority, with the help of psychiatrists Wilfred Bion and Pierre Turquet. It may help us reflect upon how we are all caught up in social and emotional patterns which are hard to resist from the perspective of the group, not just from the perspective of the authority figure. I explore this as an under-represented aspect of group life in much leadership literature, rather than claiming that it is the only thing going on, but it might be helpful to look more broadly at the dynamics of leadership more from the group perspective.

Having undergone psychoanalysis himself at the Tavistock Institute, Bion worked with groups at the Northfield Hospital in London after the war trying to help them cope with some of the psychological distress of the trauma of having been combatants. He wrote a series of papers which were later collected into the landmark book *Experiences in Groups* (1961/2011) which was a reflection on the complex dynamics of group life, drawing from long-term groups of recovering patients he ran at the Northfield Hospital. In doing so, he contrasted what he described as the 'sophisticated and rational functioning level of behaviour' present in a group focused on a task, which he termed a 'work group,' with a 'basic assumption group,' which was a state of distress experienced by the group which made them unable to focus on the task. Bion's three basic assumptions, dependency, fight/flight and pairing are emotional states which seize the group when it becomes anxious and interferes with the group's ability to function. Later, Pierre Turquet (1974) added a fourth basic assumption, oneness. These basic assumptions may alternate, or one basic assumption might take hold of the group for long periods of time. I explore all of these later.

Dependency is pattern of relating in an anxious group, which then looks to an idealized leader to help them out of a crisis. The group itself may become passive and docile and overly respectful of the leader. This is a pattern I notice whenever I meet a new group of students, or managers in an educational setting, particularly if they are young. I might experience a lot of very basic questions about things which have already been explained, or may manifest as an oversolicitousness about my opinion on what we are about to talk about. At the beginning of the pandemic, and in my institution, a relatively mundane e-mail from a manager to all staff setting out what the department should be working on elicited some members of staff to reply that they found the instructions 'inspirational.' This kind of response told me as much about how people were feeling in my business school as it did about what the manager wrote.

So, in situations of crisis, according to Bion, we are likely to become highly dependent on our leaders and to invest heavily in their actions and words. They may become idealized or if they are unavailable, we may to look to others to lead us. This can be dangerous territory both for us and for leaders if they come to believe in this idealization of themselves. Bion comments on the kind of leader that an anxious group might look to:

> In my experience most groups, not only patient groups, find a substitute that satisfies them very well. It is usually a man or a woman with marked paranoid

trends; perhaps if the presence of an enemy is not immediately obvious to the group, the next best thing is for the group to choose a leader to whom it is.

1961/2011: 67

It is not difficult to notice these kinds of dynamics writ large in global politics at the moment and not least in the United Kingdom. There has been a long, slow socio-economic crisis in the United Kingdom, particularly since the financial collapse which has widened inequalities further and has led to the suffering of already marginalized communities as state and municipal provision has been withdrawn. Nationalist politicians are then able to blame others for poorer communities' distress, even if the blame is contradictory. On the one hand, we are asked to believe that EU migrants are coming to the United Kingdom and living on state benefits and yet on the other we are asked to believe that they are coming here and taking all the jobs and driving down wages. In either case, a group in an anxious state of uncertainty becomes paranoid about the 'other,' or unites around a leader who is paranoid on their behalf.

The second basic assumption fight/flight is where group members find enemies within the group, fight among themselves, avoid talking about what is important, disrupt the functioning of the group and become aggressive. They are likely to rally round a leader who can mobilize this hostility or can join them in flights of fantasy about avoiding thinking about the situation altogether. I have sometimes wondered whether the tendencies to shock or clown around demonstrated by President Trump and Prime Minister Johnson are located in this basic assumption, the first figure constantly picking fights, or aligning with other people's fights and the second uncontrollably escaping into japery as a form of distraction from the seriousness of what he should be talking about.

The third basic assumption, pairing is an expression of hope for the future of the group and occurs when members look to two people in the group to produce offspring, in Bion's terms, perhaps the Messiah, who will save the group. In group life, members may sit back while two members of the group do all the work to help them out of their dilemma. Thinking more broadly, it may also help explain the British public's preoccupation with, say, royal babies particularly at times of national suffering. We can survive the present distress if we focus on hope for the future in the shape of the reproduction of an idealized family. Alternatively, we can think of it in our own terms as a form of regression, standing back and hoping that mum and dad will take over and sort things out for us. When students are on the point of leaving the research group that I run with colleagues, they often ask about the pipeline of new students who might come on to the programme, perhaps as a way of coping with the anxiety of leaving.

Oneness is a basic assumption in a group which encourages an undifferentiated feeling of wholeness in order for the group to preserve itself and is a very common and complex state which we can see manifested in lots of different locations. At the same time as encouraging a sense of a whole, this feeling makes it difficult to examine assumptions or call things into question. Many organizations make an appeal to oneness with their values statements, where all employees are expected to 'share the values,' even when it is not in a particularly disturbed state. But in times of crisis like the present, we are encouraged all to pull together, not to criticize the government or our senior management team, which is said to be doing its best. During the long years of austerity following the banking crisis, we were constantly reminded that 'we are all in this together.' In terms of the recent pandemic, even a cursory scan of the statistics reveals that this is not the case. However, BAME communities and health professionals have suffered a disproportionate numbers of deaths, as have poor areas of the country, as have the old and vulnerable, and not just because they were old and vulnerable, which is exactly Peter Marris' point about the uneven burden of uncertainty which is experienced more by marginalized groups. Equally in organizations, it is usually the employees on temporary or part-time contracts who are in the first wave of redundancies when organizations shrink. To explore these social effects means taking a stand and potentially putting yourself in opposition. The appeal to oneness is not just enjoined by authority figures, but we are likely to encourage each other not to let the side down, and not to be negative. The price we pay for falling into this basic assumption is an absence of critical thinking.

This sense of oneness can be experienced as regression into a primitive state by large populations of people, according to psychoanalyst Vamik Volkan (2001). Volkan's work is aimed at understanding the aspects of personality which I have referred to elsewhere, drawing on Elias, as the 'we' identity, the layer of our personality structure which reflects our allegiance and belonging to groups. Having worked for many years with populations who have gone to war with each other, Arabs and Israelis, Turkish and Greek Cypriots and Croatians and Serbs, Volkan noticed that when opposing communities are drawn into dialogue they take refuge in the 'tent' of their trauma, usually an event which has taken place in the past and is communicated intergenerationally, and which he terms a 'chosen trauma.' It is chosen in the sense that there may have been many episodes in a community's history which were traumatic, but it is one particular incident which comes to represent the people involved. By linking psychoanalysis and history, he argues that the actual detail of a chosen trauma becomes less relevant than its symbolic and unifying value and is adopted by the large group as a defence. In the paper I reference, Volkan gives an account of the way in which Milosevic mobilized the Serbs around their chosen trauma of the battle of Kosovo against the Turks. There are many episodes in history where a leader emerges to speak to this trauma for their own advantage and with horrific results for the community or communities which are considered to be 'the other' by the mobilized people. As McAfee states, 'peoples are at risk of breakdown when they adamantly deny any contingency to their own collectivity, when they insist that their group really is singular, unique, and real, rather than a happenstance of history' (2019: 61). From a US and a British perspective, we might understand our 'tent' not so much to be one of trauma, but of exceptionalism. The movement to withdraw the United Kingdom from the European Union was often couched in terms of a desired return to Britain's perceived greatness, and we are blessed with a prime minister who wrote a biography of Winston Churchill and is very keen on flags.

Both the pragmatists and Norbert Elias wrote about the dynamics of creating in-groups and out groups. In two articles (1914 and 1932), Mead wrote about what he termed 'cult values,' which I introduced in the introduction. Cult values are an idealized and imaginative construction of the unity of experience of what it means to be a 'whole' community. This is a familiar pattern in organizations when members of staff are invited to believe in the mission or values of the organization or take them up in their everyday activities. Equally, national politicians may invite us to make America great again, or believe in Global Britain. These values, which are on the one hand the most precious expression of who we believe ourselves to be, are at the same time a cult in the sense that they provide the criteria for inclusion and exclusion from the group. Cult values contribute to our feeling of an enlarged sense of self as members of the heroic group. So, in this respect, they are a key contributor to our sense of identity. At the same time, the appeal to heroic 'we-ness' can cover over critique and questioning. To ask questions about the values, or the leader expressing them, can be deemed to be an offence against the community as a whole.

Meanwhile, Norbert Elias was keen to make clear that when he talked about *The Civilising Process*, which is a treatment of how societies become more and more interdependent, he did not consider becoming civilized as meaning that difficulties in groups had been resolved. Rather, the bruises and wounds of becoming part of a highly interdependent society were internalized and operated semi-automatically in guiding our behaviour by 'rising tides of guilt and shame' (2000: 416). Neither did he consider the civilizing process to be linear or inevitable. *The Germans* (1997) explores exactly the opposite process. How is it that the civilizing process can go into reverse and descend into barbarism?

As a Jewish refugee from Nazi Germany, this was clearly a matter of direct personal concern for Elias. As for his compatriots and fellow Jews, Hannah Arendt and S.H. Foulkes, making sense of the dualisms of human behaviour, processes promoting humane ways of coexistence or the opposite, tyranny and barbarism, became a lifetime preoccupation. Elias argues that the ascendancy of the middle class to positions of national leadership from the 18th century onwards deemphasized the role of the king or prince in people's allegiances. The practice of politics and power required other ways of uniting citizens in large collectivities where people could not know each other directly, nor could they simply identify with a symbolic figurehead alone. What is needed, then, is a way of talking about the collectivity, the nation, which revolves around certain words and symbols, which foster emotional collective bonds between large numbers of people who are strangers to one another in the same country:

> So, the emotional bonds of individuals with the collectivity which they form with each other crystallize and organize themselves around common symbols which do not require any factual explanations, which can and must

be regarded as absolute values which are not to be questioned and which form focal points of a common belief system. To call them into question – to cast doubt on the common belief in own's own sovereign collectivity as a high, if not the highest possible, value – means deviancy, a breach of trust; it can lead one to become an ostracized outsider, if nothing worse.

1997: 146

Elias notes that nationalism is one of the most powerful group experiences of the 19th and 20th centuries. However, once unleashed, these feelings can be self-amplifying and are no longer under the control of individuals or groups who seek to recruit them to their cause. They elicit not only a kind of love of the collective, but also a form of self-love: anyone who feels, for example, intensely British is at the same time revering themselves for being part of the heroic group. The creation of an in-group also produces an out-group through exclusionary processes which involves scapegoat-seeking and may even cause violent behaviour to protect the sanctity of the heroic group.

Summing up the importance of group process in thinking about leadership

A great deal of scholarship focuses on the role of the leader, whether it is to promote the ubiquitous discourse of the heroic, unique individual or to critique it. Whichever turn one takes, even engaging with the ideas seems to proliferate more leadership concepts. In the earlier section, I have tried to approach the exercise of power and authority from the perspective of groups. The point of doing so is to make the case that the social conditions chose the authority figure as much as the authority figure shapes the social conditions. There are powerful processes of inclusion and exclusion, dependency and avoidance in groups, which are particularly prominent if the group is anxious and will condition expectations about what is needed of the leader, and which may play to the leader's own fantasies.

This has been true of human beings in groups since time immemorial. But in the early 21st century we seem to have co-created the *habitus* where so great is the dynamic of social acceleration and change that we are in a state of frenetic stand-still, according to Rosa (2013), which are ideal conditions for accentuating our feelings of anxiety and dependency. Rather than improving the human condition as some advocates of globalization and technology promise, in our accelerated state of change, we encouraged to look to ourselves as resource to take personal responsibility (as we explored in Chapter 4). Or alternatively, we choose national leaders who amplify our state of dependency, or who are chosen for us in organizations to best respond to the conditions of greater competition. The discourse on leadership has generated more heat than light, and there is little about our experience of leadership in organizations that might convince us that we are better led than previously.

I introduced group analysis in the last chapter, which we might think of simply as a group practice which encourages people to meet together with no particular end in view and to talk about what matters to them. It is governed by a different idea of leadership authority. Given his history, Foulkes was concerned to develop a different understanding of the role of the leader, one which rejects the dependent fantasies of the group and avoids the temptation of indulging his/her own fantasies about leadership. The facilitator of a group is referred to as a conductor rather than as a leader, and the term evokes the role of a conductor of an orchestra, where their authority is used to bring out the best in the group. In a group run along analytic lines, the conductor works with dependency to bring the members of the group to a more mature understanding of their own agency:

> What does the leader in group analysis do on this level? Briefly, he accepts his position in order to use it in the best interests of the group and eventually, to wean them from the need for authoritative guidance. What does this imply? First of all, that he must recognise the situation for what it is … He does not step down, but lets the group, in steps and stages, bring him down to earth. The change which takes place is that from a leader of the group to a leader in the group. The group, in its turn, replaces the leader's authority by that of the group.
>
> *Foulkes, 1964: 60–61*

Foulkes had normative ambitions for the role of the conductor in a group analytic context, aspiring to moral and democratic ideals in the process of exercising authority in a group. Of course, the conductor of the group is responsible for what happens, but s/he is working as part of the group, first among equals, aiming to move themselves out of the way if the group is functioning well. Foulkes considered that it was equally possible to adopt this perspective in non-therapeutic groups too as has been my experience both on the research programme I direct and working with groups of managers. There is sometimes a hesitation, a holding back, on the part of group members when they expect me to direct proceedings, but once they realize that whatever happens does so partly as a result of the quality of their own participation, then they quickly learn to benefit from a different way of proceeding.

Of course, there is a certain naivety about Foulkes' aspirations for a new kind of leadership. In a therapeutic context, the function of the conductor is to put the interests of the group first for its better therapeutic functioning, both for the individuals in the group and for the maturity of the group as a whole. However, in an organizational context, people put themselves forward to be leaders for a whole variety of reasons, including ambition, greed and a sense of superiority. To accept this is merely to accept that we are human. I do so as a counterweight to the current hysteria about the role of leaders rather than with any naivety that I am putting forward an alternative model: what I suggest drawing on Foulkes, is countercultural.

In what has preceded, I have tried to deflate the overblown discourse on leadership both by pointing to its sociohistorical roots and the function it might play in political economy and considering the relationship from the other way round. Instead of thinking about what leaders do for groups, what is it that group processes demand of leaders? The implication is that leaders are more shaped than shaping. I do not deny, however, that astute political leaders can manipulate the very group dynamics to their own advantage.

In what follows, I continue to explore the phenomenon of leadership understood as a relational and social process, a dynamic which creates and recreates the exercise of authority.

Recognizing and being recognized – the leader and the group, the group and the leader

In Chapter 5, we explored Mead's theory of communication which involves bodies gesturing and responding to each other at the same time as they gesture and respond to themselves. This allows us to anticipate the anticipation of others and reveal ourselves to ourselves as we reveal ourselves to others. Elsewhere in *Mind, Self and Society*, he wrote about the reciprocal gesture and response which enacts the phenomenon of leadership. He had in mind exceptional leaders, geniuses he calls them at one point, that one encounters once in a generation, rather than the way leaders and leadership have been written about routinely. (Although I am sure that many overpaid CEOs may consider themselves to be the kind of geniuses that Mead had in mind.) But nonetheless, he gives us some insight into the social process of group formation and development:

> Persons of great mind and great character have strikingly changed the communities to which they have responded. We call them leaders, as such, but they are simply carrying to the nth power this change in the community by the individual who makes himself a part of it, who belongs to it. The great characters have been those who, by being what they were in the community, made the community a different one.
>
> *1934: 216*

It is important to understand that Mead considers the development of the genius/ leader also to be a thoroughly social process, their behaviour is 'socially conditioned.' The leader takes the generalized attitude of the community to himself just as we all do, and the attitude of the group towards any project they have in common. However, because of their unique social experience, the world leader is able to respond in a unique and original way that surpasses an ordinary person's response. One way of thinking about this ability, then, is as a highly social sensitivity to and insight into the organized attitude of the group, which allows everybody, including the leader, to enter into a different relationship with each other. In doing so, they enlarge the community. History shows that this can be done both progressively and regressively, if we think that to a degree Prime Minister Jacinda Ardern and President Trump are mirror images of each other. There is nothing about the genius of bringing a society into a different relationship with itself that this means it is necessarily for more humane and progressive social ends. For every Nelson Mandela, there is a President Bolsonaro. Each in their own way was able to speak in terms recognizable by a sufficiently large group of people to get elected. Sometimes, this involves a leader bringing groups into relation who are normally marginalized or excluded:

> Figures of that sort become of enormous importance because they make possible communication between groups otherwise completely separate from each other. The sort of capacity we speak of is in politics the attitude of the statesman who is able to enter into the attitudes of the group and to mediate between them by making his own experience universal, so that others can enter into communication through him.
>
> *1934: 257*

I think Mead is pointing to insight that world leaders, statesmen or women have an ability shared in common with great artists, or writers because it has the paradoxical quality of particular universality about it. This is the dialectic I was pointing to in the last chapter on complex knowledge where leaders are able to express something about their own experience which calls out recognition in the communities into which they are speaking. There is a process of mutual recognition which transforms both parties and brings about an enhanced ability of members of the community to participate. In organizations, this is likely to mean navigating between different and sometimes opposing groups, particularly in times of crisis of conflict. What Mead's insights into leadership don't bring out, then, are the political skills needed of a leader, if not to bringing into relation all of the people all of the time, but enough of the people for enough of the time to sustain confidence in the exercise of authority.

Social psychologists Haslam et al. (2020) have developed an experimental basis for explaining this group process which Mead identified nearly a century ago, illustrated with historical and contemporary examples of leaders acting in groups. They argue that successful leadership involves embodying and representing what the group stands for, standing up for and acting as a champion for the group, encouraging cohesion and an understanding of what it means to be a member of the group and arranging activities and events to help group members understand what it means to be a member of the group (2020: 198). They term this their Identity Leadership Inventory. The kinds of skills that Haslam et al. identify that leaders need are some of those that we have already noted in different chapters in this book but have not just ascribed them just to leaders, but to anyone who wants to notice and participate more skilfully in groups. They argue that leaders need:

> linguistic prowess, rhetorical sophistication, poetic expression, choreography, spatial design, architectural vision, organizational acumen and social insight. But for all this diversity there are two constants that run throughout … The first is that leaders do not simply need to be artists, impresarios and engineers.

They need to be artists, impresarios and engineers of *identity* – specifically of a social identity which is shared with their followers. Social identity, then remains the key unifying construct.

2020: 165

The second constant that Haslam et al. identify is that achieving all of this is hard work: they see it as an ongoing improvisation of constantly making concrete in particular contexts the more abstract and nebulous concepts of 'who we are' and 'what we stand for.' In the book, the authors draw on the example of St Paul, who converted from being a persecutor of Christians to becoming the embodiment of a Christ-follower (according to the biographer of St Paul, Philip Esler, 2003). In this sense, and making the link again to Mead (1938), the leader in this sense is a kind of social object. By social object, Mead didn't intend an object in nature, but a pattern on relating between people: the tendency to act in particular ways by large numbers of people which we recognize and respond to. According to Haslam et al., and using my interpretation of Mead, St Paul was able to define himself as the epitome of what a follower of Christ should be and how they would act: a social object of the disciple. The importance of this insight, and one which I have made in a variety of places in the book, is the idea of paradox: the authority figure is able to link the particularity of their identity and history to say something about the identity of the group, and in the process transform both.

Summary of complex authority – implications for managers

There are any number of commentators who have noted that our preoccupation with leaders and leadership, the amount of time we spent teaching it, deconstructing, reconstructing and reinventing the ideas over the last 40 years or so, has not resulted in a demonstrable benefit to organizations or to society (Kellerman, 2012). And yet, it is hard to dislodge as a taken-for-granted assumption about its importance to organizational life. In this chapter, we have tried to decentre leadership, to better understand the conditions in which it seems to have become preeminent and understand it as a complex group process, a dynamic, improvisational relationship between the authority figure and the group in which they participate. These dynamics are guided by powerful group identifications, idealizations and processes of mutual recognition, particularly in highly volatile situations where people experience anxiety. There is enormous potential for authority figures to act into such conditions both for the good and for the bad. Following on from the chapter on the complex self, how the way we understand ourselves is conditioned by the world we are born into, I wonder whether we now live in a highly individualized world where our identities, our sense of self, is much more predisposed to a relationship of dependency with charismatic leaders.

Inquiring into the experience of leading produces insights which still leads me to have some hope that leaders are alert to the complexities of leading others. A piece of research I undertook with colleagues (Mowles et al., 2019) with senior managers in the higher education sector indicated that exercising authority in today's organizations throws up all kinds of ethical and political dilemmas, and a good deal of ambivalence in those who are asked to lead. We found that leaders may or may not have a vision and may feel conflicted about the changes that they are in charge of implementing. Some were conscious that leading involves an ability to dwell in uncertainty and to demonstrate what the poet Keats referred to as 'negative capability': that is, 'when a man is capable of being in uncertainties, mysteries, doubts, without any irritable reaching after fact and reason' (1899: 217). To maintain this involved our respondents in a good deal of practical judgement, which I deal with in Chapters 5, 6 and 8 about when to disclose this uncertainty and when not to, when to intervene and when not to. Inevitably, in trying to bring different points of view into relation with each other will involve the ability to endure conflict and negative feelings, particularly as we have reminded ourselves again in this chapter, our relationship to authority is likely to call out strong feelings of dependency in us. Being in a position of authority can provoke strong projections and idealization, and thus its reverse, potential disappointment, in those being led. A good leader would be wise not to play into these feelings, or, as Foulkes recommends, to step down gently from the pedestal upon which one has been placed so that participants in a group begin to realize their own agency and maturity. All in all as rhetor, as politician, as storyteller in chief helping the group better underhand 'who we are' and 'what we stand for,' the leader can sometimes be at the very heart of the push and pull of strong group dynamics which shape much more than the leader can shape them.

None of what I have written earlier is to imply that we don't need leaders, or that it isn't a very difficult job or that I have something against leaders. I am much more interested in deflating yet complexifying the concept of leadership.

In the next chapter, we investigate some of the ethical themes we have peppered throughout these chapters and those preceding it.

Notes

1 The last decade or so has seen the election of a number of high-profile national charismatic leaders, a quality which seems to cover over their everyday incompetence in the eyes of the majority of the electors.

2 A survey conducted by Hansard in the United Kingdom in 2019 revealed that more than half of the population wanted 'a strong leader who is prepared to break the rules' so disaffected had they become with the political process. https://edition.cnn.com/2019/04/08/uk/hansard-strong-leader-brexit-poll-gbr-intl/index.html.

3 One of the favourite authors of a number of company leaders who consider themselves heroic and charismatic is Ayn Rand. Her novel *Atlas Shrugged*, which propounds a version of heroic individualism based on the idea of rational self-interest and against any form of collectivism, seems to offer such entrepreneurs a mirror through which they see themselves reflected back. Rand had a big influence on Alan Greenspan, long-term head of the Federal Reserve and long-term advocate of low taxes and minimal state intervention.

4 This phrase is said to adorn the office of Mark Zuckerburg, Facebook CEO.

References

Alvesson, M. and Sveningsson, S. (2003a) The great disappearing act: difficulties in doing 'leadership', *Leadership Quarterly*, 14(3):359–381.

Alvesson, M. and Sveningsson, S. (2003b) Managers doing leadership: the extra-ordinarization of the mundane, *Human Relations*, 56(12):1435–1459.

Alvesson, M., Blom, M. and Sveningsson, S. (2017) *Reflexive Leadership: Organising in an Imperfect World*, London: Sage.

Bion, W. (1961/2011) *Experiences in Groups and Other Papers*, London: Routledge.

Boltanski, L. and Thévenot, L. (2006) *On Justification: Economies of Worth*, Princeton, NJ: Princeton University Press.

Davies, W. (2014) *The Limits of Neoliberalism: Authority, Sovereignty and the Logic of Competition*, London: Sage.

Dewey, J. and Bentley, A. (1949) *Knowing and the Known*, Boston, MA: Beacon Press.

Elias, N. (1997) *The Germans*, Cambridge: Polity Press.

Elias, N. (2000) *The Civilising Process*, Oxford: Oxford University Press.

Esler, P.F. (2003) *Conflict and Identity in Romans: The Social Setting of Paul's Letter*, Minneapolis, MN: Fortress Press.

Ford, J. and Harding, N. (2007) Move over management: we are all leaders now, *Management Learning*, 38(5):475–493.

Foulkes, S.H. (1964/2002) *Therapeutic Group Analysis*, London: Karnac Books.

Giddens, A. (1993) *New Rules of Sociological Method*, Stanford, CA: Stanford University Press.

Harvey, D. (2011) *The Enigma of Capital: And the Crises of Capitalism*, New York, NY: Profile books.

Haslam, S.A., Reicher, S.D. and Plastow, M.J. (2020) *The New Psychology of Leadership: Identity, Influence and Power*, 2nd Edition, London: Routledge.

Keats, J. (1899) *The Complete Poetical Works and Letters of John Keats, Cambridge Edition*, Boston, MA: Houghton Mifflin Harcourt.

Kellerman, B. (2012) *The End of Leadership*, New York, NY: Harper Collins.

Khurana, R. (2007) *From Higher Aims to Hired Hands: The Social Transformation of American Business Schools and the Unfulfilled Promise of Management as a Profession*, Princeton, NJ: Princeton University Press.

Learmonth, M. and Morrell, K. (2019) *Critical Perspectives on Leadership: The Language of Corporate Power*, London: Routledge.

Marris, P. (1996) *The Politics of Uncertainty: Attachment in Private and Public Life*, London: Routledge.

Martin, G. and Learmonth, M. (2012) A critical account of the rise and spread of 'leadership': the case of UK healthcare, *Social Science and Medicine*, 74:281–288.

Masua, D., Mowles, C. and Sarra, N. (2019) What we talk about when we talk about leadership in South Sudan, *Development in Practice*, 30(1):1–11.

Mead, G.H. (1914) The psychological bases of internationalism, *Survey*, XXIII:604–607.

Mead, G.H. (1932) Scientific method and the moral sciences, *International Journal of Ethics*, XXXV:229–247.

Mead, G.H. (1934) *Mind, Self and Society from the Standpoint of a Social Behaviourist*, Chicago, IL: Chicago University Press.

Mead, G.H. (1938) *The Philosophy of the Act*, Chicago, IL: University of Chicago.

McAfee, N. (2019) *Fear of Breakdown: Politics and Psychoanalysis*, New York, NY: Columbia University Press.

Mowles, C., Filosof, J., Flinn, K., Mason, P., Culkin, N., Andrews, R. and James, D. (2019) *Transformational Change in the Higher Education Sector: An Inquiry into Leadership Practice*, London: Leadership Foundation for Higher Education.

Rosa, H. (2013) *Social Acceleration: A New Theory of Modernity*, New York, NY: Columbia University Press.

Tourish, D. (2013) *The Dark Side of Organizational Leadership: A Critical Perspective*, London: Routledge.

Turquet, P.M. (1974) Leadership – the individual in the group. In: Gibbard, G.S., Hartman, J.J. and Mann, R.D. (eds.), *Analysis of Groups*, San Francisco, CA: Jossey-Bass.

Volkan, V.D. (2001) Transgenerational transmissions and chosen traumas: an aspect of large-group identity. *Group Analysis*, 34(1):79–97.

8

COMPLEX ETHICS

Widening our circle of concern

In May 2017, the then British Prime Minister Theresa May was asked by an interviewer whether it was wrong that nurses were paid so little that they had to use food banks. She struggled to answer. Finally, in response she argued that 'there are many complex reasons' why nurses might need to use food banks, but obviously not earning enough money was not one she wanted to admit to.[1] As someone interested in thinking about social complexity, I was intrigued to hear the argument put the other way round. In much of the more orthodox literature on complexity and organizations, many scholars cannot resist the temptation to blunt the radical implications of the complexity sciences by arguing that you can 'create the conditions' for the right kind of complexity to happen; you can 'embrace' emergence, or you can harness complexity as though it is an unalloyed good. Under the guise of writing about complexity, the fantasy of managerial control is smuggled in. To an extent, I understand this as an attempt to offer something to struggling managers that all is not lost. There are still tools and techniques, privileged points of view and ways of thinking which can make the complex less complex. Here, on the other hand, is an example of complexity being mobilized to encourage a kind of fatalism, which I first drew attention to in discussing Hayek in Chapter 4. The complex of social relations is so overwhelming that there is nothing we can do but retreat into ourselves, poor people have made bad choices or have not taken personal responsibility, or we can blame mysterious forces: there is nothing you can do to contain the market since the alternative, state intervention, is worse. Elsewhere, I have pointed to the limitations of the idea of 'personal responsibility' if we take a highly social view of the self. But however limited our actions may be in the web of other people's actions, to be aware of the limitations of individual choice is not the same as saying that we have no agency.

I have heard the same argument used in organizations too, either in defence of some action or lack of action, that the situation was just too complex for an

DOI: 10.4324/9781003002840-8

authority figure to have acted at all, or they followed blindly what they were told to do. Alternatively, responsibility is abstracted – it's 'the university' which requires me to do this, or 'the organization,' and offered as a defence made in the face of overwhelming complexity. A third retreat from questions of responsibility, of doing good by one another is to argue that the end justifies the means: a manager's responsibility is to do with meeting the targets, making the numbers and any damage along the way is unfortunate, but there is no other choice since to take conflicting conceptions of the good into account is just too confusing. This is one of the criticisms that the moral philosopher Alasdair MacIntyre (1985) had of modern management: that in eschewing a public discussion of values, what we hold to be good, it simply becomes manipulative justifying unacceptable practices by pointing to 'results.' When management is considered to be a technical discipline, then valuations of the good are thought to concern only individuals and their private worlds, rather than the community of the organization as a whole. This is a condition that MacIntyre called emotivism which he was keen to argue against, holding that discussion of the good always involves a community.

One of the original pioneers of complexity theory in organizational scholarship, Paul Cilliers, whom I wrote about in Chapter 2, became increasingly preoccupied with the ethical implications of how we deal with complexity. His concern was to do with the consequences of taking the complexity sciences seriously. If we do, and since in complex reality there is a limit to how much we can know, so the assumptions and reductions we make have ethical implications:

> We cannot know complex things in their complexity. We have to reduce the complexity in order to grasp anything. Since there is no meta-position from where the reduction can be done objectively – the 'framing' problem – we have to make certain choices. These choices introduce a normative component into our very understanding of complexity. What we leave out may seem trivial, but since the remainder (the 'supplement' in deconstructive terms) has a nonlinear relationship with the rest of the system we cannot predict the magnitude of the error produced by the reduction in time … we are not simply engaged in a technical task, we are ethically involved.
>
> *2011: 150*

I share a number of Cilliers' assumptions about social reality: that there is no position outside the complex dynamic to have a God's eye view, that taking an abstract position, a universal rule, may or may not help us in the particular circumstances we find ourselves in with others and that we cannot foresee the consequences of our actions. Nor can we escape our prejudgements, and at the same time we cannot know all there is to know about circumstances which are in flux and change. Cilliers frames the dilemmas in terms of complexity similar to the problem set out in the Chapter 6 on complex knowledge: if our social dilemmas are rich and complex and there is no ground to stand on, how should we proceed together? But unlike the retreat beaten by the then British Prime Minister, it is not enough in organizational life for managers to claim that they are unable to act because the situation is too complex, or at least they shouldn't get away with this as an excuse for long.

In this chapter, I develop the idea of emergent ethics which attempts to hold the contradiction together: the world is radically unpredictable and we can't know the outcomes of our actions, but we are still responsible for them anyway, at least as far as working through the consequences. I think it means paying attention to concrete experience as John Dewey recommends:

> Upon the whole, the forces that have influenced me have come from persons and from situations more than from books – not that I have not learned a great deal from philosophical writings, but that what I have learned from them has been technical in comparison with what I have been forced to thinking upon and about because of some experience in which I found myself entangled.
>
> *Dewey, 1930: 155*

But also taking a granular approach, noticing the detail of our interactions with each other as the necessary data for reflecting on how to go on together, I find myself agreeing with the English poet, William Blake in this regard:

> He who would do good to another must do it in Minute Particulars. General Good is the plea of the scoundrel, hypocrite, and flatterer; For Art and Science cannot exist but in minutely organized Particulars.
>
> *William Blake, Jerusalem, 1801*

I also want to try and frame the question in terms of the structure/agency, individual/group question which we have been pursuing throughout this book to explore what ethics might mean if we try to hold onto the paradox. To do so, I would like to explore a concrete situation.

Ethics in the concrete and the minute particulars

I was invited to co-convene a group in a department in a public sector organization where a staff survey had shown that over half of the staff who had taken the time to respond to the questionnaire indicated that they felt unsafe to speak up. The question was aimed at eliciting how comfortable staff felt contributing their point of view in public meetings or with their managers. My co-facilitator was someone I had worked with before and who had a lot of experience of running groups.[2]

Previously there had been several changes in ways of working in this particular department following the appointment of a new senior manager. Under the previous senior manager, the organization had drifted along in a condition of benign neglect. As long as employees got on and did their work, kept their heads down, nobody would ask them about what they were doing. This may or may not have contributed to a poor rating in the last national assessment exercise, with the department, and the organization in general, tumbling down the national league tables in terms of performance, but it was certainly understood as such. Under the new regime, the senior manager expressed a desire to raise standards and to put the clients first, even to think of them as customers. The public sector was a market-place and it was time for the department to work out a proper response to this, and one way was to introduce metrics to measure staff performance. A variety of strategies were commissioned, all of which would be managed against metrics, and one particular strategy led to eight prominent managers being told that their jobs no longer fitted with the new orientation. They were made redundant. Even the senior manager who instigated these redundancies acknowledged that he had not handled this process well, the redundancy was protracted, painful and difficult, and the reverberations were felt throughout the department in the form of gossip. As a result of the redundancies, and the way they were dealt with, union membership increased.

In the years that followed, there was a long tail of mostly older employees who had been present during the previous regime and retired early, got other jobs or simply left. They gave a variety of reasons for leaving, including not rec-ognizing themselves in the new regime. The new concentration on metrics and 'performance,' with senior staff now being appraised twice a year against indi-vidual performance targets set a new managerial environment in which to work. Second-tier managers were summoned on a regular basis to defend themselves if their areas of activity slipped into the red in the red, amber and green traffic lights system of monitoring how satisfied clients were with the services they received. The new performance-oriented environment was less surprising for new, perhaps younger members of staff because this may have been the only kind of environ-ment they had ever worked in, but for older members of staff it felt like a very new regime.

Over time, the regular discussions between union representatives and manage-ment became polarized around a number of matters, including the fear of speaking up, with the union representatives claiming that they had evidence from direct testimonies from individual members of staff about being bullied. These members of staff were, however, reluctant to identify themselves for fear of retribution. The managers claimed that they were concerned that staff should feel insecure about speaking up, but that there was nothing they could do without concrete evidence. The situation had reached a stalemate with rumours of bullying and bad treatment of some staff by some managers circulating in the department, but no action was taken either by the senior manager or the senior team, apart from making the kinds of statements about acceptable and unacceptable behaviour one might expect to hear in any organization. Indeed, some of the senior team were implicated in the accusations of bullying.

Against this background and history, the invitation to run what we called the 'being more open' group was an attempt to find a different way of discussing the difficulties arising in the department that would escape the binary of management vs unions, managers vs staff and he said/she said. The group was run along the lines of an Institute of Group Analysis experiential group that I explained in Chapter 6 – an hour and a half session with no one in charge, no agenda and nowhere to get to, held regularly. It is an experiment and trying to work with whatever members of the group have on their mind, and to explore the implications together. It is predicated on meaning-making and uncovering the complexity of the situation we found ourselves in as a community of inquirers and to work out possible next steps. An experiential group is a collective attempt to say out loud in public what people were saying to themselves, or to each other privately. Given the background of what had happened in the department, to attend and speak out involved a degree of risk. The irony of inviting people to a public meeting to speak up about a lack of confidence in speaking up was not lost on the convenors.

The first meeting was well attended, around 25 participants, although some people had expressed to me in confidence that they were reluctant to attend a meeting when the senior manager of the department and other senior managers from his team might be there. Nonetheless, as we felt our way into this first meeting, participants began to warm to the task of talking about their experience of working in this particular department. Even in the first meeting, one participant, who had recently found out that his temporary contract was not being renewed, opened up to the group about his experience of working with one particular manager, who wasn't present, but who would have been known to everyone sitting in the room. He claimed that his last three years had been a living nightmare; he had felt blocked and frustrated at every turn and had nothing to show for it, and nothing to put on his CV for a job in his next organization. Although he had tried to engage with his manager about how to do what was required of him, he had felt not just disinterest from him, but active obstruction at every turn. He had felt powerless and helpless. Coincidentally, the senior manager of the department found himself sitting next to him, and as he spoke with great force and passion, close to tears, the senior manager began to lean away from him in his seat involuntarily as though he felt the power of her emotion bodily. Other members of the group began to chime in with their own experiences of the same manager in a way that suggested a pattern of bad behaviour that had gone unchecked.

More members of the group spoke out about other events. One young black member of staff spoke about what she described as daily micro-aggressions, incidents where she had felt ignored, excluded or disrespected, not by managers as such, but by her colleagues. She pointed out that although this department, this organization, claimed as many institutions do that they stand against discrimination and embrace diversity, nonetheless her everyday experience told her something different. This made her feel uncomfortable and made it difficult for her to speak up. Some managers in the room spoke defensively about what they had heard. Others said that they were shocked by what they had heard because they had always considered the department as a good place to work where in their experience the relationships between people were mostly generative.

We continued meeting in this fashion every week until the pandemic forced us to move online, when we began to space the meetings biweekly, then monthly.

Here is my attempt to sum up some of the themes which emerged as a consequence of meeting together over a period of months which started with the permission of managers, but not at their instigation. The meeting was trying to avoid the usual binaries of more formal dispute resolution procedures in organizations involving human resource professionals and the usual policies and procedures. It seemed to me that there were clear examples of bullying from certain managers towards members of staff. These were widely known about, but not universally experienced. In general, the department had become a work environment where there was much greater surveillance, with more emphasis on individual performance and the importance of metrics. It also emerged that the inhibition to speak out was not only just a manager-managed phenomenon, but also involved other hierarchies such as race, age and gender. For example, the young black woman's testimony in the first meeting was not unique: other young women and people of colour spoke movingly about the experience of being ignored, actively excluded or intimidated in some way. Equally, there were testimonies from managers about how they had felt harassed by an overreaction from someone they were managing, which might have expressed in aggressive terms in an e-mail or face to face. We didn't explore the extent to which these last accounts, aggressions against managers, cut any ice with those present, or whether it was just heard as an excuse that 'both sides' are to blame. Nonetheless, over many weeks, it became clear that whatever had caused the response to the staff survey, and despite whether it was an accurate representation of what was happening in the department, was a complex phenomenon involving the way that power and authority were exercised between people trying to get things done together. Sometimes, this was to do with the more formal exercise of power and authority by those invested with a particular position in the department by the institution, and sometimes it was to do with fault lines of race, class and age, gestures from those who felt part of the established towards those they regarded as the outsiders (Elias, 1994). This complexity became an explicit theme to discuss together.

The biggest factor that affected my own continued participation in this exercise when my co-facilitator and I came to review whether and how to continue after the summer holidays was the fact that we had all heard a variety of stories of the way that inclusion and exclusion works in this department. We had gained much greater insight into the 'culture' of this particular organization in the sense that it was a whole department phenomenon, something for everybody to be working on if people were to feel more free to speak up. We might come to this conclusion and still not be utopian about the stresses and joys of working together: sometimes we can harm each other without meaning to, and with the best of intentions. However, it seemed to me that some people, senior managers, had more responsibility than others in addressing the more egregious stories of bullying that we had all heard. Although whatever happens, happens as a consequence of what everyone is doing or not doing, as we learned in our review of complexity models in Chapter 2, it is not the same as saying that everyone is equally responsible. As I began to see the way in which managers began to refer to the group as evidence of their taking the issues it raised seriously, while not tackling the managers who continued to bully others, it seemed to me that the group was being used as a cover for inactivity. Rather than acting on what they had heard, I began to feel that the group was becoming part of an excuse for not dealing with the problems which came to light. For this reason, I decided not to go on facilitating the groups, although the colleague I started with did.

As co-facilitators, we discussed the implications of my not continuing. On the one hand, I felt that to do so was to collude with a situation which made me increasingly uncomfortable. On the other, not to do so would be to let my colleague down and the members of staff who continued to attend the meetings, even though they had moved to video meetings, and who still found the group a resource. If I had lost confidence in the group, what was I signalling to others?

I'd now like to reflect on this narrative and explore some of the implications for thinking about ethics as a complex social phenomenon. Returning to the two quotations which I used at the beginning of this chapter, the narrative tries to convey concrete experience and to do so in the minute particulars. I mentioned in the introduction that I have heard it said by other complexity scholars that if you are not doing computer-based modelling with complexity, then you might just as well just call yourself a social theorist rather than adducing the complexity sciences. As we explored in Chapter 2, to model, you need to reduce and simply ascribe rules to abstract entities which act according to your commands (even if they then go on to take a life of their own). We might think about organizing a group, and then writing a narrative about it, as another form of modelling in the sense that we attempted to experiment with a different way of proceeding together to see what happened, and I have a given an account of what I think transpired. Just as more formal computer-based models have their strengths and limitations, so does what I have just done. This I now go on to explore.

Thinking sociologically about ethics

In Chapter 6, on complex knowledge, I wrote about C. Wright Mills' formulation of the need to combine 'the personal troubles of milieu' and the 'public issues of social structure' if we are to more fully understand what we are caught up in (1959/ 2000). Reminding ourselves of the complex adaptive systems models covered in Chapter 2, we need to consider the global pattern alongside the local interaction as they interrelate paradoxically. In doing so, I attempt to understand more fully how these ethical dilemmas arise in the first place.

One broad trend in contemporary organizational life, then, which constrains and enables the way we go on together, and which figured prominently in this particular narrative, is the relentless focus on metrics as a way of managing. We have discussed this phenomenon throughout the book as one manifestation of the development of thinking since the Enlightenment where we champion reason as a way of mastering our environment. We have no need to put our trust in the authority of the king, or the authority of the clergy or even the authority of specific experts in the professions, if we can put our trust in numbers (Porter, 1995). The development of the natural sciences, Porter argues, depends upon generalized methods which rely less and less on the subjective opinion even of the professions and can generate knowledge relatively independent from the groups which produce it. We would not have enjoyed the massive benefits of modernity without the ability of the natural sciences to predict and control nature through the use of numbers.

A similar argument is made by those advocating for more measurement in education in contemporary society. Measuring performance makes education visible at a distance and enables managers to compare and contrast, rank and evaluate. However, since the Romantic period, there has been resistance to the idea that all qualities can be resolved into quantities. This is not to decry the achievements of science but to consider their limitations in terms of making sense of what it means to be human. And this is not a new struggle. Jerry Muller (2018) recounts how the Victorian educationalist and poet Mathew Arnold opposed a 'reform' put forward by Liberal politician Robert Lowe that schools should be evaluated and rewarded according to measurable results: if school pupils could not demonstrate that they understood mathematics and reading according to a standardized test, then a small amount would be deducted from the school's budget. The idea was to link education both to science and to the market. We might understand the contemporary preoccupation with metrics in exactly the same light. To create a marketplace for education at the tertiary level in the United Kingdom, where all educational institutions can charge the same, something has to approximate to a price mechanism to distinguish one establishment from another. Metrics are a form of internal and external comparison, as well as a mechanism for disciplinary control. Arnold opposed the reform given his experience as a school inspector where he found that education was 'far too little formative and humanising … much in it, which its administrators point to as valuable *results*, is in truth mere machinery' (quoted in Muller, 2018: 31). Contemporary educators might recognize what Arnold complained about, where students can cram, recite and pass exams but can't necessarily think for themselves.

Metrification doesn't just have implications for students, but also for those required to administer the system. My colleague Emma Elkington (2021) recently completed her doctoral thesis from the perspective of a senior middle manager who is required to manage others and to be managed according to performance targets. She writes about the way it puts her in a double bind: she can't live with the shortcomings of metrics and the dilemmas that she has to deal with, and at the same time she can't live without them because this is the game she is in, in her particular institution. The metrics tell her something about what she has to manage but is only the start of the conversation. She concludes that a means of managing which has an ostensible claim to be objective, rational and factual actually provokes rivalry, anxiety and rebellion among those caught up in administering it. It allows the management team to a degree to *See Like a State* (Scott, 1998), that is, manage at a distance. It can also amplify some of the fissiparous dynamics of group life in those who are being judged as a consequence, both students and teachers (Elkington,

2021). As I noted in my last book (Mowles, 2015), the substitution of *techne* for practical judgement, or phronesis, where practical judgement is required to decide in particular circumstances the particular goods in play in a concrete situation, can give rise to all kinds of irrationalities in work, as the hermeneutic philosopher Hans Georg Gadamer noticed. Writing about the rise of the 'functionary,' by which I take him to mean manager, in organizational life he observed:

> In the scientific, technical, economic, monetary processes, and most especially in administration, politics, and similar forms, he [sic] has to maintain himself as he is: one inserted for the smooth functioning of the apparatus. That is why he is in demand, and therein lies his chances for advancement. Even when the dialectic of this evolution is sensible to each one who asserts that ever fewer people are making the decisions and even more are manning the apparatus, modern industrial society is oppressed by immanent structural pressures. But this leads to the degeneration of practice into technique and – through no fault of the experts themselves – to a general decline into social irrationality.
>
> *1993: 74*

What I think Gadamer is getting at here, as an example of a wide variety of scholars who champion reason in its broadest human sense rather than just a narrow rationality (Toulmin, 2003), is that the variabilities of particular circumstances requiring particular human judgement are irreducible if we are to continue to acknowledge each other in the process. To standardize and proceduralize, to rely too heavily on abstract quantification is to restrict the scope for ethical action. Nor does it fulfil what it is supposed to as the philosopher Onora O'Neill pointed out in her Reith Lectures of 2002: despite the avalanche of information about public sector performance, the public have no greater trust in the services than they did when such information was not available. I think the 'social irrationality' that Gadamer points to is experienced a lot these days where adherence to the needs of the organization trumps basic humanity. Anyone dealing with a large bureaucracy has probably come across this.

The philosopher of recognition Axel Honneth reaches similar conclusions when he reflects on the processes of reification, turning processes into things, which afflict contemporary society. Drawing on work by John Dewey and Heidegger, Honneth reminds us that abstracting from primary human experience is a necessary cognitive process to make better reflective sense of it. However, and after Dewey, Honneth thinks that we can become so committed to our schemes of thought that we lose sight of qualitative reasons, the primary human impulse, why we were interested to inquire in the first place. We may fall into inattentiveness regarding what we are concerned about, and the people who merit our concern:

> in the course of our practices we might pursue a goal so energetically and one dimensionally that we stop paying attention to other, possibly more original and important motives and aims.
>
> *Honneth, 2005: 130*

In the process of systematically following abstract schemes of thought, Honneth argues, we may fail to recognize each other and thus do each other harm. Put simply, what I think Honneth is saying is that if we focus too much on frameworks and metrics, we might be hitting the target but missing the point, if the effect is to create an organization where the employees are hypervigilant, mutually competitive and anxious about speaking out. A second example is where employees rigidly follow the rules to the exclusion of using their practical judgement. We have probably all come across colleagues like this (and do they usually work in finance?) where a slavish adherence to a policy or procedure actually makes work for everyone, including the person insisting on following the rules.

What I'm trying to point to in the tools and techniques of performance management in contemporary organizations, drawing on Elkington, Gadamer and Honneth, is that it is a generalized way of managing in which people cease to recognize each other fully, because they prioritize abstract ways of knowing. Among other motives, management metrics are intended to improve the quality of work but may do so at the expense of our recognizing each other as individuals, as members of a community where there are a variety of ways of belonging and participating and various goods in play. What we bring in our uniqueness is reduced to just one thing: whether we have met the target or not. Such a way of thinking may be inherent in an approach to management that treats employees as 'human resources,' and can be understood as another development of Taylorism. On the one hand then, the experience in the university school that I describe is not unique to them alone: it is consistent with experience of many, many organizations where individual performance is primary and measured by metrics. This is a repeating pattern in contemporary organizational life which catches everyone up but is not deterministic. Staff in such organizations are continuously judged against abstract standards which are set outside the context of their action. In this sense, they are subject to a particular power regime and ideology, one which privileges the imposition of quantifiable standards undertaken in the name of improving quality.

It does leave managers with particular dilemmas about how to act in these circumstances; however, if they are not to be left with ex-Prime Minister Theresa May's defence, that there are many complex reasons why people might feel scared to speak out, but, by implication, there is nothing they can do about it. Not to play the game of metrics is to invite exclusion, or to exclude oneself. To speak out might provoke a similar outcome. Another good in play is the ability to have a career and be recognized as a manager. There are very few organizations where managers fully agree with everything that the regime of managing requires of them.

Having attempted to sketch in something of a background against which the events have taken place and thinking back to the narrative I describe above, there are a variety of goods being negotiated, not just the fear of speaking up which is attributable to what we might consider a more managerial environment. It would be easy to reduce the ethical questions and their causes to just one thing. For example, it didn't surprise me to learn that women, particularly younger women, and people of colour felt misrecognized in the school, metrics or no metrics. Equally there are

all kinds of hierarchies and politics which play out between people in any organization, and I would not want to give the impression that the time before the current
regime was all sweetness and light.

On deliberation in groups – revealing competing goods and becoming visible to each other

A complaint that I hear again and again about an invitation to inquire further into
complex reality is that it doesn't promise anything practical. If people are looking
for advice for what to do in the form of a grid or a framework, then I see their
point – at the very least you could say that in the context of management, reflection and deliberation in groups is unfamiliar, the two-by-two Cartesian diagram
familiar. It is difficult to know whether the group my colleague and I ran made any
difference to the relationships between people in this particular school,[3] but here
are some of the motivations for doing so focusing on the ethics drawing on pragmatic arguments.

I have explained how I think throughout this book that a particular ideology
is dominant in organizations which privileges metrics, marketization and focuses
on the individual. This is by no means the only point of view as I discovered
when I undertook some research into senior management teams in UK universities
(Mowles et al., 2019). One of the ethical challenges in management, then, is how
to recognize different valuations of the good about, say, what a university should be
for, even though the dominant ideology may still prevail. Of course, even this may
be opposed: I have heard some managers say that it is a kindness not to entertain
other points of view since a particular strategy may already have been decided. To
allow for difference would simply be frustrating and encourage false hope about
alternatives.

But I argue that we may not understand or agree with each other, no matter
how patiently we listen to each other, but this is no argument against continuing
to try. In trying, we may be able to recognize each other sufficiently to increase the
scope for action and to humanize the work place. In our current situation, I think
this is particularly difficult, not just in organizations but more widely, where groups
of people may hold points of view which are not just different to our own, but
which we find morally repugnant. There is an increasing propensity in contemporary society to become polarized and to be unable to find common ground. This
can be exacerbated by social media which seem algorithmically driven to create
polarizations to drive traffic. The capacity to find sufficient ground for exploring
our differences, then, becomes imperative if we are to deal with the large and
intractable problems with which we are faced.

The group we convened in this particular school was an attempt to work differently than just meeting through formal channels, management and unions, or
revising policy or looking at 'best practice' in other organizations so that it could
be imported. I am not suggesting that any of these other options is not worthwhile. But it was an active intervention to try and explore and discuss, together,

acknowledging all the difficulties of doing so, to find the extent to which we could entertain and engage with the manifold interpretations of what it meant to work in this community.

One of G.H. Mead's central insights about ethics, which he claims is consonant with scientific method, is that in any given situation we need to take as many points of view as possible into account:

> You take into account, in other words, all the values that arise, even when you reject certain values for the sake of others. You have to bring them all into the account. Your position in this field is like the position in the scientific field, where you have to take all the facts into account. The scientist that does not do that is morally wrong. On the valuational side, too, you must take into account all the values; you are morally wrong there if you refuse to consider certain ones. So the imperative you are under is to take into account all the values involved in the problem as far as it appears.
>
> *1938: essay 24, 462*

Ethical engagement with others is a creative and imaginative act which involves inquiry into the points of view of others, and, according to both Mead and Dewey, it involves a change in our own identity:

> Sympathy is the animating mold of moral judgement not because its dictates take precedence in action over those of other impulses (which they do not do), but because it furnishes the most efficacious *intellectual* standpoint. It is the tool, *par excellence*, for resolving complex situations. Then when it passes over into active and overt conduct, it does so *fused* with other impulses and not in isolation and is thus protected from sentimentality. In the fusion there is broad and objective survey of all desires and projects because there is an expanded personality.
>
> *Dewey, 1932/1998: 333*

Both Dewey and Mead encourage us to lean towards complexity, to understand different valuations of the good in the plural. The movement is to the social: we can only begin the process by responding in our own terms, and according to our own experience to what is required. But our ability to transcend narrow self-interest involves taking the perspectives of the particular others involved in grappling with a specific dilemma. It is a route to being able to adopt become more detached about involvement, in Elias' terms, which does not completely eschew the subjective point of view. The pragmatic view does not leave the interests of the individual out of the picture. Mead reminds us that there are asocial and social aspects of the self (1934: 321) and the asocial aspect of our personalities is the most precious part of who we are. According to Mead, it needs to be transcended but not ignored. He reminds us that there is nothing more irritating than someone who is constantly trying to do good by other people: 'there is no more distressing person to have about than one who is constantly seeking to assist everybody else' (1934: 276).

What the pragmatists recommend here is a contextual and emergent understanding of ethics. I think the first point of departure is to deflate the idea that there is a universal, neutral and ahistorical framework in which all points of view can be adequately translated so that we can evaluate different validity claims. This is true too, for metrics, which tell us some things about the work, but not everything we need to know. To make an argument simply on 'the facts' is never going to cut it for anyone working in organizations who may feel unrecognized by such a claim.

To argue that there is no universal point of view, quantified or not quantified, is not the same as saying that anything goes, and it's your point of view against mine. If we take a pragmatic perspective on this, some points of view are more useful than others in helping us to go on together. This still leaves questions open about how we establish usefulness, particularly when the pragmatic position is that we do so in a community of engaged inquirers where there are a variety of points of view. We can evaluate different claims but using a variety of methods and with interpretative sensitivity and imagination, which is possible in a reflective group, particularly if it is facilitated well. Elsewhere, I wrote about how the biologist Richard Dawkins had argued that the referendum in the United Kingdom on whether to leave the EU should only have been conducted on 'the facts' alone. I noted that this would have been a difficult undertaking given how much of the political contestation revolved around questions of identity and themes of inclusion and exclusion. There were few available facts about a proposal to withdraw from the EU which had never been attempted before by any other country. More evaluative methods were required by all of those involved in the debate than the simple finding of facts. We should also acknowledge, however, that increasingly in contemporary society, there are groups of people who believe in fantastical conspiracy theories or who adopt a contrarian point of view on the grounds of 'free speech' who may never accept the exchange of reasons. Some scholars call them 'denialists' (Kahn-Harris, 2018), and we shouldn't be naïve that a simple exchange of views would change someone's mind, or that even such an exchange is possible. It is also the case that today disinformation is produced on an industrial scale and deliberately spread by states wishing to destabilize other nations with a view to finding people predisposed to believing their disinformation to further their political ends. The disinformation is not necessarily aimed at getting people to believe a particular thing, but to disbelieve everything. As Hanna Arendt has pointed out, these are the preconditions for totalitarianism.

A deliberative group is usually possible because there are overlaps in our different interpretations of the world. I think Kahn-Harris makes this case well when he points to the idea that we all deny the obvious and may all entertain desires which cause us shame, whether we consider ourselves denialists or not. The experience of desire is shared, though the object of desire is plural and may also be of a morally repugnant nature. We also experience many different valuations of the good. But we may have to face the practical possibility that we may fail to understand 'alien' traditions in terms of the tradition to which we belong. This possibility of failure places an ethical obligation on us to listen carefully, but in doing so, there may be a temptation to recategorize what we hear in terms of what we already understand without doing justice to what is genuinely different in what's being said. This may lead us either to try and colonize it ('they agree with us, they just don't know it') or dismiss it as exotic nonsense. I think Richard Kearney (2002) makes a similar suggestion about the importance of standing one's ground, but at the same time being radically open to the otherness of the other. It is too easy to fall into monstering those we disagree with, even though their point of view may be monstrous. I would add a caveat that even if one concludes that other points of view are exotic nonsense, this should not block further inquiry as to the role this particular nonsense plays for the person entertaining it.

Within a given language or tradition, people are already making claims which transcend their context. Even the idea that there is an elite conspiracy of experts, big government, big pharma and neoliberal politicians, who set out to cheat 'the people,' is more than just a local claim and may be something to work with. The meeting of different valuations of the good makes it harder to not only present one's own position in a simplistic way, but also to understand another's position in the same terms. Gadamer's insight remains true that when we undertake to fully understand someone else, we end up by understanding our own position better.

In a further reflexive turn, I want to reflect on what I have done in this chapter in terms of illustrating complex ethics by writing a narrative about an episode of organizational life I have been involved in. I consider this a meditation on research method, which might provoke insights for managers if they continue to take an interest in what is going on in their organizations. The beginning of inquiry might be to ask what stories are being told and by whom?

The complex characteristics of narrative as a medium for exploring ethics

Narratives have been used for as long as there have been humans living in groups as a method to find out about what it means to be human and to make sense of our lives together. The first observed use of a form of narrative in European languages is found in Old French of the 15th century: *narracion* is an account, a statement, a relating, a recounting, a narrative tale and probably comes directly from Latin *narrationem* (nominative *narratio*) a relating, a narrative, a noun of action from the past participle stem of *narrare*, to tell, relate, recount, explain, literally to make acquainted with. The Oxford English Dictionary defines narrative as an account of a series of events, facts, etc. given in order and with the establishing of connections between them. Narrative has always been associated with knowing, then, and, in particular, a way of bringing diverse things together in a particular order and showing the relationships between them.

There is now a good deal of organizational literature establishing narrative as a suitable medium for conveying complex experience (Tsoukas and Hatch, 2001; Rhodes and Brown, 2005; Thomas, 2010; Cunliffe and Coupland, 2012; Gorli et al., 2015). Narrative features prominently in the hermeneutic and phenomenological philosophical traditions, particularly in the works of Paul Ricoeur (1990) and Hannah Arendt (1958), in Alasdair MacIntyre's virtue ethics (1985) and in the work of philosophers such as Gadamer and Charles Taylor (1989) who are inspired by Hegel. Any scholar interested in experience and the way that human beings become is inevitably drawn to the story of that becoming. This is in contrast to schools of thought which may proceed from the idea that we arrive on the earth fully formed and that research is concerned with the unfolding of what is already there. Equally, it is at odds with a perspective on ethics that adopts an abstract, universalist position, aiming at valuations of the good which any person using their reason would reach. What I explore here is an emergent and contingent discussion of ethics which aspires to be as complex as the narrative I tell.

The first thing to notice is how narrative, ethics and complexity are closely interwoven. The narrative above has a complex time structure. To tell the story, I have to give some background, I go on to narrate some events and imply causality, how one thing might have led to another. There is a history prior to the story unfolding, there is then the story I tell and there is an implied and open-ended story which I don't tell about what happened to the group once I left as co-facilitator. In the pluperfect, I describe what had happened, I relate the narrative in the past perfect and imply a future. In writing what I do now and reflecting on it, I create a narrative of the whole exercise to engage the reader's reflective capacity alongside my own to evaluate what I have said previously. But the history I tell also raises questions of ethics. In telling the story as I do, I am adopting a point of view. Just as Cilliers noted, the details that I choose to bring in to the narrative say as much about me as they do about what happened. So as a reader, you are immediately confronted with the question of my reliability as a narrator (Ricoeur, 1992). As a reader, you don't have much to go on, depending on how you have experienced me as a narrator up to this point in the book. Implicitly, perhaps explicitly, you are likely to have informed an opinion about my ability to be fair in the representation of other people's points of view up to this point, including the narrative I set out earlier. Throughout this book, I have made the point that there is nowhere to stand outside experience to take up a detached or 'objective' position: we explored the ramifications of this in Chapter 5 on communication in arguing for rhetoric as an engaged form of persuasion, and in Chapter 6 where I put forward the idea of the imperative for becoming more detached about our involvement with one another. In discussing the narrative I have set out earlier, I am trying to make some of my assumptions clear so that I also say something about my valuations of the good in the situation in which I find myself with others (Ellis, 2007).

So continuing to the second potential strength of narrative for exploring ethics, there can be many points of view in a narrative, not just my own. The differing world views are not given equal prominence, however, and have been filtered, selected and presented by me. I have a responsibility to do justice to other people's positions because we have been in relation and may continue to be so (Lapadat, 2017). Each perspective carries with it an evaluation of the good: the union representatives defending their members who claim to have been bullied are seeking redress, meanwhile managers don't want others to be accused of something unsubstantiated. The new senior manager of the school wants to raise performance so that it does better the next time there is a national research assessment. Narrative allows me to hold these competing valuations, including my own, in some kind of tension. This points to the dialectical and emergent nature of knowledge of human affairs, which we explored in Chapter 6, which is different from scientific knowledge of an object. Scientific knowledge is aimed at fully understanding an object independent of the point of view of the person trying to understand. What I try to do here is to investigate the relationships and differing points of view which may be in conflict. In this sense, ethics can never be guided by natural science methods (which for some can be construed as a weakness of narrative rather than a strength).

A third characteristic of narrative is that what I describe is concrete and involves particular actors who do and say particular things. In other words, the reader isn't asked to grasp these in the abstract as though representative of experience everywhere, but experience is tied to this specific community. The detail of what I describe might produce resonance, either similarities or differences with experience for the reader: in other words my intention is to draw you into a relationship with me and what I am describing. When I turn to doing more interpretative work, evaluating what I think is going on and what is important for me, the reader may then be provoked into doing interpretative work for themselves, both of what I offer and of their own experience. To what degree is my interpretation plausible and convincing? I don't make any claims to be describing the truth of what happens, but this doesn't mean that what I have written is just made up, fiction. The question for the reader, according to psychologist Jerome Bruner (1986) is the extent to which my narrative evokes verisimilitude.

A fourth characteristic of narrative for its adherents is its incompleteness. There is much that is unresolved about my narrative. What happened to the group after I left it: did participants go on attending and where did my departure leave me with my co-facilitator? Did the staff returns on their next survey indicate an improved sense of being able to speak out? Did bullying continue, and was it really bullying? So there are very few binaries in a good narrative, and no Hollywood endings. Indeed, a good narrative needs a good plot, a mystery that needs inquiring into (Alvesson and Kärreman, 2011): in most cases, if we know how the story is going to end, then there is no tension, no need to inquire. For some, this incompleteness might be frustrating if there are no heroes and villains, or if we cannot fully understand the situation. As I continue to explore this narrative in this chapter, I try to maintain a fallibilist position, that is, where I don't hide from expressing a point of view, but give ground to the claim that this is the truth, or a final version of what has been going on, a matter to which I will return.

Narrative enables a rich picture of identity, the narrator's and the key protagonists in the story, because the stories intersect and inform each other. Identity is multi-perspectival: we have stories about ourselves and our history, which we renarrate and update to relate to others. For the moral philosopher Alasdair MacIntyre (1985), our stories about ourselves can never be complete because we are always part of other people's stories, which is an observation I drew attention to in Chapter 3 using the work of Hannah Arendt. Reflecting on these stories gives us clues to moral action: 'I can only answer the question what am I to do if I can answer the prior question, of what stories am I part?' (1985: 216). But we can never fully understand ourselves or give an account of ourselves as the feminist philosopher Judith Butler argues (2005), because there is no beginning to our story. One thing we have in common with everyone else we are struggling to make sense with is that none of us can give a full account of ourselves. With narrative and identity, we are never dealing with absolute goods.

Concluding thoughts on complex ethics and the implications for managers

MacIntyre, whom I mentioned earlier, considered the relationship between institutions, ethics and professions in his book *After Virtue*. Following on from Aristotle, he puts forward the idea that a community sustains itself on the basis of a discussion of goods inherent to that community. The development of a sense of professionalism arises in a complex relationship of virtues, institutions and practices. Without institutions, practices are unsustainable: nonetheless, without a discussion of virtues within the emerging professions, institutions can corrupt practices.

Entering a practice involves first engaging in a discipline with all the meaning that this word implies: a disciple is someone who follows. Becoming a practitioner will mean submitting ourselves to the best standards that have been achieved so far by other practitioners. In other words, all organizations need to cohere, and to do so means that we have to accept to a degree the discipline of meeting organizational expectations. But this discipline is not slavish: practitioners are also a community who discipline each other by entering into discussion with a sense of justice, courage and truthfulness. This enables them to go on re-establishing the practice and the new rules and practices that need to be created if the practice is to continue to be relevant to the society it serves. MacIntyre argues that a profession is concerned with producing goods which are intrinsic to the community of practitioners who make up that profession: for example, let's say that civil servants are committed to the idea of public service, which then becomes an organizing principle of the discussion which helps to form the civil service as a discipline. The pursuit of external goods, such as personal wealth or creating wealth for shareholders, is an extrinsic good incommensurable with the practice under discussion.

In the narrative I describe earlier, there seemed to be too few opportunities to discuss what it meant to be members of this particular community until my co-convenor and I created a group to do so. There were too few openings to explore who the members of the community thought they were and what was valuable to them in working together. In this sense, it was difficult for people to take responsibility for developing the community of which they were part and this is one of the reasons why they found it difficult to recognize themselves as members of it. I am not making a naïve call for democracy or for every member of the school to call into question every decision that was made. However, an organization where people become reluctant to speak out in public describes an environment where politics, the everyday exercise of power between people, has retreated, and where people are no longer prepared to make themselves visible to one another or are unconfident about how to do so. As I described in Chapter 3 drawing on Hannah Arendt, the alternative to being able to negotiate power publicly between us is to retreat into the private, which allows for the potential of tyranny. In this chapter, I drew attention to a generalized phenomenon in organizations dedicated to measuring performance with metrics, which some people can experience as oppressive because it covers over their unique qualities as individuals. Employees are measured against numerical targets and made commensurable with one another, with the implication that they are only as valuable as the contribution they make to the organization understood as enterprise.

Arendt speaks to the paradox of individual and group which I have been exploring throughout this book; it is only through recognizing our uniqueness as individuals, our plurality, that we can become free, but this is only achievable through speaking out and acting in a group. The Arendt scholar Sophie Loidolt expresses her interpretation of what Arendt means by politics and freedom thus:

> It is a notion of the political that empowers the individuals to seize their worldly possibilities of existence *together* – and that makes clear that freedom is to be found in nothing other than in those experiences where we actively relate to the world and visibly take positions, no matter what the 'realistic' chances of 'success' are.
>
> *2018: 265*

So, the implications for managers are that creating opportunities for exploring new ways of going on together, strategies, is not the same as allowing a democratic vote on whether the changes should go ahead or not. Rather, it is a chance for people to recognize each other and their differences in the collective responsibility of developing a shared community and as a means of making the workplace more human.

Notes

1 A Conservative MP, who currently serves as the UK Foreign Minister, claimed that people using food banks weren't necessarily poor, they were just experiencing cash flow problems. So one way of thinking about poverty from a particular perspective is as a permanent

individual cash flow problem, not as a socio-economic pattern where some groups are privileged and some not, which demands a larger policy intervention.

2 My co-facilitator Kevin Flinn's book on leadership development is worth reading (Flinn, 2018).

3 As time has passed, there has been a much greater focus on what is known as the 'inclusion agenda' in this particular school, by which is meant paying attention to policies, procedures and practices that allows for the diverse employees more fully to recognize themselves as equal members of staff.

References

Alvesson, M. and Kärreman, D. (2011) *Qualitative Research and Theory Development: Mystery as Method*, London: Sage.

Arendt, H. (1958) *The Human Condition*, Chicago, IL: University of Chicago.

Bruner, J. (1986) *Actual Minds, Possible Worlds*, Cambridge, MA: Harvard University Press.

Butler, J.P. (2005) *Giving and Account of Oneself*, New York, NY: Fordham University Press.

Cilliers, P. (2011) Complexity, poststructuralism and organization. In: Allen, P., Maguire, S. and McKelvey, B. (eds.), *The Sage Handbook of Complexity and Management*, London: Sage, pp. 142–154.

Cunliffe, A. and Coupland, C. (2012) From hero to villain to hero: making experience sensible through embodied narrative sensemaking, *Human Relations*, 65(1):62–88.

Dewey, J. (1930). From absolutism to experimentalism. In: Adams, G.P. and Pepperell Montague, Wm. (eds.), *Contemporary American Philosophy: Personal Statements*. New York: Russell and Russell, pp. 13–27.

Dewey, J. (1932/1998) Moral judgement and knowledge. In: Hickman, L.A. and Alexander, T.M. (eds.), *The Essential Dewey: Ethics, Logic, Psychology*, Vol. 2, Indianapolis, IN: Indiana University Press, pp. 328–340.

Elias, N. and Scotson, J. (1994) *The Established and the Outsiders*, London: Sage.

Elkington, E. (2021) *Subjugation and Subterfuge: Struggling with Metrics as a Middle Manager in a UK Business School*, Unpublished Doctorate of Management Thesis, University of Hertfordshire.

Ellis, C. (2007) Telling secrets, revealing lies: relational ethics in research with intimate others, *Qualitative Inquiry*, 13(1): 3–29.

Flinn, K. (2018) *Leadership Development: A Complexity Approach*, London: Routledge.

Gadamer, H.-G. (1993) *Reason in the Age of Science*, Cambridge, MA: MIT Press.

Gorli, M., Nicolini, D. and Scaratti, G. (2015) Reflexivity in practice: tools and conditions for developing organizational authorship, *Human Relations*, 68(8):1347–1375.

Honneth, A. (2005) *Reification: A Recognition-Theoretical View*, The Tanner Lectures on Human Values, Delivered at University of California, Berkeley, March 14–16.

Kahn-Harris, K. (2018) *Denial: The Unspeakable Truth*, London: Notting Hill Editions.

Kearney, R. (2002) *Strangers, Gods and Monsters: Interpreting Otherness*, London: Routledge.

Lapadat, J.C. (2017) Ethics in autoethnography and collaborative autoethnography, *Qualitative Inquiry*, 23(8):589–603.

Loidolt, S. (2018) *Phenomenology of Plurality: Hannah Arendt on Political Intersubjectivity*, London: Routledge.

MacIntyre, A. (1985) *After Virtue*, 2nd Edition, London: Duckworth.

Mead, G.H. (1934) *Mind, Self and Society from the Standpoint of a Social Behaviorist*, Chicago, IL: Chicago University Press.

Mead, G.H. (1938) *The Philosophy of the Act*, Chicago, IL: University of Chicago.

Mowles, C. (2015) *Managing in Uncertainty: Complexity and the Paradoxes of Everyday Organisational Life,* London: Routledge.

Mowles, C., Filosof, J., Flinn, K., Mason, P., Culkin, N., Andrews, R. and James, D. (2019) *Transformational Change in the Higher Education Sector: An Inquiry into Leadership Practice,* London: Leadership Foundation for Higher Education.

Muller, J. (2018) *The Tyranny of Metrics,* Princeton, NJ: Princeton University Press.

O'Neill, O. (2002) *A Question of Trust: Reith Lectures 2002,* Cambridge: Cambridge University Press.

Porter, T.M. (1995) *Trust in Numbers: The Pursuit of Objectivity in Science and Public Life,* Princeton, NJ: Princeton University Press.

Rhodes, C. and Brown, A.D. (2005) Narrative, organizations and research, *International Journal of Management Reviews,* 7(3):167–188.

Ricoeur, P. (1990) *Time and Narrative,* Vols. I–III, Chicago, IL: University of Chicago Press.

Ricoeur, P. (1992) *Oneself as Another (Blamey K, trans.),* Chicago, IL: University of Chicago Press.

Scott, J.C. (1998) *Seeing Like a State: How Certain Schemes to Improve the Human Condition Have Failed,* New Haven, CT: Yale University Press.

Taylor, C. (1989) *Sources of the Self: The Making of Modern Identity,* Cambridge: Cambridge University Press.

Thomas, G. (2010) Doing case study: abduction not induction, phronesis not theory, *Qualitative Inquiry,* 16(7):575–582.

Toulmin, S. (2003) *Return to Reason,* Cambridge, MA: Harvard University Press.

Tsoukas, H. and Hatch, M.J. (2001) Complex thinking, complex practice: the case for a narrative approach to organizational complexity, *Human Relations,* 54(8):979–1013.

Wright Mills, C. (1959/2000) *The Sociological Imagination,* Oxford: Oxford University Press.

9

CONCLUSIONS

Towards greater humility and humane ways of working

Whether they are explicit to us or not, our actions in the world are guided by theories about the way the world works, as the economist J.M. Keynes (2016) once observed.[1] This is no less true for the way people practise as leaders and managers than it is for any other area of social life. On entering an organization, a manager or consultant brings with them their own understanding of the world forged not just in other organizations but from their experience of their life in its entirety and the theories that they have picked up along the way. For example, their attitude to authority is likely to be shaped as much by their early family and school life as it is from any management course they have been on. But, whether they have been on management courses or not, and whatever they bring, leaders and managers will take up their roles in organizations where particular ways of managing are taken for granted, and because they may have informed thinking and acting for some considerable time in that organization, they are hard to resist. New entrants to organizations are more shaped than shaping because of the powerful influence of accepted ways of managing in the institution they join, which is probably shared equally by other institutions involved in similar activities.

This is an interesting phenomenon to pay attention to, which I have done throughout this book, because the insight I offer about being strongly influenced by the network, of which one is part, suggests the complete opposite to much orthodox organizational literature where there is an encouragement to 'choose' your management or leadership 'style.' The latter idea suggests that it is in a person's gift to decide how they are going to manage or intervene in the organization. Claiming the reverse that the organization a person joins will have much more effect on the way they manage than vice versa is not the same as implying that they have no choice at all. So one of the central tasks of this book, drawing some of the insights from the complexity sciences, has been to argue that our position in the social network in which we participate helps define us but doesn't entirely

DOI: 10.4324/9781003002840-9

limit us in terms of agency. Exploring managerial/consultant agency is a theme that has run throughout this book as we have tried to think together about the relationship between the individual and the group. What lies at the heart of this exploration is an interest in the complex dynamics of organizational life, to try and notice how things are done in organizations, to think about what intellectual assumptions inform how things are done and to notice the push and pull of trying to cooperate with others.

Although this book is focused on understanding complexity in organizations, a perceptive reader will have noticed that I have made wider claims at the same time. I claim that the theories I draw on to try and explain some of the key tenets of leadership and management refracted through the complexity sciences apply more widely to what human beings get up to more generally. Organizations are sites where we spend a great deal of our lives, whether as employees or consultants, and are particular environments where there is a developed sense about what leaders and managers should be doing. What they should be doing is contested, of course, but day-to-day practice is informed by more than a hundred years of management theory developed in business schools where there is a good deal of convergence in thinking. This has developed into something of an orthodoxy.[2] But neither universities nor theories of managing are separate from wider sociopolitical and economic thinking and events and they mutually inform each other. Some of the dilemmas and debates about human action, the predictability or otherwise of human affairs, stability and change have been going on for thousands of years. The discussion has grown in nuance and detail but there is a case for arguing that we are still exploring the different poles of the philosophical positions of Heraclitus, who argued that all is flux and change, and Parmenides, who held that despite the appearance of flux and change, there is an unchanging reality which underpins all things. How things change, or stay the same and the role humans have in affecting this are questions which have exercised us for a very long time, long before we had a notion of the complexity sciences or management theory.

Just as organizations and the ideas from business schools about how to lead and manage are not isolated from societies in which they are embedded, it is also the case that over the last 30 years or so, there has been a much greater blurring of the boundaries between places of work and society: society bleeds into organizations, and organizations bleed into society. We live in a highly economized, and marketized society where management ideas and vocabulary have spilled out beyond the boundaries of organizations, fusing with our everyday ways of describing ourselves and what we are doing. In contemporary life, we are encouraged to think of ourselves as a business with an inducement to constantly 'upgrade' our skills, so we are thought to need constant self-management in the form of anger management, time management and stress management and to monitor our everyday activity and heartbeat with digital watches: there is very little that we are involved in as humans, the idea goes, that can't be managed with a plan and some targets. The notion of being 'businesslike' often turns on the assumptions of the rational autonomous individual, setting themself goals, being positive, being future-oriented and being completely focused on maximizing their utility and measuring their success. These basic assumptions pervade much orthodox management theory, and so too are they mobilized in daily life.

Coming to terms with the radical insights from the complexity sciences challenges many of the taken-for-granted assumptions about who we are, how we function and the limits to our knowledge. It places uncertainty, unpredictability and unmanageability back at the heart of questions about how we go on together. Here is a reprise of what I think I have been saying, drawing on the body of work termed complex responsive processes of relating (Stacey et al., 2000).

On the strengths and limitations of models

When I introduce complexity models and explore their implications to groups of managers, I sometimes experience scepticism from some people in the room. Some of this scepticism I understand as a healthy response to a discipline which is riven with fads and fashions and a preoccupation with the next best thing. In a world where there are increasing demands on our attention and more and more efforts to get us to subscribe to a particular point of view by being controversial, I can't blame questioning managers who might have been round the block a few times and are inured to the offer of new ways of managing, or five- or eight-step processes which will transform their lives. In this volume, I have taken a stand in favour of critical engagement, exercising our judgement about what goes on around us. Another form of scepticism emerges from managers who may have been on a lot of management courses where there is a preoccupation with prediction and control. If as a manager, you can't control things, then is that the same as saying that managers or management doesn't matter? Perhaps the insight that managers are in charge but not necessarily in control is too decentring a thought for managers who want to believe they stand on solid ground.

In Chapter 2, I reprised the variety of complexity models from most to least complex in terms of the assumptions that they make about the phenomena they claim to be modelling. The simpler they become, the more they average away the detail of what they draw from. This makes them more manageable and likely to offer a more limited range of options if they have been commissioned by those wanting to make policy, for example, but to do so they get further and further away from the blooming, buzzing confusion of life. I indicated that the models which interest me the most in terms of their implications for social life are complex adaptive systems (CAS) models with large numbers of diverse agents acting in non-average ways. There are five characteristics of these models which I claimed have implications for understanding day-to-day organizational life and the implications for management. These are as follows:

1. The model is in constant motion and never at rest, and never reaches an equilibrium state. It demonstrates qualitative changes over time, so history is important.

2. The model demonstrates a quality of predictable unpredictability, or stable instability with recognizable patterns which repeat, but never quite in the same way. When the agents are diverse, and when they interact in non-average ways, it's possible for completely novel forms to emerge. Because the agents' interactions are governed by non-linear equations, the amplification of small differences can escalate into population-wide changes.

3. There is no 'centre' to the model: no controlling agent or group of agents which dictates the activity of all the other agents.

4. The agents interact locally with other agents placing 'constraints' on each other. They are said to be 'self-organizing,' which is not the same as saying they are random, or are somehow unconstrained, but is a combination of local negotiation of constraints combined with the characteristic earlier, that there is no controlling agent or group of agents.

5. The population of agents demonstrates a paradoxical quality of forming and being formed with the global pattern of agents arising from the aggregation of local agent activity, at the same time as the local activity is constrained by the global pattern.

I hope that I made my assumptions clear in claiming that this is a computer-based model and, therefore, has the limitations of all modelling, but nonetheless I wanted to argue by analogy that it offers helpful insights for thinking about social life. I feel unabashed by making such a claim in the sense that there are many assumptions informing more orthodox theories of management which may be less spoken about because they are dominant. In pointing this out, I am also saying something about the way ideology works. A coherent set of ideas which informs many management programmes implies that managers can predict and control, and that there are universally applicable tools and techniques which can bring about improvement irrespective of context. In offering a challenge to the orthodoxy, one is often asked for a burden of proof greater than that offered by the established way of thinking. As managers sometimes ask when I introduce the ideas – why should we believe what you are saying? The implications of taking the insights of the complexity sciences seriously are unsettling, whether one 'believes' them or not.

The first characteristic that the model is constantly in flux and never reaches an equilibrium state is a profound challenge to the equilibrium models which dominate more orthodox management thinking, for example, unfreeze, change and refreeze. A three- or five-year strategy makes explicit assumptions about organizational beginnings and endings and linear causation between one stage and the next – if the world is in constant flux, how will we know when the strategy has begun and when it has ended? Carving up the world, pretending this is the beginning of a process might be necessary not only to make sense, but also carries with it its own fictions. A manager interested in complexity might become more awake when colleagues around them declare that they are looking to achieve balance in the order of things and insist that if we are going to make an organizational journey, we need to map out all the stages in advance. They may also take an interest in how things have become as they are: what were the qualitative changes over time, rather than just taking an interest in an idealized future. Our discussion in the present about an anticipated future is always informed by our interpretation of the past.

The second characteristic that complex models demonstrate predictable unpredictability, stable instability brings some managers relief and others anxiety. For those experiencing relief, the models offer an explanation about why things may not work out as intended. This doesn't have to be because of a failure of management. The second group might feel that the models offer an excuse to those who are insufficiently attentive to detail, or weak on implementation. The potential for the amplification of small differences points to how important diversity among agents and agent behaviour is to the emergence of novelty. This is in contradistinction to the emphasis placed in many organizations on agreement and alignment, and perhaps leaving politics at the door. In the models, history is important, not just how we proceed towards an idealized future.

The third characteristic that there is no centre of activity, or controlling node of agents, deflates the ubiquitous and inescapable idea of leadership and perhaps our dependency on leaders. If leaders can't bring about as much as the discourse assumes that they can, this has big consequences for leadership studies, leadership consultants, coaches and all of us if we are waiting passively to be led.

Fourth, the insight that local, self-organizing activity shapes the 'whole' organization through the negotiation of competing constraints may encourage us to pay attention to what is happening between people acting locally, and how power and authority is mediated. Rather than struggling with the abstract and the macro, we may focus just as much on the particular and the micro to understand some of the patterns of behaviour which are going on in organizations.

And lastly, the paradoxical quality of a CAS might make us curious about dialectic and the co-presence of opposites. Projects are never only successful, organizational changes are likely to advantage some and disadvantage others; people come to work both to compete and co-operate.

What is it that I claim is radical in how I set out this interpretation, given that there are a variety of schools of thought which draw on the complexity sciences? From the perspective of qualitative researchers, it isn't such a radical claim to try and harness the prestige of the natural sciences to bolster the claims of social science. It may sound to them like a form of camouflage. However, there are a variety of schools of thought which try to reduce the radical implications of the analogies I make by claiming that social life is only complex some of the time, or is so at times of the manager's choosing. Then there are traditions of thought offering tools and techniques of complexity, and even franchised training in complexity specialisms. I make no suggestion that complexity and emergence can be harnessed, embraced or otherwise turned to the good. As frustrating as it may be in a discipline developed out of a desire to make things cohere, the sense we make, the potential we have to make a difference to the order of things, will depend on context, history and the interweaving of intentions.

In this book, I do offer something of a framework, a way of categorizing and making sense of how complexity might affect our everyday reality, by claiming that there are seven types of complexity.

Complex action

If we persist with a theory of the social world which arises from non-linear, local interactions which have a history, where constraints are negotiated and where small differences can escalate into population-wide changes, then this suggests a more complex theory of action than sometimes informs more orthodox theories of management. Instead of assuming that change arises as a result of the magical properties of individuals, their charisma perhaps or their unique insight into the future which galvanizes others, or through the aggregation and disaggregation of discrete individual entities bumping into each other with linear cause and effect, we have searched for a theory which helps us understand dynamic process. Whether we think of it in terms of Deweyan transaction, or refer to it as Stacey et al. (2000) do as transformational teleology, the point of reaching for a more processual understanding of action is that it helps us understand how we are caught up with others in a particular place at a particular time trying to make sense of how we go on together. Location, participants and time are all entangled with the potential for repetition or transformation both at the same time.

A variety of sociologists use game analogies to represent the dynamic properties of social life which are always in flux. There is an evolving set of rules which govern our actions to a degree, but which evolve in the playing. There is no rule so precise that it dictates our every move and as Bourdieu (1992) in particular has observed: excellent social practice consists of improvisation on the rules which could not have been predicted in advance, an improvisation which takes place with all sides negotiating the rules, or constraints, and making them work. And Elias and Mead help us understand how it is that we have a sense of how to play the game at all. We are born into a world where a particular game of games is already going on, at a particular time and place with a particular language and all the cultural associations that go along with that. As we develop from children, we internalize a sense of the 'generalized other' so that a general sense of how our society works becomes part of our personality structure. This allows us to anticipate what is expected of us, and what we might expect of others; we develop a 'feel for the game' (Bourdieu, 1990), all of which evolves from our evolving participation in social life. We develop self-control from our internalized understanding of the rules of the game which, for Elias are self-policing through rising tides of guilt and shame. We discipline ourselves to avoid exclusion from the groups we belong to: self-control goes hand in hand with social control.

Negotiating the constraints of our particular work contexts points to the importance of noticing power relationships. Sometimes power is undiscussable at work for a variety of reasons: because we pretend we are all in the same boat, because we are told that this is just the way things have to be or because we are all invited to align with the 'vision.' But, according to Elias, Foucault and other scholars I draw on in this book, power enables as well as constrains, it is productive as well as destructive and is a quality of all human relating. We are interdependent and need one another, and so we are inevitably caught up in negotiating our conflicting needs according to who needs whom more, and to negotiate inclusion in a group. This negotiating is often undertaken in public, as Hannah Arendt reminds us, and this we call politics. If it doesn't take place in public, or perhaps doesn't take place at all, then the alternatives can be violence or tyranny. Power also operates necessarily in the shadows in organizations through the medium of gossip with both the powerful and the less powerful participating. Speaking out, making ourselves visible to one another, is how we recognize each other as unique individuals engaged in a collective undertaking and gives us the possibility of starting something new. In keeping with the focus of this book, Arendt reminds us that a small group of people acting together can have large effects (and presumably vice versa) and that we cannot know the effects of our actions which ripple out interminably.

Complex selves

One question which dominates sociological thinking is whether the individual or the group is prior: are individuals formed outside in, or is society formed inside out? I try to cleave to the idea, as in Elias and Mead's understanding, that both I and we (I and the groups I belong to), I and me (I and a generalized sense of other selves), are two sides of the same coin. But I also take the position that the group is prior; it precedes us. Our sense of self has a history and it is only recently in human history that we have come to think of ourselves as being discrete and cut off from one another, a phenomenon which seems to have accelerated particularly in the last decades of the 20th and early 21st centuries and particularly in the Global North. We are interdependent with others, and it is our place in the network of relationships that makes us who we are. This is not to deny individuality but to explain how it is that individuality arises.

Many orthodox theories of management proceed from the perspective that the individual is prior, which is no surprise given that socio-economic ideologies proposing a similar point of view have come to dominate many societies, particularly in the Global North. Saying that they have come to dominate is not the same as claiming that they are uncontested or play out everywhere the same. But in general, I claim that there has been a retreat from the collective and argue that this creates a variety of pathologies as well as some opportunities. Our sense of self and our possibilities are shaped and informed by discourses which have real effects in the social world.

Starting with the positives, for some, the idea of the entrepreneurial self is liberating. The possibility of remaking ourselves, being the entrepreneur of our own lives has enabled recent generations to escape what they might understand to be the constraints of tradition and family expectation to live lives in which they see themselves more fully reflected. This is not just a phenomenon of their own choosing but is mainly due to social acceleration and the fragmentation of long-term work and careers, as Hartmut Rosa has demonstrated (2015). However, there are a number of scholars who have drawn attention to the stresses and isolation of having to reinvent yourself over and over in the work place and beyond, and to continuously pull yourself up by your own bootstraps. If everything is to do with personal responsibility and the choices we make, then the ideology of the entrepreneurial self can blind us to the more objective social structures which shape and constrain us. Organizations can feel like lonely places where we are in permanent competition with other self-optimizing individuals, and where there is little emphasis placed on solidarity. Performance metrics can sometimes contribute to this experience, although some people find them galvanizing.

There are strong tendencies in contemporary society to reduce all human endeavour to economics and the marketplace: we might be encouraged to market ourselves as a brand, to treat our friendships as a business or to treat our students as customers. We can become caught up in endless demonstrations of adaptability so that we suffer from indeterminacy, not recognizing ourselves because we feel cut off from others. Organizing everything around market dynamics can not only be invigorating, but it also has implications for our sense of self and our relationship with others.

Complex communication

The chapter on complex communication makes the case that language, meaning, is always unstable, revisable and emergent. Meaning emerges from the ongoing gesture and response between highly social selves, where there is a possibility of surprising ourselves and each other in our mutual communication. At work, the organization is talked into being by people trying to make sense together about what's going on, what's important and what it means: negotiating the work also involves negotiating individual and group identity. As one of my previous colleagues used to say,[3] the three most important questions in organizations are: who are we, what do we think we are doing and who are we becoming? The ethnomethodologist Deirdre Boden (1994) claims that the organization is created inside out – in other words, not in large airy abstractions that are often used in speaking about organizations but in micro-interactions where people are fiercely committed to work out how to go on together from within the context they find themselves. They are more or less completely absorbed in the game. To work out how to go on together, they have to take up organizational abstractions, strategies, policies, managers' injunctions and work out what they mean for the here and now.

I take the idea of the sociality of self and action further by claiming that knowledge is also produced in groups of people in dialogue and discussion with each other, where the conversation is never at rest and never concluded. Scientific knowledge emerges in exactly the same way, in dialogic practice.

I have pointed to the role of power relationships in forming what Elias referred to as figurations, particular patterns of durable flexibility that emerge in society more generally and in organizations. The credibility of certain discourses and ways of speaking prevail in organizations according to who is speaking and what their power position is. Oppositional power may be exercised in more hidden ways through gossip, but those in charge also reinforce their power through gossip too. In managerial organizations, there is often an appeal to metaphysics, the vision or the mission, or to metrics, which has taken on the mantle of incontrovertibility. To take an interest in metrics is to claim that you are managing 'objectively' and not just based on 'gut feeling,' as one manager I know expressed it. This is an appeal to evidence. Alternatively there are a variety of organizational development processes which see themselves as against hierarchy and against the myth of leadership which try to proceduralize communication between employees on the claim that this sets politics aside.

As an alternative, I make the case for the virtues of rhetoric, persuading and being persuaded, as a form of activity which keeps the messy reality of humanity alive and appeals to emotions as well as judgement. It provokes what I have already claimed is important in the mediation of power relationships – making ourselves visible to each other and our uniqueness. Deliberation in groups allows for keeping competing goods in dynamic tension and provokes critical judgement in a community of inquirers into what this community needs to take the next step together.

Complex knowledge, complex knowing

To take the complexity sciences seriously calls into question how much we can know about our social reality, and which methods serve us best in finding out what's going on. I wonder if it is taking liberties to claim that management and organization studies in orthodox form is slightly envious of the natural sciences, wishing it too could claim an evidence base. If it is to be a science, then perhaps it is a science of uncertainty which requires paying attention in different ways.

The traditions of thinking brought into this book value criticality, calling things into question, including the assumptions of the person trying to find things out. There is no starting position from which to proceed, no solid ground upon which to pitch one's tent, just good enough ground for now; a perspective known as post-foundationalism. There are a variety of schools of thought which value interdisciplinarity, borrowing from whichever systematic thinking helps us shed light on what we are trying to find out about in our relationships with each other and our environments. They share some concerns about the importance of history, the importance of overcoming unhelpful dualisms like subject and object, knower and known (leadership and management). The traditions I have found particularly helpful are interested in ways of speaking about flux and change, rather than entities at rest, and what we might think of as the engine of change between human beings, the fluctuating interdependencies we experience through our power relationships with each other. I am not so interested in abstracts like truth and certainty, although this is not say that everything is equally reality-convergent or that we should doubt everything all of the time. But like the pragmatists, I have valued ways of knowing which help shed light on practical difficulties when we get stuck in organizations.

What has helped me best illuminate my dilemmas at work is hanging on to what Elias referred to as the perspective of the airman and the swimmer (2001: 12), able to take a more detached view of the landscape at the same time as having direct knowledge of the currents, eddies and flows of the river that we all find ourselves swimming in. The eminent sociologist C. Wright Mills (1959/2000) described the same paradox as taking an interest in 'the personal troubles of milieu' and the 'public issues of social structure.' The kind of knowledge that we need to better understand our workplaces has the personal inflection of direct experience but tries to generalize against a background of wider social, political and organizational concerns.

I make a case for the importance of honing our critical reflexivity through practice in groups: given how much time we spend in groups, the best place to practice noticing how we show up and how we make sense of other is in a group. Group analytic practice (Foulkes and Anthony, 1984 [1957]) is an experimental discipline which allows participants to try out different strategies of participating in a group and is a good place to take oneself as an object to oneself, to become reflexive. If what happens in organizations, happens as a result of what everyone is doing, then having enhanced skills in noticing and making sense of what everyone is doing may make one a more skilful manager.

Complex authority

There is something about our highly individualized age that privileges and celebrates the role of highly charismatic individuals, often men, and assumes, perhaps encourages, our dependence on them for finding a way through our difficulties. A society of highly atomized individuals unused to looking to groups as a resource may indeed seek out heroic individuals to remove some of the responsibility of working out problems together. As our society speeds up through technology, global integration and competition, we create the very circumstances which amplify uncertainty and provoke our feelings of dependency. However, despite the proliferation of theories of leadership, courses on leadership and consultancy on leadership, it still feels as though we haven't yet reached peak leadership; we dig more holes rather than hanging up our shovels. Leadership has become associated with everything important and good in organizations, and every social dilemma we face can often be attributed to a failure of leadership. Who would want to be a transactional manager if one could be a transformational leader? There is little evidence that this avalanche of thinking about leadership has resulted in better leaders helping us deal with our difficulties more skilfully.

If we take seriously one of the insights claimed from the complexity sciences that there is no central site of control in a CAS, then, this might lead us to deflate the swollen discourse on leadership and think instead about the role of leaders and groups. This is not to be anti-leadership or to deny the importance of leaders, but simply to put the other side of the argument that groups chose their leaders as much as leaders choose their groups. This then problematizes the notion that a leader can choose her style of leadership rather than being shaped as much by the group she is brought in to lead. There are very strong emotional currents in groups which can disrupt our ability to focus on what's important and instead distract us with unhelpful longings for certainty. In these circumstances, we might choose the very people who are most harmful to our circumstances, uniting us against a phantom enemy or promising certainty when this is least available. The very strong emotional ties, which might unite us around an inflated and heroic 'we' identity, are unstable and unpredictable and can also take on a life of their own in dangerous ways. The storming of the Capitol in Washington, DC in 2021 is a very good example of this.

Group analytic practice, based on different assumptions about power and authority, is a discipline which actively seeks to wean participants in a group off their dependency and encourages group members to have a greater sense of their own agency in affecting what happens, no matter how insignificant our contribution might feel. Meanwhile and from a pragmatic perspective, a good leader is someone who through their process of socialization is exceptionally adroit in bringing people into a different relation with each other and with the leader, and in the process, transforming both. A good leader is someone who can speak and act in a way in which the majority can recognize themselves, at the same time as recognizing the leader. They become, in Mead's (1938) terms, a social object, and embodiment of what the group can be. The leader is in the group, but the group is also in the leader.

It might be more helpful to think of leadership as an improvisational activity which takes place in groups involving the negotiation of power and identity through processes of mutual recognition.

Complex ethics

Taking an interest in complex social life brings into sharper focus the ethical choices we make in simplifying and categorizing to make good enough sense of the world. In a way, this is no different from assuming that the world is predictable and controllable but becoming aware that you are simplifying a rich hinterland of complexity makes the process become much more obvious and thus perhaps more burdensome. I know lots of unreflective managers largely untroubled by uncertainty who make decisions, propose and dispose as though what they do is rational and obvious. To a degree, we all proceed ideologically as though the world is as we see it. Introducing uncertainty, doubt, criticality and foregrounding practical judgement can make a manager self-conscious.

Complexity can also be used as a refuge. The world is just too complex for us to take responsibility for our actions, or the forces we faced were just too great for us to overcome. There are many complex reasons why people use food banks as a previous British Prime Minister once said.[4]

I try to explore the case that the world may be complex; we may even do some justice to more fully understanding the complexity by deliberating in detail about the concrete and particular circumstances and investigating further, but we still have responsibility to act.

Ethical dilemmas themselves take place within broader social processes. I make the argument that hypercompetitiveness, individualization and marketization in organizations are likely to create their own pathologies, particularly when they weaken the bonds of solidarity and staying in relation. When we are judged against metrics, an abstract and commensurable standard, rather than recognized as human beings, it can lead to feelings of oppression and alienation. Those obliged to manage within a performative regime may find themselves caught up in a double bind and dealing with feelings of rivalry, shame and anxiety, feelings which the scheme of managing according to metrics is supposed to do away with. But it would also be a mistake to reduce everything that is going on in an organization to just one thing. There are patterns of discrimination and injustice between groups and within groups which have been repeated for centuries, racism and gender discrimination, for example, which continue to show up in different ways.

The pragmatists recommend that we may do greater justice to competing goods in communities systematically not only by taking into account as many views as possible, through imagination and empathy, but also by acknowledging our own interests. This may involve making our interests and position clear, but being radically open to the other at the same time, which is easier said than done.

So what does it mean for managers to take complexity seriously?

Management is an instrumental discipline. It aims to control, to put things under one's hand (manus, from the Latin). For this reason, I think the idea of complexity that the world is stable and unstable, predictable and unpredictable both at the same time can be a bit of an affront to what managers think they should be doing. Of course, we need managers – it would be very hard to make organizations cohere without them. But what kind of managers do we need if our starting point is that the world emerges in unpredictable ways through the quality of our participation in it?

In this book, I introduced the work of the sociologist Hartmut Rosa, who has developed a detailed taxonomy of our contemporary dilemmas in a body of work (2015, 2019, 2020). He claims that over the last three centuries, we have accelerated, fragmented and instrumentalized our world. The same disciplines of mind that enable us to abstract from ourselves, from nature and from our social reality leading to highly developed societies and, in general, more comfortable lives have paradoxically caused the problems of environmental degradation, frenetic social standstill, increased inequality and an inability to find resonance in our relationships. This is because we refuse to accept that the world is uncontrollable. He describes our relationship to the world as aggressive, because the methods we have developed try to make things visible, by making them visible we try to control through mastering and managing, and by managing them, we try to make them useful. The difficulty he perceives is that usefulness is not the only criterion which renders the world vibrant and worth living in. Transformation, which is sometimes talked about in organizations as though it can be designed and planned, is a state where both we and others are transformed in the interaction: it involves mutual responsiveness, not just actor and acted upon. Uncontrollability is the price we pay for novelty and freedom. If we are trapped in the endless pursuit of bringing more and more things within our reach to subdue and appropriate them, the result he claims, is that we become alienated. We turn the world into a dead world of things of use, which means we lose the world and in the process become disenchanted. Quoting Hannah Arendt, he argues that we are in danger of being in a 'relation of relationlessness' (Rosa, 2020: 27) in a lifeless world.

In the review of the seven types of complexity (and bearing in mind there are 'types of complexity' that we barely touched on like time) I tried to draw attention to how our lives keep escaping our attempts to manage them; our actions don't work out as we intended, we are misunderstood despite giving very clear instructions, we behave in ways which surprise even ourselves, we are in charge but can't bring about what we wanted, we cause harm even when we intended to do right by others. People, things, circumstances fight back. Despite the managerial quest to run things effectively and efficiently there is a huge chasm between expectation and reality. Instruments of control like performance management metrics provoke gaming activity from staff and elicit strong feelings of shame, rivalry and anxiety, the opposite of what 'managing objectively' is supposed to bring about. Our fitbits and digital projects of self, parenting apps, dating apps, make us wary about ourselves and distrustful of our own judgement. In our personal lives we experience surprise, disappointment and spontaneity, whereas at work we might be blamed for failing to anticipate or plan, for bringing about the wrong kind of novelty, or in the case of a number of critical management scholars recently made redundant at the University of Leicester, for failing to produce the right kind of research which falls within the objectives of the new research strategy. It seems that we expect a different kind of causality and experience in our personal lives from the one we anticipate in organizations.

Taking complexity seriously is an invitation to pay attention differently. There are variety of perspectives, which I have partially explored in this book, such as critical management studies, which also destabilize, denaturalize and problematize what we may take for granted, particularly if we have had a more orthodox management education. What distinguishes the perspective I have written about is that it does draw on the minority but substantial disciplines of the complexity sciences and tries to take them up in social terms, arguing by analogy. In this sense it is interdisciplinary and pluralistic. In being pluralistic it is critical of the idea that there is just one way of managing: there are multiple possibilities of staying in relation in organizational life.

I think assuming that social reality is predictably unpredictable deflates the claims of managers and management, but certainly doesn't make managers unnecessary. You don't have to be a Zen monk or nun to expect the unexpected and unwanted, but it might make you more humble, more realistic perhaps, in any change initiative or project, and less likely to blame others, or yourself, if things don't work out as planned. If change is dialectical, then there will always be winners and losers, those who recognize themselves in a new regime and those who don't. It will achieve some of the things which are expected, and will have adverse negative effects as well. Even those who don't feel recognized in the decisions about change will need recognizing in some way, and even further acts of recognition may not prevent them opposing what's going on. This is not the same as a manager changing their mind about a decision taken. Acting into a web of other people's actions and intentions is likely to disrupt existing power relations between groups, fears about being included and excluded so employees will dig in, support the changes, resist, argue, lobby and act politically. Any manager implementing changes, or just doing their day-to-day job, is also acting politically, whether they do so consciously or not. Thinking about how to manage well involves exercising practical judgement in the productive use of power.

So working in an organization is severely provoking to our sense of identity, who we think we are, because who we think we are is tightly bound up with the membership of groups we belong to. And what we do matters to us, and we are invested in it. Today's managers could wise up about the pressures in many organizations to proceduralize, to measure and to individualize achievement, even if in general they think of these trends to be a good thing. The pressure on employees is endless to adapt and be flexible and to take personal responsibility to look to themselves as the primary resource will not be alleviated by sending them on resilience courses. This is because we are social animals who come to know ourselves and deal with our problems in groups. Whichever way we choose to manage will provoke strong feelings towards the authority figure, and/or because of the shifting power figurations and because we feel more or less recognized or perhaps misrecognized. So there is no optimum way of working with others, just different sorts of dynamics with different patterns of feeling and response. All ways of managing involve assumptions about how change happens which are more or less reality-convergent, and enact ideologies about authority and what this particular group should choose to value. Sometimes a group is trying to deal with circumstances which it has never faced before, which will involve, in Hannah Arendt's words, thinking without a bannister.

We talk organizations into existence by making broad, abstract generalizations which can only be taken up locally with each other to work out what they mean for how we go on together. In the deliberation there will be lots of opportunities for misunderstanding and misinterpreting, so the researcher-manager will find it helpful to listen to how people talk about what they are doing. In reflecting back what they hear, by interpreting, managers may become editors in chief of the organizational narratives. It will help them to persuade using rhetoric, and, in turn, to be persuaded if this is helpful to what they want to achieve. There is no communication so clear and no rule so precise that it won't need exploring and repeating before the manager and the managed have a good enough understanding of what is intended. And as that good enough understanding is established, so it will break open into new possibilities and new understandings with the passing of time.

In organizations which are predicated on speed and action, taking time to think, and to deliberate with others is one of the most helpful ways of trying to explore what's going on around here. We can't call into question everything all of the time, but pausing to think about particular difficulties may help groups better understand what they are not seeing. Sometimes the only way to realize what we think is to hear ourselves say it out loud to other people, and to see ourselves reflected back in the way people to respond to what we say and who we are. A group may help managers better understand what they take for granted and thus to see a situation as more plural than they had originally thought. Making the organization more plural might make it feel like a more humane place to work.

A thoughtful manager/leader will be wary of the projections of strong feelings towards them from others which always arise from being in a position of power. The ability to endure the sometimes negative feelings of others towards the manager and what is going on, particularly in conditions of uncertainty, sometimes even to encourage the anxiety and negative feelings to be expressed, is part and parcel of doing the job. A leader/manager may be able to live longer with uncertainty, contradictions and doubt, and bear this for others. It may be helpful to reveal one's own doubt about what happens next, but this depends on context. Perhaps people in positions of power can be more cautious about the inflated claims of transformation which accompany important positions in organizations and can pay attention to the way the group shapes them as much as they shape the group, forming and being formed. A good place to start is to notice what is important to the group, and how a leader/manager can speak in a way in which the majority can seem themselves reflected. A good question might be to ask what the leader/manager needs of the group and what the group needs of the leader/manager right now.

A manager is in an unenviable position of having to obey multiple obligations: the organization which employs them, the people they manage, the profession of management and one's own conscience. This is likely to lead to ambivalence at the very least towards some of the things they are asked to do. Just as there are conflicting tensions arising from multiple goods, so there are multiple points of view in a group. To a degree, it is important to do justice, or at least to recognize, as many of them as possible, whether it affects decision-making or not. In the end, managers have to be able to live with themselves, go home and be able to look themselves in the mirror.

Notes

1

> Practical men [sic] who believe themselves to be quite exempt from any intellectual influences are usually the slaves of some defunct economist. Madmen in authority, who hear voices in the air, are distilling their frenzy from some academic scribbler of a few years back.

> J.M. Keynes (2016), *The General Theory of Employment, Interest and Money*

I think Keynes would have been alive to the irony that the effect he describes was just as likely to be the case for his own theories of the economy.

2 Two critical volumes on the evolution of business schools and the development of leadership and management theory are Khurana (2007) and Cummings et al. (2017).

3 Prof Doug Griffin was one of the original founders of the Complexity and Management Group at the University of Hertfordshire and a key contributor to the perspective of complex responsive processes of relating. He was also my principal supervisor. He died in 2015.

4 As explained in Chapter 8 on complex ethics.

References

Boden, D. (1994) *The Business of Talk*, Cambridge: Polity Press.

Bourdieu, P. (1990) *In Other Words*, Stanford, CA: Stanford University Press.

Bourdieu, P. (1992) *The Logic of Practice*, Cambridge: Polity Press.

Cummings, S., Bridgman, T., Hassard, J. and Rowlinson, M. (2017) *A New History of Management*, Cambridge: Cambridge University Press.

Elias, N. (2001) *The Society of Individuals*, Oxford: Oxford University Press.

Foulkes, S.H. and Anthony, E.J. (1984 [1957]) *Group Psychotherapy: The Psychoanalytic Approach*, London: Karnac Books.

Keynes, J.M. (2016) *The General Theory of Employment, Interest and Money*, Hinsdale: Dryden Press.

Khurana, R. (2007) *From Higher Aims to Hired Hands: The Social Transformation of American Business Schools and the Unfulfilled Promise of Management as a Profession*, Princeton, NJ: Princeton University Press.

Mead, G.H. (1938) *The Philosophy of the Act*, Chicago, IL: University of Chicago Press.

Rosa, H. (2015) *Social Acceleration: A New Theory of Modernity*, New York, NY: Columbia University Press.

Rosa, H. (2019) *Resonance: A Sociology of Our Relationship to the World*, Cambridge: Polity Press.

Rosa, H. (2020) *The Uncontrollability of the World*, Cambridge: Polity Press.

Stacey, R., Griffin, D. and Shaw, P. (2000) *Complexity and Management: Fad or Radical Challenge to Systems Thinking*, London: Routledge.

Wright Mills, C. (1959/2000) *The Sociological Imagination*, Oxford: Oxford University Press.

INDEX

Printed in the United States
by Baker & Taylor Publisher Services